Jarrow

0   40

0   80   160 Kilometers

•YORK

akefield/
rnsdale

• Brinsworth
•
Tinsley

*Sherwood
Forest*

N O R T H
S E A

• Leicester
• Peatling Magna

• Ramsay

E N G L A N D

Thames

uucklebury

LONDON•

•Winchester

Canterbury•

In Search of England

Journeys into the English Past

MICHAEL WOOD

University of California Press

BERKELEY   LOS ANGELES

University of California Press
Berkeley and Los Angeles, California

Published by arrangement with Penguin Books Ltd

ISBN 0−520−22582−1

Set in 12/14.75 pt Monotype Bembo
Typeset by Rowland Phototypesetting Ltd, Bury St Edmunds, Suffolk
Printed in Great Britain by Clays Ltd, St Ives plc

9 8 7 6 5 4 3 2 1

Contents

PART THREE
Landscapes and People

List of Illustrations

SECTION OPENINGS

Myth and History
Sir Bedivere throwing Excalibur into the lake, miniature in a compilation of the *Saint Graal*, fourteenth century. Add. MS 10294 (British Library).

Manuscripts and Mysteries
Frontispiece from manuscript of Bede's version of St Cuthbert's *Life* showing King Athelstan offering the book to the saint, *c.* 934. CCC. MS 183, f.1v. (Reproduced courtesy of the Master and Fellows of Corpus Christi College, Cambridge).

Landscapes and People
Sower at work, marginal decoration from the Luttrell Psalter, a Latin manuscript written and illuminated *c.* 1335–40 for Sir Geoffrey Luttrell. Add. MS 42130, f.170v (British Library. Photo: Bridgeman Art Library, London).

Introduction

In the Dark Ages, when Celtic bards sat round their fires and told tales, 'The Matter of Britain was the chief object of care'. By that they meant the great theme of Celtic British history: the dispossession of the lowland Celts by the invading English, the myths of Arthur and the rest, the loss of Celtic Britain. This book looks at some aspects of what one might call the Matter of England. It is a series of stories which, directly or indirectly, touch on some questions of English history and identity and the transmission of tradition. They are stories which have particularly fascinated me over the years of making films and writing books about history. The book is a miscellany, then, but one which I hope adds up to more than the sum of its parts.

My title is borrowed from the account of H. V. Morton's journey written seventy years ago, a story which is the subject of one of the chapters in this book. My search for England, though, is very different from Morton's: where he journeyed the length and breadth of the land and took a broad-sweep view, here I offer a few close-up details, deep sections of English history, taken at different places and different times. My emphasis is in the Early Middle Ages, the ninth and tenth centuries, when the English State was created, and when certain crucial elements become apparent in the English identity. Some stories in the book touch on the great divide of English history, the Reformation of Henry VIII in the 1530s, when an awareness of the Old English (or Anglo-Saxon) past was rekindled, and its manuscripts and monuments began to be recovered, but when also the greatest ever destruction of heritage in these islands took place. But these are contemporary journeys too, for as Great Britain begins to recede, and as the break-up of Britain is dissected by the pundits, older regional identities are reasserting themselves, and new myths are being created to serve them. So the process of history continues all around us: 'History is now, and England' as T.S. Eliot said.

I have divided the book into three sections which I should briefly explain. The first section looks at the transmission of our ideas about history, identity and communal experience through myth, for myth plays just as important a part in the construction of identity as does historical fact – indeed it is often difficult to tell them apart!

The second section is more precisely about texts and old manuscripts (which I confess hold a particular fascination for me). These chapters look at the way our early history has been recovered by piecing together fragments, sometimes literally. For example, the key accounts of two of the greatest figures in our history, Alfred and Athelstan, are based on manuscripts which no longer exist. Chapter Ten examines what kind of stories can be recovered from an old book: a tale quite in keeping with the sleuthings of the medieval detective William of Baskerville in *The Name of the Rose*.

In the third section we move out of the library into the landscape: to Devon and Yorkshire, to Durham, Berkshire and Leicester. These chapters look at particular places over time: a house, a wood, a church, a village. For landscapes too constitute a kind of text, which can be deciphered.

Whether about myths, texts, or landscapes, I hope it will become clear that these tales do not just concern the transmission of information. For in recovering them, we learn not only about the past, but about ourselves. The medieval past is not a dead subject.

Finally, these stories are full of detail, from marks in burned manuscripts and medieval tax returns, to cigarette cards and cartoons. Curiously, I feel impelled to apologize for this. I can only say in my defence that it is the detail which really fascinates me. Contract lawyers and diplomatic negotiators have a saying that 'the devil is in the detail', but to my eyes so are the angels: winged messengers from the past who bring these faint and fragile intimations from past lives every bit as interesting and worthwhile as our own, if not more so. This whole book is assembled from such fragments, for that is the nature of the sources for the first centuries of English history. No one grand narrative of those times will ever be possible; all we can do is use the fragments to conjure up that long-dissolved world which happens to have made us what we are. But perhaps, in the end, that is the most satisfying way to convey the texture, the intricate connections of that lost whole. As a now often maligned but still acute observer of English history, Rudyard Kipling, said:

> If England was what England seems
> And not the England of our dreams
> If she was putty, brass and paint
> 'Ow quick we'd drop her . . . but she ain't.

Acknowledgements

The origin of these pieces is various. Some, like chapters two and seven, are fresh looks at subjects I have covered in TV documentaries. Some are the by-product of the writing of a book on King Athelstan and his times which has yet to see the light of day. Chapter nine has been delivered as a lecture to the London University Medieval Seminar, to a conference on Athelstan at Manchester University, and to the Eton College History Society, and I would like to express my thanks to the organizers and participants who suggested improvements; and also to Patrick Wormald, Jinty Nelson and Rod Thomson, whose helpful criticisms improved a much longer academic version: needless to say, any errors which remain are mine. Chapter three started life as a programme made for BBC Radio 4. My interest in the Barbudans in Chapter fifteen first saw light in a film for the BBC's Domesday series in 1986: my belated thanks to Margaret Tweedy in Cheltenham, and of course to the Barbudan community in Leicester, especially to Brillheart James. Thanks too to the Ramsay family of Bury Barton, Devon, to Miriam Harte at Jarrow, to the Reverend Colin Gibson at Tinsley, and to Professor Malcom Todd for answering my queries about his digs around Lapford. Obviously much of the detail in a book of this kind is based on the work of professional scholars in the field, and the reader will find my main debts in the bibliography. James Ravilious and John Davies kindly provided me with prints of their photographs. The staff at the British Library Students' Room were unfailingly courteous and helpful: access to that unrivalled treasure trove is one of the greatest privileges one could wish for. At Maya Vision, John Cranmer was always at hand with his computer expertise. Prue Cave was an invaluable support once more, correcting the whole text while I was shivering with a film crew in the mountains of Peru. At Penguin, Kate Samano expertly did the final edit of a rather dense typescript. Grainne Kelly found the pictures and Tony Lacey offered much kind support, patience, and good advice which greatly improved my text. Thanks to my agent, Lavinia Trevor, who first suggested putting my English 'roots' pieces together as a book. My last debt is to my family, who put up with obsessive hours spent on medieval texts on top of the often considerable pressures of making films in a small independent film company in the world of late-nineties television: to them my heartfelt thanks, for this, and for everything.

PART ONE
Myth and History

Sir Bedivere throws Excalibur back into the lake, from a
fourteenth-century miniature.

1. The Norman Yoke

'My son,' said the Norman Baron, 'I am dying and you will be heir
To all the broad acres in England that William gave me for my share
When we conquered the Saxon at Hastings, and a nice little handful
    it is.
But before you go over to rule it I want you to understand this:-
The Saxon is not like us Normans. His manners are not so polite.
But he never means anything serious till he talks about justice and
    right.
When he stands like an ox in the furrow with his sullen set eyes in
    your own,
And grumbles, 'This isn't fair dealing,' my son, leave the Saxon
    alone . . .

        Rudyard Kipling, *Norman and Saxon* (AD 1100)

When we are young we are all affected by certain incidents, stories or images from the past which, consciously or unconsciously, we carry into adult life. They may be disturbing, they may be inspiring; we may learn from them, they may drag us down: so at least the psychologists tell us. Nations are the same, I suspect, wounded or inspired by incidents in their birth and early life, reshaping and encoding them as myths which are handed down to serve as warnings or exemplars in later life. And they matter: for just as the healthy integration of one's past failures is held to be important in growing up to be an adult, so sociologists tell us one of the key factors in the creation of national identity is the facing up to disasters and the achievement of a sense of a shared past. This is not a literal past, of course, save, possibly, in a biological sense. It is images of the past: often as highly structured and selective as myths –

imprinted, almost in the manner of genetic information, on our sensibility. So each new historical era mirrors itself in the picture and active mythology of its past. Hence the French still metaphorize 'the Revolution'; the Americans 'the Civil War'; going much further back in time, traditional Iranians still bemoan 'the Arab Conquest' which may have brought them Islam, but was still, they feel, the defeat of an ancient and superior civilization by a Johnny-come-lately. For the English, for nine hundred years it has been the Norman Conquest which has been one of the greatest sources of myth. In fact, it is a remarkable thing that when an English person (though not Scottish, Welsh or Irish, one should note) refers to 'the Conquest', even now, he or she can mean only one date: 1066.

When I was a child, there was a boy's weekly paper called *The Eagle* which published a comic-strip version of the Norman Conquest. It was gripping stuff: the tragic story of the flaxen-haired Harold, who finally falls heroically to the crop-haired and fascistic Duke William. At the end of the final episode, the king's loyal friend the thegn Ulric of Glastonbury carries the king's body, wrapped in the 'national' flag, the Golden Dragon of Wessex. He staggers towards the shore, all hope lost. Then suddenly the clouds part over the sea, and across the sunset sky Ulric sees a vision which (with hindsight) uncannily recalls the pageant of English history on the posters for the 1924 Empire Exhibition at Wembley: 'A Glorious Body of Men'. For riding on the night skies were the ships of Drake and Nelson, the Thin Red Line, the Tommies of the Somme and D Day, the Hurricanes of the Few. Above it the caption read 'Saxon England was gone but a greater one would rise'. It was a view of British history suitable for children of the 1950s: that even as the empire was being 'given away', English/British history still had a manifest destiny. And it also, one might add, had the added advantage of getting over what the Hollywood moguls call the 'negative-ending problem': when the hero dies and the good guys lose!

I have to admit that I never quite got over reading the story of Ulric the Saxon at the age of ten or eleven. I am sure that subconsciously it shaped my view of Saxons and Normans at least as much as did Sir Frank Stenton, whose great book on Anglo-Saxon England was our bible in the sixth form, a work whose laconic prose suggested a knowledge far greater than could ever be put between the covers of a single book. Stenton's vision, it has to be said, was not completely divorced from the vision of Ulric the Saxon. His book came out in 1943, and could not fail to be touched by wider events. Unlike many academic books, it was written with the heart and the spirit as well as the intellect. Its patriotism is unmistakable, its view of the origins of England undeniably teleological. Stenton believed in the continuity of English history. He was a Nottingham-shire man, from the old Danelaw, who as a boy was fascinated by what then were still visible living connections: 'My father,' he wrote, 'who was steward of the soke or "liberty" of Southwell, held in that capacity courts which represented the same rights possessed over his estates by Osketill, Archbishop of York, in the tenth century.'

Stenton saw the rise of England to unity as an inevitable process, and at times the reader may still detect a whiff of wartime spirit, a little touch of Harry in the night, for example in the passage describing Alfred as the founder of the British Navy, in which battleships of gun-metal grey seem to hug the Saxon horizon just as Ulric the Saxon saw them. Stenton's book described the high culture of England before the Conquest, and in particular the administrative skills of its rulers. In his appreciation of Old English art and literature he seemed to be saying something about our own ancestors; and when he said of the Norman conquerors that 'politically they were masters of their world', we knew what he meant. Though the modern revolution in Anglo-Saxon studies would begin only in the 1970s, Stenton's was a defining moment in our perception of the Old English past. (Not least, as it turned out, because his was the last gasp of the Victorian idea of the continuity of English history which he had grown up with. The sixties would see this go, as indeed did the study of English medieval history itself in the new redbrick universities of Harold Wilson.)

At any rate, in 1966 the 900th anniversary of the Norman Conquest was celebrated with much brouhaha. Stenton had retired

and was too old now (at eighty-six) to participate in the junketing.
Most of the magazines ran big features on the story of 1066: the
satirical magazine *Punch* did an issue as if William had lost. On TV,
pundits tramped over the battlefields of Hastings and Stamford
Bridge. Early in the year, the *Sunday Times* set out the agenda with
an essay in its colour supplement by Field Marshal Montgomery,
the British war hero of El Alamein and D Day, who often appeared
in the press and on TV in those days. Montgomery's position was
essentially that of Thomas Carlyle: 'Without the Normans what
had it been? Tribes of Jutes and Angles wandering around in
pot-bellied equanimity.'

In other words, the Saxons were hirsute backwoodsmen whose
achievements were as nothing till the Normans brought discipline,
organization and European civilization. To Montgomery, a military
man, the Battle of Hastings was proof of it: Harold's absurd strategy
and non-existent tactics, charging all that way from Yorkshire to
Sussex only to stand on a hill and be cut down; stoically resisting
while the Conqueror's New Model Army in their short haircuts
wheeled in parade-ground cavalry manoeuvres and jabbed them to
defeat. It was a victory of new technology over old, of forward-
looking Europeans over backward-looking provincials who had
probably stayed up all night quaffing flagons of ale (a nod there to
the Victorian historian Freeman's famous picture of the last night
of Saxon England). All in all, a victory for discipline and modern
technology: 'And a damn good thing too,' you could almost hear
him saying.

Sitting in Cuthbert Seton's medieval history class next day, I
was emboldened to pen a reply to Field Marshal Montgomery.
Struggling to find the right tone, I eventually hit on writing in the
first person from King Harold. 'I am amazed that your distinguished
correspondent failed to see what I was doing in October 1066,' I
began, and gathering courage I went on to berate his complete
failure to understand 'my' campaign: 'It is nonsense to suggest that
I was trying to fight a defensive battle, my plan quite simply was
this . . .' The following Sunday my piece was published under the
title 'King Harold on the Defensive'. A day or two later I was

standing mud-streaked on the football field when one of the head
prefects called me over:

'High Master wants to see you.'

I went in. He was holding a letter from Montgomery. 'What's
this, Wood?'

The tight lip hovered, slightly amused. I read the letter. The
tone was slightly irritated and one could almost hear the famous
clipped tones: 'I gather that King Hawold in another incarnation
is a schoolboy at Manchester Gwammar School.' He summoned
me to come down and 'debate' the matter with him in the House
of Lords. Good, I thought. Ulric the Saxon still mattered.

With some trepidation I took the train to Euston and the Underground to Westminster. I presented myself to the policeman under
King's Tower and was ushered into the presence. It turned out to
be a strange day. The 'debate', if one may call it such, was a damp
squib, of course. I was overawed and quickly retreated under the
blast of his experience. Over parboiled vegetables in the House of
Lords restaurant he was more concerned to hammer out to me the
lessons of modern history. To this schoolboy he poured out his
heart on the betrayals of 1944; on what he saw as the disastrous
conduct of the last phase of the war. Like many of his generation
(and he had also fought – and been badly wounded – in the First
World War), he was dismayed by the partition of Europe, which
then must have seemed permanent, and by the threat to the humanistic tradition of the West represented by the Cold War and the
nuclear arms race. They had never taken his advice, he felt, and
this still hurt him.

He was small and dapper with a beaky nose; a lonely sort, I
guessed. He lived in a mill in Hampshire with his wartime caravan,
his mobile HQ, still parked at the bottom of the garden, with faded
photographs on the wall of his great adversary, Erwin Rommel.
He was, as I remember, a fitness fanatic; and he had lost none of
his concern for discipline in the ranks. He started off by grilling me
in that sharp, clipped military voice one had heard so often on old
black-and-white newsfilm.

'You don't smoke, do you?' he began brusquely over the soup.

'No, sir.'

'Good. Neither do I. Never have. Disgusting habit.' He leaned back. 'Do you drink?'

'No, sir. Well, not really.' (I fibbed: illicit pints of mild with English teachers on trips to Stratford surely didn't count?) 'Well, only in moderation . . .'

'Harumph . . . Never touched a drop all my life. Temperance is one of the cardinal virtues. Self-control is as important as prudence and fortitude in leadership, and it has been throughout history . . . just as the life of William the Conqueror shows.' He put his hands together and leaned forward. 'Now about your piece in the *Sunday Times*. You see, my boy, before the Normans, the English had no real civilization: they had been living in the Dark Ages, after all. They had had some good leaders: Alfred the Great, for example, he was a good chap. When he made peace with the Danes it was a great act of statesmanship . . . years ahead of his time . . . the sort of leadership we are desperate for today.' He threw a glance towards the lower chamber: he was evidently not a fan of Harold Wilson. 'But the Normans brought ordered government. Look at the Domesday Book. Ordered government, you see, is the basis of freedom. The Conquest was a great boon to this country . . . it welded together the nation . . . set it on the road to empire and the world influence it has had . . .'

I felt Ulric the Saxon's friendly spirit on cue tapping at my shoulder: 'Hang on, sir, the Domesday Book is English, isn't it, sir? It's organized on the English system of shires and hundreds. They must have done that sort of thing many times before. And wasn't the scribe an Englishman? Sir Frank Stenton says . . .'

'It was a Norman work,' he interjected. 'King William sponsored it, Norman acumen made it possible.'

'I suppose so,' I said and sank back, blushing furiously. Evidently we were not going to see eye to eye.

Then, looking at him over the table as he spoke, it suddenly clicked. Of course! He was a Norman! His ancestor Roger of Montgomery had commanded one wing at Hastings. In gratitude the Conqueror had gifted him vast tracts of the Welsh borderland which had once belonged to English thegns (men like dear old Ulric of Glastonbury). There Roger founded a Norman new town in the lovely parish which still bears his name. Studded the place with castles, even though he probably spent more time on his estates in Normandy or safe on the south coast near Brighton. The Field Marshal may have been a national war hero, but to me that particular war was far away and long ago: much longer ago than 1066. From that moment, as far as I was concerned, he would always be a Norman.

'You see, my boy, the greatness of England would never have been possible without the Normans.'

I tried a last desperate, outflanking move. 'But they were just a bunch of Vikings who had only learned to speak French a generation or two back. They learned everything from us.' (By now the gloves were off: it was 'us' and 'them'.) 'Our civilization went back over 500 years. Our missionaries like Saint Boniface had converted Germany. And look at our beautiful manuscript painting . . .'

He would have none of it. Fine as they were, manuscript paintings were not the defining marks of history as far as he was concerned. And looking back, I suppose in a way he had a point. Who had cared about the manuscript paintings in Chartres or Dresden? He had earned the right the hard way to see war as the motive force in history: the destroyer or protector of liberty. In the end, it felt as if our little 'debate' was a gross mismatch. What did I know about history? What *could* I know? He gently brushed my arguments away with his napkin while a black-dressed waitress spooned more disintegrating potatoes on to his plate. And that was that. After lunch, he introduced me to the former prime minister Clement Attlee, who had led Labour to victory in 1945. Now frail and bent, Attlee smiled when he heard my reason for being there. 'Ah, the Norman Yoke,' he chuckled. 'That old chestnut.'

I took the train back up north that evening. I think the Field Marshal genuinely thought me a misguided youth, though later he kindly sent me his books, inscribed 'Hoping you may find in these pages something of value in your study of history.'

The brush with fame got me a minute's notoriety when I went up to university, where Billy Pantin, a delightful old medievalist, said at our first tutorial, 'We were amused by your ideas on the Anglo-Saxons. Especially at your attempt to revive the Norman Yoke.'

Now I confess, embarrassingly, I had no idea what the Norman Yoke was, let alone that that was what I had been trotting out. At university I soon discovered. The late sixties, of course, were the time of radical student movements: Che, Vietnam, the Paris riots. Even students like me, who were not particularly political, were touched by them, for these ideas were everywhere in the air, and they fed the study of history. This was the time of the rediscovery of the English radical tradition, and one of the great figures was Christopher Hill, whose lectures were packed by many people who were not even doing the history course. His brilliant books uncovered a forgotten history, a vast ferment of ideas: Levellers, Diggers, Muggletonians, all dealing in myths of history, parallel visions of English history – and surprisingly, they had a lot to say about the Norman Yoke. Indeed, for them it was the central myth of our history.

In a nutshell, the myth was this: England had free institutions before 1066, which were lost to William the Conqueror. All laws made since the Conquest were therefore illegal: so from 1066 till 1642 (and indeed afterwards), the English had lived under the Norman Yoke. English law had been superseded by laws written in Norman French and interpreted by Norman lawyers; the Old English custom of local government, with local hearings in the vernacular, had been done away with; the feudal system had dispossessed the free-born English. The Conquest had also strengthened the ties of the English Church with the papacy, where before 1066 the English Church had enjoyed independence from Rome. In 1646, the New Model Army was awash with these ideas. As one said: 'What were the Lords of England but William the Conqueror's Colonels?'

In his lectures and books, Hill showed that this had been one of the greatest, most long-lasting and most fertile myths in English history. In Oxford, right up to that time, it had been taught as part of a seventeenth-century antiquarian controversy: just the nutty theories of a few left-wing extremists in the English Revolution.

But Hill argued that it was part of the fibre of Englishness, and in particular part of a radical attempt to reimagine England. An England not made by the rulers, an England not created, as the likes of Namier and Plumb imagined, in the country houses of the rich, but by the people themselves.

Take this from the greatest of the Levellers, Gerard Winstanley, the Wigan-born son of a draper who led the communistically inclined Diggers on to St George's Heath in Surrey in 1649 to take over the common land:

England, you know, hath been conquered and enslaved divers times, and the best laws that England hath (viz. Magna Charta) were got by our forefathers' importunate petitioning unto the kings, that still were their task-masters; and yet these best laws are yokes and manacles, tying one sort of people to be slaves to another . . . The last enslaving yoke that England groaned under (and yet is not freed from) was the Norman, as you know; and since William the Conqueror came in, about six hundred years ago, all the kings did confirm the old laws, or else make new ones, to uphold that Norman Conquest over us; and the most favouring laws that we have doth still bind the hands of the enslaved English from enjoying the freedom of their creation.

You of the gentry, as well as we of the commonalty, all groaned under the burden of the bad government and burdening laws under the late King Charles, who was the last successor of William the Conqueror: you and we cried for a Parliament, and a Parliament was called, and wars, you know, presently begun, between the King, that represented William the Conqueror, and the body of the English people that were enslaved . . . and William the Conqueror's successor, which was Charles [I], was cast out; and thereby we have recovered ourselves from under that Norman yoke. *An Appeal to the House of Commons (1649)*

Some took it even further. John Hare, for example, wanted not only the Lords thrown out and their lands expropriated, but the laws redone in English, and French words expunged from the language! Political dynamite. And the fascinating thing is that the Levellers believed it: for them it was not just a metaphor, but a historical fact that our liberties were lost in 1066. The controversy touched the rank and file too, among whom were literate radicals deeply concerned about how to reinterpret the pattern of English history. The Army debates at Putney church in the autumn of 1647 reveal the undercurrents bubbling below the surface of the Puritan revolution – here the stenographer has recorded the actual words of Cromwell, Ireton and the rest in heated debate with rank-and-file Levellers in the Army. Take this exchange between Ireton and one of the Leveller officers, who had argued that the Commons had been represented before the Norman Conquest:

NICHOLAS COWLING: 'Since the time of the Conquest the greatest part of the kingdom was in vassalage.'

IRETON (who is clearly perplexed by this question of history before the Norman Conquest): 'We should not seem to derive all our tyranny from the Norman Conquest. If subjection to a King be tyranny, we had a King before the Norman Conquest. I cannot but wonder at the strange inferences that are made. He tells us that there is no memory of the Commons having any interest in the legislative power till Edward the First's time . . . and yet would certainly have us to believe that the Commons had all the right before the Conquest.'

COWLING: 'In Alfred's time the Commons had all the power, and the King, before the Conquest, hanged forty-three judges in one year.'

Cowling had got this story about Alfred (which is fiction, by the way) from Andrew Horne's *Mirror of Justice*, a late-thirteenth-century poem in French which circulated among the leaders after it was printed in 1642. But Ireton was right to be sceptical. As history, of course, Cowling's remarks are nonsensical: late-Saxon government was at times ferociously oppressive, inflicting blinding, mutilation and branding as punishment, and sending out government snoopers (*exploratores*), who strangely bring to mind Elizabeth's 'thought police', her pursuivants who hunted down Jesuits and miscreants. But the beliefs of the seventeenth-century radicals about the Old English past were not entirely ridiculous. It is true that the English tradition of local representation was derived from pre-Conquest institutions, in particular the shire, hundred and parish, and they did use the vernacular: the law was English. But most particularly, of course, the idea of Englishness and of allegiance to the English state derived from before 1066.

From the Civil War, the myth can be traced as a continuous radical motif down to our own time. Think of Tom Paine's scintillating passages in *Common Sense* ('A French bastard landing with armed banditti and establishing himself King of England, against the consent of the natives, is, in plain terms, a very paltry, rascally original. It certainly has no divinity in it.') and in *The Rights of Man* ('If the succession runs in the line of the Conqueror, the Nation runs in the line of being conquered and ought to rescue itself.') As late as 1911, a pamphlet on the last Liberal government asked, 'Who shall rule: Briton or Norman?' and argued from a series of maps that south-east England, the Tory heartland, is Norman England! As a young journalist, I remember hearing Arthur Scargill, the then firebrand President of the Yorkshire Mineworkers and a well-known left-winger, say the same sort of thing jokingly in a diatribe against Parliament which one could say broadly sympathized with Guy Fawkes.

In popular culture, the tale has lasted much longer. Comics, novels and stories still evoke the Norman Yoke, with plucky free Saxons pitted against regimented Continental despots: William's troops with 'polished leather boots with pointed toes', as Julian Rathbone's latest novel, *The Last Saxon King*, has it. The formula still works in the movies, every time Robin Hood stands up for the rights of the oppressed Saxons against the wicked Sheriff of Nottingham. We could, of course, dismiss it all as a Tudor myth, created in the sixteenth century to justify and underline the break with Rome, an especially potent myth after Henry VIII's reign. Coincidentally, at that time the rediscovery of the Anglo-Saxon world began, with a flood of manuscripts from the dissolution of the monasteries, and with the publishing of Old English works to examine the question of the English Church before 1066. All were used by polemicists, whether Catholic or Protestant, to underline their own interpretation of contemporary history.

This view of the Conquest, coloured by the publication of Anglo-Saxon texts in the Tudor period, became widespread. The growth of literacy in the sixteenth century and the opening of free grammar schools meant the currency of this debate was sold to the educated middle classes as a vision of our history. Hence its appearance in the portfolio of the radicals. Tyndale in the 1530s and Spenser in 1590 attributed every kind of evil to the Norman Conquest. But is it just an antiquarian fable? Could there have been some continuity of these ideas between the eleventh and the seventeenth centuries? Could a folk memory even have survived? What if this idea was not just a literary motif, but had been handed down in the very fibre of English people?

As I remember it, these questions were asked by Christopher Hill in his lectures during the late sixties, but he confessed he couldn't answer them either way. The evidence was simply not available. The research had not been done. At that time, when the ideas of the seventeenth-century radicals were being uncovered, a link might perhaps have seemed unlikely, but the more we know about these things, the more surprising it would be if there was no continuity of ideas. Something which has struck me forcibly during a lifetime of travelling in other cultures, especially in Asia, is the tenacious persistence of oral traditions. A prima facie case, one would think, that the tale of the Norman Yoke may not be merely a Tudor antiquarian controversy, but might perhaps also be the product of an oral tradition transmitted in English over the centuries when English was not the official or literary language: a tradition of a real event.

Going back to the event, there is no question that it was a most terrible time. For a start, the Old English ruling class was decimated. Many were killed in the three battles of 1066, others in the guerrilla warfare, purges and killings which followed. In 1069, the Rising of the North saw Northumbria devastated (the aftermath recorded for all to see in the pages of Domesday Book seventeen years later). There were many dramatic individual cases of resistence, such as the revolt of Hereward the Wake, which culminated in the siege of Ely, the implacable Conqueror driving siege causeways through the fens whose remains are still visible today near the villages of Willingham and Over.

That was only the beginning. Twenty years on, as Domesday Book shows, only two of the 1,400 English tenants-in-chief were left. The ruling class had been removed wholesale. Even more interesting is the evidence now emerging of a stark social divide between Normans and English which persisted for several generations, with the English living as second-class citizens in their own land. A remarkable new study by Katharine Keats-Rohan has shown that the gulf between the one-and-a-half million Anglo-Saxons and the twenty or thirty thousand Normans was far greater than historians had ever suspected. Surprisingly, in the hundred years or so after the Conquest, there was virtually no intermarriage between the Norman aristocracy and the English. In the ten top Norman families there was no intermarriage at all for over two centuries. Among a further 2,000 Norman families, the intermarriage rate was less than 5 per cent for four generations. This stands on its head the old assumption that from the start there was substantial intermarriage between the conquerors and the conquered. In reality, it would appear that the Normans considered themselves to be socially and ethnically superior, and practised a form of social separation which Dr Keats-Rohan considers 'a medieval forerunner of apartheid'. No wonder the 'myth' of the Norman Yoke can be found as early as the late eleventh and twelfth centuries, among chroniclers like William of Malmesbury and Orderic Vitalis, who strangely enough were both of mixed parentage. 'This was a terrible havoc of our most dear country,' Henry Huntingdon wrote, 'five plagues were sent to Britain by God . . . the last was the Normans, who still hold the English in subjection.'

They all wrote within a few decades of the Conquest. What is surprising is to find so many writers saying the same thing at the end of the thirteenth century, two hundred years on, still speaking from the standpoint of the oppressed. Two hundred and fifty years after the Conquest, men like Andrew Horne were persistently railing against the occupiers. So, although the myth is in some sense an antiquarian creation of the sixteenth century, there is no denying that it is a persistent underlying theme in English literature from the Norman period onwards. And one of the most interesting modern discoveries, as the literature of the twelfth to fourteenth centuries comes to light, is how the growth of the sense of Englishness is tied up with the bitter wound of the Conquest.

In the thirteenth century, for example, a constant theme is the sense that England has been subjugated, and that painful and humiliating ethnic divisions, signalled by language, which stemmed from 1066, are still clear:

The Normans could then speak nothing but their own language, and spoke French as they did at home and also taught their children. So that the upper class of the country that is descended from them stick to the language they got from home: therefore unless a person knows French he is little thought of. But the lower class stick to English and their own language even now.

Robert Manning in 1295 is similarly anti-Norman. He talks of the enslavement of his audience brought about by William and his followers, 'who have held the English in subjection ever since'. He sees the present feudal system as a consequence of the Conquest. 'For all this thralldom that now on England is, through Normans it came, bondage and distress.' The tale is clearly so ingrained by now that it is capable of being used as metaphor which can be applied to contemporary history.

We must take this sort of thing with a pinch of salt. Like radical language of any period, including our own, much of the polemic is self-evidently specious and over-simplified. Horne's breakdown of the languages is a simplification of a much more fluid situation. Similarly, though some Norman families evidently liked to boast of their descent from companions of the Conqueror (as they still do!), by Horne's day others liked to point to Saxon heroes in their pedigree. Indeed, by the thirteenth century there is some evidence that among the yeomen class people couldn't tell French from English any longer. By then, perhaps, the wound was fading and the myth beginning to take its place.

The myth was especially useful when economic times were hard, as in the late thirteenth century when boom turned to bust and poor smallholding freemen (who were usually of Old English descent) found themselves in dispute with big lay or Church land-owners, and when feudal lords attempted to reassert their traditional authority and exact ancient dues from a society changing rapidly and fundamentally. To explain their oppression in simple historical terms and to characterize the oppressors as foreigners was obviously an attractive strategy. But the point is that the myth is constant here, and surely a link with our Levelling heroes. There seems at least to be a case for thinking that the Norman Yoke is a continuous literary and folk theme from the eleventh century to the Tudors, continuing on to the radicals in the seventeenth century who picked it up and ran with it. A theme which survived till our own times, one of the most potent English myths.

But the myth was surely a reflection of real events. Modern historians have compared the experience of the Conquest to that of Nazi-occupied Europe. The recurrent message in the sources is a sense of the horror of occupation. When we read in eleventh-century sources of the killing of rebel communities, including their women and children, the analogies suggested are with the 1990s world of ethnic cleansing in Africa or the killing fields of Bosnia and Kosovo. For the English, 1066 was a shattering event − the most cataclysmic in their history − and like many shattering events, the story was handed down as a communal memory. The terrible first decades were etched into the national experience: castles were built in every village, whole areas of towns were demolished to make space for Norman garrisons, and resistance provoked ferocious reprisals. Along with the wholesale removal of the ruling class, even the comfortable old Saxon minsters in the little rural towns (as William of Malmesbury put it) were torn down and replaced by huge Romanesque cathedrals which still stand as memorials to the Norman victory. Of the feelings of the ordinary people we know little. Just the odd note, like the Domesday entry for Marsh Gibbon in Buckinghamshire, where the 1066 freeholder Aelfric now holds his land rented from William, a Norman, wretchedly and with a heavy heart (*graviter et miserabiliter*).

Of course, in the end it would be English – the lower-class language – which would win out. But it took nearly three centuries for Englishness to re-emerge as the national culture: a movement signalled by the revival of English vernacular literature in full power in the fourteenth century – a demonstration of the ability of English to stay underground and metamorphose. Today we are still an English nation, not French.

There's a tailpiece to this story which takes me back to the story of my schooldays brush with Field Marshal Montgomery. Some years ago, I made a film for the BBC about the Norman Conquest, and I decided to explore his ancestor's roots. Roger of Montgomery was one of the conquerors of 1066; he gave his name to a shire and its county town, a name that remains until today. He seemed a fitting symbol of the story, especially in the long relationship of Normandy and Britain. I traced Roger back to an overgrown ring work in dense woods at St Etienne de Montomery in the Camembert region, and I followed him out to the Welsh border where he carved out his vast Marcher lordship in the years after 1066: to Montgomery.

It's a heavenly spot; one of those places where you could almost tell the whole history of the island through one parish. The hill was inhabited in the Iron Age (you can still see the great banks of the fort). From the top there's a wonderful view across the Severn into Powys, and in the evening sunlight you can make out the banks of the big Roman fort beyond the Welshpool–Newtown railway, thrown up in Ostorius Scapula's campaign against Caractacus. Looking the other way, back into England, Offa's Dyke is a mile off, and beyond the dyke you can see the tower of the old minster church at Chirbury, an Anglo-Saxon borough fortified in 915, but one which never really took off: there are still ploughed fields inside the line of defences built by the Lady of the Mercians. The Saxon town and the medieval castles were built there because this is the ancient borderland between the Welsh and the English. It's as clear as day when you look at the place names on the Ordnance Survey map: Rhydwhyman, Fflos and Caerhowel on the Severn side of town; to the east, Winsbury Marrington and

Church Stoke. And all along this border are the overgrown mottes left by the Norman conquerors. Dudston and Gwarthlow, Touchill and Brompton are all within four miles of Montgomery, part of the forward line covering the great border castles at Bishops Castle and Clun, on the ancient tradeways into Wales.

Montgomery itself is a neat, planned town of the twelfth century. It suffered Border raids through the Middle Ages, but for the most part must have been a delightful place in which to live. In the sixteenth century, the castle was the home of Magdalen Herbert, mother of the poets George and Edward. Her friend John Donne wrote 'The Primrose' here (and you can understand why, when you see the fields below Town Hill blooming in the spring).

The big stone castle still stands over the town. From there, you can look across the Severn into Wales, and in the middle distance, under a great clump of trees, you can make out the mound of the first Norman castle built by Roger, which has been identified as a place called Hen Domen by an old sunken way which crossed the Severn at Rhydwhyman. Excavations here by Phil Barker over the last twenty years are still the only detailed examination of a motte and bailey made anywhere in Britain or Europe. And they have provided us with the most detailed archaeological picture available of what it was actually *like* when the Normans came.

Phil is retired now, but the image I hold is of him out on Hen Domen hill in green wellington boots. A tall, rangy figure, with a mane of snow-white hair and the sunbeaten face of a field archaeologist who's spent most of his time in the open air through the summer digging seasons. Twinkly eyed and sceptical, he refuses to be drawn into speculations beyond what the facts allow:

'Inside was crammed with buildings. We found fifty in one half of the bailey: granaries, chapel, hall with hearth, stables. Many were two storey, all built with massive timbers. Each castle used a vast amount of wood. They will have felled the forest all around: press-ganging local labour to work for the army engineers and carpenters . . . the fill for the buildings' walls was planks and thick clay.'

The interior of the bailey was about a hundred yards across:

partly filled with the dig hut and the team's tents, which helped one imagine the scene of long ago:

'Don't imagine you could stand inside like this and see the view like some colonial on the terrace watching the sun go down over Wales with a gin and tonic in your hand. Round you were two-tiered defences, with a fighting platform probably seven feet high, which had rooms underneath, then a palisade above it, so the wall was at least fourteen feet high, standing over a bank and deep ditch. The impression I get from excavating it is quite claustrophobic.'

We crashed through brambles down into the ditch, which was still ten feet deep, and then clambered up the steep bank of the outer bailey. It was a lovely scene: the woods, dense thickets down the outer slopes, the thick grass covered with bluebells and cowslips. 'You have to think all of this away . . . you wouldn't have had any of this beautiful sylvan landscape. They were experts in scorched earth. After all, these were the people who left the whole of Northumbria wasted and famine stricken. They wouldn't have left a tree within a mile. They would have cut everything down to use for building materials, for firewood, and to prevent any Welshman finding cover. You have to imagine a raw castle; bare earth, bare timber . . . in a completely blitzed landscape.'

I asked Phil, having lived with the place all this time, what he felt he knew of the people who built it.

'For the archaeologist, this is a building designed to fulfil a function: and that function was oppression, pure and simple. Every Norman landowner had a place like this and armed men in his service – mercenaries, retainers – paid for from the proceeds of conquest. A tiny place like this was part of a pyramid of domination to keep people in the neighbourhood in check and to make sure you held on to what you'd got . . . to judge by this one place, it must have been a grip of iron.'

That night, the team lit a camp-fire by the tents and, after food, we sat round to mull over the significance of this one castle among the hundreds built across Britain. Front-line places – at first the front line was everywhere, though the borders were the most keenly fought.

'I'd say the people here lived a very hard life, and they must have been very hard people: tough, ruthless men, like a bunch of SAS who lived just to fight and conquer. Any resistance was punished by murderous reprisals against the civilian population. You know what it says in the *Anglo-Saxon Chronicle*: "they oppressed the poor people by building castles everywhere". In the ravaging of the North they systematically devastated the farmlands of Northumbria as a reprisal – so that they would never oppose Norman rule again. Simeon of Durham says that people had to sell their own children into slavery. They were left to eat rats and grass . . .'

Phil stared into the fire. He was a man used to dealing with facts, not wild theories. His revolutionary book was about the techniques of the new archaeology, a bible about soil patterns, resistivity, deciphering strata. He was not the sort to build Camelot out of a few Dark Age post holes. But his finds, I felt, cut through the myth to real events: the piles of nails, the sling shots and arrow heads; the stock of rusting spear heads, the forges with black pits of ash and charcoal. I felt I'd finally touched Ulric the Saxon and his world . . .

'We'll never know what would have been if the Conquest had never happened. Norman influence was already strong before the Conquest, and probably in the next century England would still have become part of European Gothic civilization. England, after all, always drew on Continental civilization to fertilize its own. Its most creative periods – in the eighth century, the tenth century, the twelfth-century Renaissance, the Tudors, the Enlightenment, and now – were ones where the exchanges with the Continent were most fruitful.'

'So what about the idea that only the Normans made England's greatness?'

He threw another log on the fire. 'Well, you can't go back in history. It happened. There was a high civilization in Anglo-Saxon England: beautiful, archaic and idiosyncratic. Think of the Winchester school of painting, the embroideries – of which the Bayeux Tapestry was the last, by the way. Close your eyes and listen to Anglo-Saxon Church music. I mean, it's English, isn't it? It couldn't

be from anywhere else. And no doubt a strong oppressive government was put on this little country. People read these things in
their own way. Some think that's a very good thing indeed. But
not everybody.'

He grinned. 'It was the last time the island was conquered. The
English always say that, don't they? It was that which enabled our
institutions to develop with a continuity never allowed to most
other cultures. You have to say that it probably did contribute to
our greatness. What emerged was the product of both English and
French: just look at Shakespeare's language if you want proof of
that. So, sure, it made us what we are.'

He shook his head. 'But I don't think we ever forgot.'

In the firelight, I thought I saw the ghost of Ulric the Saxon
smile.

2. King Arthur: Lost Again?

The long-awaited sign came at last in the summer of 1998. An ancient stone bearing a sixth-century inscription was unearthed at Tintagel, 'the mythical birthplace of the legendary king'. Broken up to use as a drain cover outside a sixth- or seventh-century building, the inscription had been cut in an informal Latin script. The spokesman for English Heritage who announced the discovery called it 'the find of a lifetime', which, he said, added 'a new dimension to there having been a real Arthur'. In the popular press and on the main TV bulletins, there were no ifs and buts – King Arthur had finally been tracked down. The BBC newsreader announced: 'The discovery could prove that King Arthur had his headquarters at the site of the ruined castle on the coast of north Cornwall.' A pundit confirmed the general opinion at the end of the 1990s – that Arthur had indeed existed in the late Roman Empire, fighting back hordes of Anglo-Saxons: 'As a historical figure Arthur almost certainly did exist, a successful soldier fighting battles across the country in the sixth century.'

The inscription itself is small and broken, in Roman lettering and in the Latin language. It says simply: 'Artognou, father of a descendant of Coll, has had [this] constructed' (presumably referring to a lost building rather than the drain which it ended up covering – it would, after all, be a bit of a let down to find our hero had really been a Dark Age sewerage inspector). Clearly this was a person of status; though not, it would seem, a king. His name, however, is a problem. There were many names in Celtic Late Antiquity with the first element of *Art-* ('Bear'), and this one, Artognou, is one of them. But it is not Arthur. If we would find a historical Arthur, we ought to get the name right. But the remarkable reaction in the press, and on radio and TV – almost willing it to be true – set me thinking again about the origins of the legend. Did Arthur really exist? Did the story really originate in the battles between Britons and Saxons, as is accepted these days? Is the south-west the real location of Arthur's fabled court at Camelot? And why did the British – and the English – need him?

The legend was already fixed in the popular imagination soon after the Norman Conquest. In 1113, some priests from Laon in northern France came on a fund-raising trip to Britain (their church had burned down the previous year). Their journey took them across southern England into Devon and Cornwall, and in many places they were proudly shown Arthurian relics – 'Arthur's Oven', 'Arthur's Seat' – and not just by literary types, but by the common people who crowded round them as they displayed their holy relics in market squares and offered cures and blessings in exchange for ready cash. 'You see,' said one Devonian, in an uncanny foretaste of the English Heritage spokesperson, 'this is Arthur country . . .'

When they reached Bodmin, a strange incident took place. In the borough square in front of St Petroc's church, the subject of King Arthur came up. The locals told the French priests in no uncertain terms that King Arthur was not dead but 'would return, and Britain would rise again'. One imagines the Laon monks were learned Frenchmen of the twelfth-century Enlightenment, and perhaps also shared the distaste of their upper-class countrymen for English peasants; at any rate they sneered at such stories. 'Arthur not dead? Come, come, my good fellows . . . that's just a fairy tale . . .' The irate locals erupted. When the Frenchmen refused to back down, vegetables were thrown, blows followed, and a full-blown riot was narrowly averted.

If nothing else, our tale proves that Arthur was by then a big story in southern Britain. He was already rooted in folklore; his name applied to natural features like 'Arthur's Oven', the Iron Age cromlech on Bodmin Moor. Welsh nationalists in the previous century had already spoken of Arthur in much the same terms as the good people of Bodmin, also claiming the king would one day return. At roughly the same time as the Laon visit, according to the chronicler Wace, 'marvellous stories of King Arthur have been noised about this mighty realm so far and wide that the truth has turned to fable and idle song (though such songs are neither sheer bare lies nor gospel truths)'. That was the literary judgement, but the Laon story shows us the tale gripped the common people, too.

Soon afterwards came Geoffrey of Monmouth, with the literary smash of the High Middle Ages, the *History of the Kings of Britain*. In his account, Arthur is a hero who bestrides Europe like a colossus; a Napoleon of the Dark Ages. This version, Geoffrey says (it has always been assumed with his tongue firmly in his cheek), is based on a lost manuscript, a secret history of the kings of the Britons which he alone has been able to examine.

These were not mere antiquarian issues. Geoffrey's Welsh nation-alist Arthur came at a sensitive political moment: the Welsh revolts of the 1130s had used Arthurian rhetoric, with their insistent claim that 'Britain would rise again . . .' It is hardly surprising, then, that in this climate, given Arthur's rapidly growing status as folk hero, tourist draw and political rallying cry, the establishment should try to dig him up, to hit at least two birds with one stone: prove him dead and reinvent him as a tourist event — a rather post-modern project in its way. All these ideas played their part in 1191 in the 'discovery' of Arthur's tomb at Glastonbury, one of our earliest recorded 'archaeological digs'.

Abbot Henry ordered the monks to dig on the edge of the monks' cemetery between two stone crosses bearing the names of Old English abbots. Why he chose exactly this spot is not known, but the chronicler Gerald of Wales says that the place had been revealed 'by strange and miraculous signs': monks had had nocturnal visions. There were even stories that King Henry II himself had ordered the exhumation, having apparently acquired secret information from 'an ancient Welsh bard, a singer of the past' (who said that they would find the body at least sixteen feet beneath the earth, not in a tomb of stone but in a hollow oak. 'And the reason why the body was placed so deep and hidden away is this: that it might never be discovered by the Saxons, who occupied the island after his death, whom he had so often in his life defeated and almost utterly destroyed.')

They cleared the ground and dug. And sure enough, deep down, in a hollowed oak, they found the body of a big man and the bones of a woman with him, and a lead cross: 'Here lies buried the renowned King Arthur, with Guinevere his second wife, in the Isle of Avalon.'

This is the earliest identification of Glastonbury with Geoffrey of Monmouth's Avalon. The cross has since disappeared. It was illustrated by the antiquarian Camden in 1695: judging by his engraving, it could be of the tenth or the twelfth century. Modern re-excavation of the area located the hole dug in 1191, and the remains of slab-lined graves (two or three of them) at the bottom were dated from the seventh century, two centuries later than the supposed time of King Arthur. The cemetery level had been artificially raised in the tenth century. That's as much as we know.

The discovery of the grave in 1191 took place, coincidentally or not, after a fire had badly damaged the fabric of the monastery: as businessmen, medieval abbots were nothing if not pragmatic. The restoration fund needed a big boost and finding the king's burial place at Glastonbury provided it. Proving he actually was dead at the same time may have been an intended political spin-off. But it had no effect on the spread of Arthur's cult, which was really all-pervasive from the late twelfth century onwards: a Welsh myth appropriated first by the English, then much more comprehensively by the Normans as they extended their rule over the British Isles. By the thirteenth century, Arthur had become a pan-British hero. Sites associated with him were found from Scotland to Cornwall, and the poems known as the Welsh triads asserted that he had held his courts in Cornwall, Wales *and* Scotland. Arthur had become the greatest British hero, and his tale would soon spread across Europe.

Ever since then, Arthur has been the inspiration for thousands of texts, including the great medieval romances of Chrétien de Troyes and Thomas Mallory, and the ethereal, doom-laden epics of Tennyson and the pre-Raphaelites. The myth has lost none of its appeal (and power) in modern literature, film and popular culture. It is an academic industry: the *Bulletin of the Arthurian Society* (a society which has branches as far away as Japan) is now in its fiftieth year. It lists 6–700 publications in each of its annuals, and that is only the academic end of the market. There are Arthur films from Disney and Bresson to Indiana Jones, not forgetting a memorable Monty Python ('Strange women lying in ponds distributing swords is no basis for a system of government!'). The vast number of novels about Arthur shows no sign of drying up. Bernard Cornwell is only the latest to top the best-sellers. And this is not to mention the flood of publications of an ecological and spiritual bent which connect with the Arthurian theme.

At the other end of the literary scale, serious scholars of the Dark Ages and archaeologists have now produced detailed reconstructions of the 'Age of Arthur', attempting to place him in a real history. This all began in the fifties with Geoffrey Ashe's *King Arthur's Avalon* and his later *Camelot and the Vision of Albion* and *The Quest for Arthur's Britain*. The theories written up in these books were filled out by professional academics like Leslie Alcock, head of the 'Camelot excavation committee' which excavated the South Cadbury hill-fort in Somerset. And all were outdone by the work of John Morris, who offered nothing less than a reconstruction of the whole Age of Arthur and the politics of the Arthurian empire. It is in this context that we have to place the 1998 furore over the find at Tintagel of the 'Artognou' inscription.

Meanwhile, though, there were others in the academic world who were moving in the opposite direction, cautiously attempting in small-scale discrete articles to revalue the sources for Arthur. They came up with very different results. When I made a film on the Arthur question in 1980, a small contribution to the controversy, I was guided by their minimalist approach. Looking simply at the primary sources for the fabled king, somewhat to my own surprise, I must confess, our film concluded that none of the earliest sources allowed a historical Arthur. Needless to say, this gave us our biggest postbag. Of the 3,000 letters we received, most were irate letters from Arthur enthusiasts and believers, claiming to know the location of his battle sites and even his burial place, not to mention the current resting place of the Holy Grail. There were comments in the press too: I was sent up in *Private Eye*, and taken to task on the editorial page of the *Daily Telegraph*, where Christopher Booker complained at such a nitpicking approach: who was Mr Wood to demolish our most cherished myths, which were much needed in the declining years of modern Britain, in the days when the cold heart and iron hand of Mrs T. were steering the helm of Albion? Geoffrey Ashe, the doyen of Arthurian writers, who had staked his name on the historicity of the sources, also replied, in *The Discovery of King Arthur*. He complained that as a way of judging the historicity of Arthur, my kind of source-criticism was 'ill-conceived', but he conceded nevertheless that on a strict reading of the evidence, we are forced to abandon all the key texts on which the modern picture of a historical Arthur has been built. 'Wood had a case,' he wrote, 'and I am indebted to him for prompting a reappraisal of the whole topic, leading me to a fresh conception which, I believe, in principal is the answer.' In a surprising *coup de main*, Ashe then abandoned the so-called historical sources and went back to the old trickster Geoffrey of Monmouth's famous lost book. Geoffrey really had a genuine source for the fifth century A D, he argued – and Arthur was in it.

But the idea that there is an 'answer' to the question at all is precisely the problem. If a figure only appears in sources centuries after his presumed day, and then in a semi-legendary guise, how can we justify taking him back into the real history of the earlier time when we have no evidence for it? The questions remain the same. Did Arthur exist? If so, when was he? I have already nailed my colours to the mast of the small skiff of Arthur sceptics; nothing has happened since to change my view that Arthur is fiction, not history. Except an interesting little discovery, which is the chief subject of this chapter. First, though, a brief résumé of the earliest sources for the Arthur story . . .

These sources are still used by all Arthur fans, Avalonians, Holy Grailers, believers and sceptics – and scholars too. The question, as so often in history, is one of interpretation; and in this field more than most, interpretation tends to veer sharply to one side or the other, to what one might call the maximum or the minimum.

The sources are still what they always were. There are only three of them. Earliest as it stands is Nennius' *History of the Britons*. This famous text was composed around 829. Nennius wrote it as a riposte to the patronizing attitude of the English towards Welsh history, and mixed history and myth with abandon: 'I made a heap of all I could find,' he says of his method. No early manucript of Nennius survives. The best text was in an eleventh-century manuscript in Chartres, which unfortunately was totally destroyed in 1944 when the Germans bombarded the town, but from photographs one can see that the manuscript was copied from an earlier Welsh exemplar. The date of the events Nennius describes appears to be the late fifth century A D, during the period when Germanic warrior bands were sailing across the North Sea to harry the people of the former Roman province of Britain:

On Hengest's death his son Octha came down from the north of Britain to the kingdom of the Kentishmen. Then in those days Arthur fought against them with the kings of the Britons, but he was commander in the battles.

This is apparently the earliest mention we have in any source of Arthur. Nennius goes on to give a list of Arthur's twelve battles, which scholars think was culled from a bardic poem about the hero's deeds: a battle at the mouth of the river *Glein*; four battles on a river *Dubglas* in the region of *Linnuis*; a sixth battle on a river called *Bassas*; a seventh in the 'Caledonian forest'; further battles were fought at *Guinnion* fort; the 'City of the Legion'; at the river *Tribruit*; on a hill called *Agned*; and the twelfth at a place called *Badon* (which Nennius elsewhere identifies with the hot springs at Bath). The location of these battles has been, and is, hotly argued, and they have been placed all over Britain. Some, though, are clearly in the north: the Caledonian forest and Fort Guinnion among them.

For two of the battles, Nennius adds further details. At the eighth battle, at Guinnion fort, 'Arthur carried the image of the holy Mary, the everlasting virgin on his shield, and the heathen were put to flight on that day and there was a great slaughter made on them through the power of Our Lord Jesus Christ and the power of the holy Virgin Mary his mother . . .' At the twelfth battle, Badon Hill, 'nine hundred and sixty men fell in one day, from a single charge of Arthur's, and no one laid them low save he alone, and he was victorious in all his campaigns'.

A slightly different version of Nennius survives in a Vatican manuscript. It uses a later ninth-century Welsh edition, but the text as we have it was written in England in 945. This adds a small detail, shown here in italics, to the original:

Then the warrior Arthur, with the soldiers and the kings of Britain, used to fight against them [i.e., the Saxons]. And *though there were many of more noble birth than he*, he was twelve times leader in war and victor of the battles.

At the end of the original text, the author goes on to talk about the natural marvels of Britain, and identifies some places associated with Arthur in folklore, which suggests that Arthur was already by then viewed as a folk hero. So it is safe to conclude from Nennius that by the ninth century Arthur was already famous, and the subject of song. Though that does not, of course, prove he was a real person.

The second source for Arthur is *The Annals of Wales*, which are older than Nennius in origin, incorporating some genuine notes from the fifth and sixth centuries. But the text as it stands survives in a manuscript dating from the twelfth century, which in turn is a copy of a compilation made in South Wales only in 955. In it there are two references to Arthur, which, it should be remembered, cannot safely be taken back before the mid tenth century. The references are as follows:

516 – The battle of Badon, in which Arthur carried the cross of our Lord Jesus Christ for three days and nights on his shoulders and the Britons were the victors.

537 – The fight at Camlann, in which Arthur and Medraut fell; and there was plague in Britain and Ireland.

The next entry '547 – A great mortality' (i.e., plague) probably refers to the great plague which swept the Roman Empire in the 540s and which is known from historians such as Procopius. The original annals would have been written in Latin. However, the story about Arthur bearing the cross on his back (or perhaps on his shield), which is paralleled in Nennius, sounds as if it was taken from a poetic source in Welsh. It doesn't fit with the otherwise very brief notes in the annals, and most scholars think it was probably added later. The set of annals was originally laconic in the extreme and may have simply noted the fact of Badon and possibly the Camlann battle, though interestingly that entry, too, uses a Welsh word, suggesting it is a later interpolation.

The third and last source on Arthur is the *Gododdin*, a wonderful poem composed in the Cumbrian area in the sixth century. It concerns an ill-fated and ultimately tragic attack on Catraeth (Catterick), in which 300 British heroes died. Among the heroes, one is praised for his bravery, 'though he was no Arthur'. If we could prove this line was written in the sixth century, then obviously we would have an important pointer to the early date of the Arthur story, but unfortunately this phrase is not in early versions of the poem and was clearly added at a much later date: probably in the ninth century.

Not much to go on then: on close inspection we appear to lack any primary source for our hero. So how did the idea of a historical Arthur come about? The vexed question of the historicity of Arthur already exercised John Leland in the 1530s, but was seriously mooted only in the late nineteenth century, at a time of great interest in the Arthur myth, as we can see from Tennyson and his Victorian contemporaries, and artists like Burne Jones and Dante Rossetti. This was the time of the rise of scientific archaeology. In Greece and Turkey, Heinrich Schliemann had shown that myths could, in some sense, be 'true': that the places named by Homer, for example, were indeed important places in the Bronze Age. Troy had really existed. It appeared that this was what archaeology could do, and in Britain the hope arose that it might be possible to fix Arthur in place and time.

The key was the connection made in both Nennius and the
Annals between Arthur and the Battle of Badon. For this was
unquestionably a real battle. It was fought at the end of the fifth
century A D, when Anglo-Saxon barbarians were attacking the
former Roman province of Britain, and when a number of battles
took place between Saxons and Britons in the south-west. This
surely (it was thought) was the context of Arthur. Badon was a hill,
perhaps in the Bath region, and most likely an old Iron Age hill-fort
like those at Barbury Castle and Old Sarum in Wiltshire and Dyrham
in Gloucestershire, where other battles of the time had taken place.
If Arthur existed, then on the basis of *The Annals of Wales* and
Nennius, historians looked to put him into this real history of the
late fifth or early sixth century. Surprisingly, if he was a deadly
enemy of the invading Angles and Saxons, he is not mentioned
anywhere in the *Anglo-Saxon Chronicle*, but that is not as serious as
it might appear: the *Chronicle* was written much later, and has the
barest notes for this period, naming few Celtic leaders. What was
needed to construct this 'real' history of Arthur was a contemporary
source for the period around 500. And, as it happens, there is one:
our only primary narrative source, and one of the most important
sources in all British history: Gildas' *On the Ruin of Britain*.

Gildas probably wrote in the 540s, though possibly a decade or
two earlier. He was perhaps from Strat Clut (Strathclyde). To
writers from later generations, such as Bede and William of Malmesbury, Gildas was simply the 'Historian of the Britons'. We know
next to nothing about him. He was later celebrated as a saint, but
he may not have been a monk – more likely he was a professional
rhetorician, a native speaker of both Latin and Welsh. His book is
the only such source to have survived. How it managed to get into
the monastic libraries of the medieval period is a very interesting
question: most late-Roman texts which have come down to us
came from Rome. Gildas' text was probably obtained from a Welsh
monastery, early enough in the Old English period to be used by
Bede around A D 700.

Gildas was not writing a history of his times, but a political tract,
a scathing attack on the rulers of his time, especially the kings of

south-west Britain, whom he saw as a bad lot bar none. He succeeded so well that he was imitated by preachers long afterwards, whenever they needed a template for a vision of a nation ruined by the corruption of its leaders and people: at the time of the Vikings in the eighth century, for example; in Ethelred's day around 1000; and even after the Norman Conquest. Gildas' story is told in an intensely dramatic, polemical style, and he adds to the feeling of intensity by frequent sermonizing. This denunciation of one of the 'tyrants' of the mid sixth century gives a flavour:

What are you doing, Aurelius Caninus? . . . Are you not engulfed by the same slime, if not a more deadly one, made up of parricides, fornications, adulteries? . . . Do you not hate peace in our country as if it were some noxious snake? . . . Why are you senseless and stiff, like a leopard in your behaviour, and spotted with wickedness? Your head is already whitening, as you sit upon a throne that is full of guiles and stained from top to bottom with diverse murders and adulteries, the bad son of a good king . . .

As the background to his attack, Gildas describes the fall of Roman Britain, looking back over a hundred years before his birth. It's our most important narrative for this critical time. After the Romans under Honorius refuse further aid to the province, as Gildas tells it, order breaks down and the situation begins to resemble a modern decolonization. After foreign invasions, the cities are abandoned and Hadrian's Wall ceases to be garrisoned. Then civil war breaks out, exacerbated by famine. Around 450, an appeal by the ruling class to the Roman consul Aetius fails. More famine and desperate warfare follow, before a period of about twenty-five years of relative peace and abundance. But this was the calm before the real storm. During this time, renewed barbarian attacks lead to stasis at home: a 'proud tyrant' (elsewhere identified as Vortigern) takes control. According to Gildas (and we are now probably in the 480s), it was the tyrant who took the fateful step of inviting Saxons as mercenaries in the north-east to repel Pictish marauders. This they do successfully, but more come after them in the hope of richer pickings, and in the end the federates rebel. War now rages across the island as far as the Irish Sea; urban life is destroyed, and the land is devastated from east to west. Then, at this desperate moment, comes the hour, comes the man. Gildas tells of the British fight back in a very famous passage which appears in all the Arthurian literature. In modern editions it begins in Chapter 25; the date is probably in the 490s:

After some time passed, when the cruel plunderers [i.e., the Saxons] had gone home, God gave strength to the survivors [i.e., the Britons fighting the Anglo-Saxon invaders]. Wretched people fled to them from all directions . . . and begged that they should not be altogether destroyed, their leader Ambrosius Aurelianus, a gentleman who, perhaps alone of the Romans, had survived the shock of this notable storm: certainly his parents, who had worn the purple, were killed in it. His descendants in our day have become greatly inferior to their grandfather's excellence. Under him our people regained their strength and challenged the victors to battle; with God's will they won the victory.

CHAPTER 26

From that time now our countrymen won, then the enemies, so that in this people the Lord could make trial (as he does) of this latter-day Israel to see whether it loves him or not. This lasted right up to the year of the siege of Badon Hill, pretty well the last defeat of the hated ones, and certainly not the least. That was the year of my birth; as I know, one month of the forty-fourth year since then has already passed.

It is a fantastically suggestive passage, but also frustratingly obtuse, riddled with ambiguity. Even the apparent precision of the dating seems on close inspection to be capable of many different interpretations, though most scholars today place Badon around AD 500. Certainly, though, the passage has the ring of a contemporary narrative, revealing all sorts of things by implication that only a contemporary would know. The role of Ambrosius' family is a case in point. But there are major problems with it: in particular, how much time is covered by the narrative? Obviously some time passes, but some would argue only a few (perhaps five) years.

There are few more important narrative passages in British history, but how can we be sure, over this long gap of time, that this is what Gildas actually said? Gildas wrote in the mid sixth century and his text was available to Bede in the early 700s. But our earliest testimony for it is a tenth-century manuscript, now in the British Library, where it has the shelf-mark Cotton MS Vitellius A vi (the book came from the seventeenth-century collection of Sir Robert Cotton, whose shelves were topped with busts of the Roman emperors, hence this was the sixth book on the top shelf under the bust of the Emperor Vitellius). So the book was written some four hundred years after Gildas' original text. Moreover, this is the exemplar of all later manuscripts, which are twelfth century or later. Unfortunately, the manuscript was badly damaged when Cotton's library was destroyed by fire in 1731, a fire that robbed us of many crucial texts for early English history, including Asser's *Life of King Alfred*. So all the modern versions of Gildas are based on a text derived from later copies, and from the two editions made in Tudor times, whose editors had the chance to view the manuscript before it was burned. As with many other stories in this book, our knowledge of key events in the British past hinges on a destroyed or lost text.

Luckily, a catalogue of Cotton's library was published in 1696. It tells us that the book had seventy-two folios, and contained these items: (1) A Hymn to the Virgin Mary; (2) Gildas; (3) A Hymn to St Theodore Archbishop of Canterbury and Abbot Hadrian; (4) A Hymn to St Augustine of Canterbury, which was at the end of the book. All the hymns, we are told, were inscribed with musical notations, and the subject matter of the hymns shows us that the text was copied in Canterbury, the oldest English foundation. This suggests that the text from which it was copied was also in Kent at that time.

In the manuscript room of the British Library it is still possible to inspect the remains. The book is inside a slipcase, in a modern leather binding; it is terribly burned. All the pages are mounted separately now: thirty-seven survive, most illegible, shrunk, shrivelled and split; some blackened and water-stained. The book was quarto size, the page size nearly six inches by eight; but some surviving folios are now shrivelled to half that. It's a sad spectacle, but in the middle one or two pages survive to show a very beautiful regular square minuscule of the mid tenth century, with a full array of punctuation, abbreviation and accent marks. An interesting feature of the manuscript which immediately catches the eye is that it has no chapter headings and divisions, so the modern division into chapters would appear to have no early authority. Obviously, there is no guarantee that the scribe who recorded our text handed it down absolutely accurately from his exemplar, but he was a good scribe, and this was a good manuscript. It is the best we have and there is no alternative but to accept its testimony.

Now by an extraordinarily lucky chance, our Arthurian crux, the section translated above from the introduction of Ambrosius to the Battle of Badon, has survived in an almost legible state. Five lines at the bottom of folio eight (verso), and parts of nine lines at the top of folio nine are still legible with the help of a magnifying glass and by viewing the page against the light. What they contain will, I think, be of interest to any reader on the Arthurian question, even with no knowledge of Latin, so I have transcribed exactly what I can see on these pages. In italics are the destroyed parts of the text which are no longer legible and which I have supplemented from the standard modern edition; I have also expanded the abbreviations. At this distance in time, this is probably as near as we can hope to get to what Gildas actually wrote:

(British Library Cotton MS Vitellius A vi folio 8 verso: bottom of page)

16 internicionem usque dele*rentur duce* ambrosio
   aureliano uiro modesto *qui solus* forte
   romanae gentis tantae *tempestatis* collisio
   ne occisis. in eadem parentibus p*urp*ura
20 nimirum indutis superfue*rat cuius nunc* tem

(folio 9 recto: top of page)

1   poribus nostris suboles magnopere auita bonitate
    degenerauit; Uires capessunt uictores prouo
    cantes ad proelium quis uictoria domino annuen
    te cessit; ex eo tempore nunc ciues nunc
5   hostes uincebant ut in ista gente experiretur
    dominus solito more praesentem is*raelem utrum*
    diligat *eum an non; usque ad annum obsession*is ba
    donici montis

Literal translation:

16 not be altogether destroyed, led by ambrosius
    aurelianus, a gentleman who alone perhaps
    of a Roman noble family the shock of such a storm
    (though certainly killed in it his parents were who the purple
20 had worn) had survived; whose descendants

1   in our own day from the excellence of their ancestor a long way
    have degenerated; our people regained their strength; the victors
    challenged to battle, to whom the victory god willing
    was given; from that time now our citizens now
5   the enemy won, so that in this people could make trial
    the Lord, as he does, of this latter-day Israel to see
    if it loves him or not; up to the year of the siege of
    Badon Hill (this lasted . . .)

Looking at the Latin text, the crucial thing here is not only the words, which survive in later copies. It is the punctuation and layout which are critical, and they are rather difficult to convey in translation because the punctuation system in early medieval manuscripts is markedly different from our own. Quiet reading was not unknown at that time, but books were also intended to be read out loud (an English writer speaks of having '*heard* the tearful passion of Boethius' in King Alfred's translation). And hence the system of punctuation marks related to the act of reading out loud. Marks were used to denote short and medium pauses and ends of sentences: a low point or comma for a short pause, a medial point (our semicolon) for a middle pause, and a high point (period) for the end of the sentence. These were not hard-and-fast rules: across the Christian Latin world they changed according to time and place, and only a detailed study of the remains of Vitellius A vi will confirm all the scribe's habits. However, the general impression, I think, is plain: the first semicolon on line 2, for example, is clear with a fine stroke down using the end of the quill; as for the crucial semicolon on line 4, only the bottom comma is definitely visible with a fine stroke down: but it can only be either a comma or semicolon. This may seem like nit-picking, but it has an important consequence which will be of some interest to Arthur watchers. Not only is there is no authority for a new beginning of chapter at *ex eo tempore* (line 4), but the punctuation suggests only a short or medium pause for breath. The passage up to the battle of Badon should therefore be part of the description of the wars of Ambrosius.

I have taken an inordinate amount of time over this passage, but it will be obvious that it is crucial to those who postulate a historical Arthur who won the battle of Badon. The key figure here, leader of the war against the Saxons, is Ambrosius. Gildas tells us he was of an important Roman *gens*, a noble family, people who had 'worn the purple'; perhaps this is merely honorific, but he may really mean what he says. Ambrosius and his family are not known from any other early historical source, but some memory of their exploits came down to Nennius, who mentions their conflict with the tyrant Vortigern, and a battle with an otherwise unknown Vitalinus at Guoloph (possibly Wallop in Hampshire).

So, according to Gildas, it is Ambrosius who is the key historical figure in the wars of the late fifth century. In this light, therefore, it is perhaps worth noting that one of the Iron Age hill-forts in southern Britain which was reoccupied in the Late Roman period was later known as the 'fortress of Ambrosius'. This is Amesbury in Wiltshire, in Old English *Ambresburh*. The name is first recorded in the ninth century, and as late as the fifteenth century the town was still described as the *burgus Ambrosii*. The fort is situated at the point where the Avon is crossed by a very ancient route from London to the south-west, now the A303. Amesbury evidently fell into the hands of the West Saxon dynasty in the mid sixth century and remained part of the ancient core of the royal demesne of the kings of Wessex and England. It was gifted in the will of King Alfred the Great (899), and again by King Eadred (946), and was later in the hands of the widow of King Edgar (979). Tenth-century kings held Christmas courts there. It was still in royal hands in the 1140s, but from then on the estate became dispersed.

But the history of Amesbury goes much further back. The parish of Amesbury contains the most remarkable collection of Bronze Age monuments in Britain, among them Stonehenge: the greatest of all monuments to the power of the prehistoric rulers of southern Britain. Stonehenge was built and developed over two millennia (3100–1100 BC) by such rulers; perhaps, then, it is no coincidence that the Iron Age fort associated with the leader of the British in the fifth century should be adjacent to Stonehenge. There is no evidence yet that the fort was occupied late in the fifth century, but as it is still largely unexcavated, this is not surprising. But in the early 1990s at Butterfield Down, only a mile east of the town, a Romano-British settlement of at least fifteen acres, and possibly larger, was excavated, revealing a hoard of 1,000 late-Roman coins, including eight in gold from AD 405. One might guess that the estate belonged to the rulers of the region for centuries before the Anglo-Saxons, and that the legend of Ambrosius and his connection with the place has a basis in fact. Driving past it on the A303 to Somerset, one goes through what is even today a great belt of Crown land west of the Avon, where the Army trains, and I have often wondered if this might be a case where the continuity of government property could be traceable from pre-Roman times. At any rate, I think it more likely that it is at Amesbury, rather than at Camelot, that the real history of the fifth-century war of resistence is waiting to be discovered.

But if Ambrosius was the leader in the war, then where does that leave Arthur? If Arthur won twelve battles which climaxed at

Badon Hill, if he bore the cross on his back and killed hordes of pagans, then it is more than strange that he is not mentioned in Gildas' account of the battle. Indeed, to judge by the text which we have recovered from the burned manuscript, Gildas viewed Badon as the climax of the fightback led by Ambrosius. It is not, I suppose, impossible that Arthur could have been a general under Ambrosius (the later alteration to Nennius, that many were 'better born than he', sounds very much like a specific response to Gildas' remarks about Ambrosius' family having worn the purple), but the importance of Badon to Gildas makes it surprising that if a leader other than Ambrosius had won the battle, he should fail to note the fact. Especially a leader as heroic as legend later portrays Arthur.

No source before the ninth century mentions Arthur, and none then in a form or context which can safely be taken as historical. Our one contemporary source from the sixth century, Gildas, does not refer to Arthur, and tells us that the British leader in the battles of the late fifth century was called Ambrosius, not Arthur. The case for a fifth- or sixth-century Arthur, then, falls apart.

Arthur, I take it, is a mythical character, like the sleeping hero of Irish legend: the focus of the revanchist hopes of British 'fellow citizens', the cymry, whom the English have ever since called Welsh (*weallisc*: 'servile ones', 'down and outs'). Stories involving other mythical characters may have become attached to his name in the eighth and ninth centuries, as the English pushed west. By the tenth century, Arthur was certainly a figure of legend, although the creation of the Arthur we know and love is Norman and post-Norman, the collective work of Geoffrey of Monmouth, Chrétien de Troyes, Mallory and the rest, leading on to Tennyson and Hollywood.

I must confess, though, to a last, lingering doubt. Why *Arthur*? Why did legend choose that name? Was there a historical personage named Arthur, even if not the one we have become used to in recent years, not the victor of Badon and the rest? Many have wondered, and it is perhaps worth a moment's playful speculation. In 1925, Kemp Malone first suggested as a model one Lucius Artorius, a Roman centurion of the late second – early third century, who led two legions from Britain against the people of Armorica (Britanny). At least this man has the right name, but that is all he shares with our hero, save an expedition to the Continent which appears in post-Geoffrey tales, but not in earlier sources. It is perhaps not totally inconceivable that tales or ballads might have gathered around such a figure, but evidence is entirely lacking, and the span of time from the third century to the ninth is rather long to bridge with pure supposition. It is difficult to imagine any circumstance in which such a figure could have given rise to such a myth so long after. But no doubt advocates of Lucius Artorius will arise in due course.

The name Artorius is evidently Roman or sub-Roman. Now as it happens, in the *Life of St Columba* written by Adomnan of Iona in around 700, there is an undoubted Arthur: *Arturius*, the eldest son and heir of Aedan Mac Gabrain, king of Dalriada, the Scottish Dark Age kingdom situated in the Clyde valley. This Arthur died tragically in battle in the 590s fighting an obscure border tribe called the Miathi. The story of St Columba's prophecy of Arthur's death in this 'unhappy victory' appears in an excellent manuscript of the eighth century, now preserved in Schaffhausen in Germany: it is the earliest surviving record to mention the name of Arthur. Moreover, this Scottish prince died in an area well known to Arthur specialists; according to Nennius, Arthur's last battle took place at *Camlann*, which we now know is Camboglanna, the 'Crooked Glen', the name of the Roman fort of Castlesteads on Hadrian's Wall which stood on a sharp curve of the River Irthing, east of Carlisle. Other battles in Nennius' famous list of Arthur's victories may also be plausibly placed in the north and north-west, in the 'Caledonian forest', for example; at the Roman fort of Bremenium on Dere Street north of the Wall; and on the River Glen near the Anglo-Saxon and British royal centre of Yeavering. This list, it is now accepted, came from a Dark Age battle poem which mixed battles from different periods and attached them to the one hero, 'Arthur'. So could it have come from one of the sub-Roman courts in Cumbria or Strathclyde, where we know late-Roman traditions hung on tenaciously for longer than in the south? Could Adomnan's prince be the starting-point of the legend; our only reference to the 'real' Arthur, whom Nennius then mythologizes more than two centuries after his day? As we have seen, there is no need for historians to look for a historical Arthur at all, but I would think it is quite likely that some of the battles of Nennius were sung in the late-sixth-century royal halls of Dalriada.

Finally though, lest I be accused once more of putting the textual critic's knife between the shoulder-blades of a hallowed hero, let me conclude with a word on the power of the myth. Critics of this kind of textual approach to Arthur are wrong to suggest that the power of the myth is diminished by exposing the nature of the historical sources. For what is at stake with the sources is the interpretation of the *history* of the fifth and sixth centuries, not the *myth* of Arthur. Whether Gildas mentions him, or whether Nennius makes him up, whether indeed he existed at all, is in the end irrelevant to the myth. For we are dealing here with what Henry Corbin called an imaginal world, in which the figure of Arthur remains, as it always will, a symbol of British history; 'the living bond between the Britons and the English', as Faulkner Jones put it in *The English Spirit*. He is the source of an inexhaustibly rich body of myth, in which Chrétien's Yvain, the Gawain poet's Green Knight, or Mallory's Elaine will always shine more intensely than Nennius' cobbled hero. For the myth-makers, New Agers and Ley-liners, that is the real point. For them, as in a way for all of us, Arthur still lives, and will one day return. As Thomas Mallory said:

Yet some men say King Arthur is not dead but had by the will of our Lord Jesus Christ into another place: and men say he shall come again and win the Holy Cross. I will not say it shall be so; but many men say that there is written on his tomb this verse: 'Here lies Arthur: once and future king.'

3. Glastonbury, the Grail and the Isle of Avalon

'And did those feet in ancient times, walk upon England's mountains green . . . ?'

William Blake, 'Jerusalem' (c. 1806)

Unlike the Celts, the Irish and the Welsh, one might suspect that the English have no real myths. There is, after all, no 'English mythology' section in bookshops alongside the Celtic, Hindu, Norse, Native American or South Seas mythologies. The so-called myths of the English, in fact, are really about the English State and Englishness itself: kings and queens, the Mother of Parliaments, the Tower and Beefeaters, Merrie England, and so on: myths which are discussed elsewhere in this book. Although the English have folk tales, such as Robin Hood, the mythology of the British Isles, in the sense of the ancient stories of mystery, all comes from the Celtic imagination. When Shakespeare wanted to use British myth – for *Cymbeline*, for example, or *King Lear* – he went back to Geoffrey of Monmouth's *History of the Kings of the Britons*.

The reasons for this lack of mythology are not hard to see. The Anglo-Saxon ancestors of the English were not native to Britain. They came to these islands in the Dark Ages, arriving into a much older culture whose roots went far back into the Bronze and Iron Ages. Compared with the Celts, then, English history is recent. The pagan English were soon converted to Christianity, starting in 597, and over the following centuries they gradually lost touch with Woden, Thunor and the rest of their gods, along with their pagan stories, except as folk tales. So for mythology they had to invent. And in that long process of invention, which is still going on, one place in particular became the most famous factory of myth in Britain: Glastonbury.

Go to Glastonbury now and you can't avoid it. Drive into town from Wells and you are greeted by a big sign at the roadside: GLASTONBURY, THE ANCIENT ISLE OF AVALON. In the town's souvenir shops, with their piles of pilgrim badges, Dunstan car-stickers and Arthurian tea-towels, you get the flavour of a little Lourdes. The myth and religious tales are everywhere. Glaston-bury's claims are many: it is the burial place of Joseph of Arimathea, the man who carried the Cross and placed Christ in the tomb; it is the site of the tomb of King Arthur, the once-and-future king; and if you believe some of its more imaginative medieval story-tellers, it is also the burial place of Ireland's Saint Patrick, Scotland's St Aidan and David of Wales. (How about that for pan-British inclusive-ness?) Still more famously, it is claimed to be the resting place of the Holy Grail, the mystic chalice used by Christ at the Last Supper: the Chalice Well, where the Grail is said to be buried, is now a place of prayer and healing. There is even an old story that Christ himself came here to Glastonbury, a story William Blake used in creating what is often described as our real national anthem: 'Jerusalem'. So when we sing 'And did those feet in ancient times . . .' at the Last Night of the Proms, we are actually celebrating a Glastonbury legend (which Elton John echoed in his song for Diana, Princess of Wales at her funeral service in Westminster Abbey). Glastonbury, then, is in some sense perceived to be a touchstone of British – and English – identity. But why Glastonbury? How did it all happen? Is it due to an authentic ancient sanctity, the 'highest soul powers of Albion' as one thirties mystical writer has it? Or did it come about for other reasons?

In the vegetarian café opposite the Avalon Bookshop I met Robert. He had been a businessman of considerable means, but at the end of Thatcher's decade he had given up the rat race in London and come to live here, drawn by the myth. He was reserved, quietly spoken, with a rather diffident manner, cautious of speaking to someone like me from 'the Media' who, in these brittle post-modern days, is expected to poke fun at such mystical quests. But when he saw that I, too, in my way, was a lover of Glastonbury, he relaxed:

'I came to Glastonbury to be with like-minded people. We had a wonderful idea: to re-establish the library: a library of British spirituality. It's a kind of spiritual restoration project. Glastonbury Abbey was destroyed in the sixteenth century, but the power of these things is still there and can be tapped again in our time. You see, there was an ancient primordial Celtic wisdom which became overlaid by Christianity and then became submerged in the modern world after the Reformation and the Enlightenment, but it has been transmitted down to modern England. These days we and our children face great threats: globalization and all that goes with it – the destruction of the climate, the landscape and all the ancient spiritual and cultural traditions. People think globalization just works on the surface of identity, but it's not true: it is now scrubbing away meanings encoded for millennia within languages and traditions. There was once a holistic vision, and they had it here. We wanted to do something to restore that vision, even if in one small place. That's why so many like-minded people have gathered here.'

'But why Glastonbury?'

'Every nation has its chief holy place. Think of Jerusalem, Delphi, Tara in Ireland. For England it is Glastonbury. It was deliberately broken in the sixteenth century, but it is still there. We just need to re-create the language and sensibility, restore ways of thinking mythically. You see, Glastonbury-Avalon is the mythic basis of our country . . . the point where British and English myths intersect and feed each other; it's a wellspring . . .'

I was doubtful. Over the years I've been to many holy places. I've climbed the Chinese Holy Mountains, and sat by the Ganges at Benares; I've walked the sacred paths of the Peruvians and the Highland Maya. Like many non-believers, I guess, I am fascinated by the power of spiritual traditions. But so far as I can see, it is the presence of the pilgrims which breathes life into a place. People make places holy; they are sacred because, as Hamlet says, 'thinking makes it so'. Glastonbury died in the 1540s, and it is its ghost which has been resurrected in the twentieth century, a ghost which only has colour because it is animated by our blood, our breath and spirit. The continuity has gone. What Christianity represents to us Europeans now, as Milan Kundera says, is 'a memory to which we all belong' – even atheists. But in the England of Thatcher and Blair, surely the language – and hence the belief – is no more?

'But it's not gone,' Robert replied. 'The pilgrims are back here now and they've never been away. The physical structure of the abbey may have been destroyed in the sixteenth century, but not the sanctity of the place. Even in the 1750s tens of thousands of people came for cures to the Chalice Well. They didn't just come for the mineral water. Holy places like this have a kind of residue of numinous power. The landscape of a sacred site exerts a kind of spiritual force-field. These are spiritual realities which go beyond conventional religion.'

'Are we talking metaphorically, or literally?'

'Why do we have to distinguish between the two?'

'But do you mean actual power-lines?'

'Many of my colleagues here would say yes.'

I frowned.

'Well, look. These are spiritual realities. It doesn't matter whether you think it's a metaphor or literal truth: it is real to those who believe in it, invest in it. You have an ancient mythic landscape next door to the town, only one step away. You should take a look.'

After lunch I went for a walk. It was a cold day, cumulus swirling over the Tor. Glastonbury was stripped of its aura, but still had its own charm: a straggle of Georgian and Victorian shops and houses, a couple of medieval churches in weathered Doulton stone, all clustered round the abbey precinct just as they had been in the Middle Ages. On the outskirts, there's the usual post-seventies ribbon development with a cavernous DIY superstore. Glastonbury has had its ups and downs since the abbey was destroyed: the canals and railways have come and gone, and the town has been left with none of the well-heeled assurance of the nearby cathedral town of Wells. But since the late sixties, the sacred centre of Glastonbury has experienced a strange new afterlife. You see it in the shop fronts: Crystal Star, the Glastonbury Healing Centre, Mystical Tours, The Glastonbury Experience, the Gothic Image bookshop. You can have aromatherapy, rune and Tarot readings and esoteric healing. It is easy to smile: for the majority of us, our sense of alternative imaginal worlds is gone. They have been reduced to mere tricks of technology. For all our boundless inventiveness, the twentieth century has brought about the end of magic.

As Robert had suggested, I went for a walk in the abbey grounds. At the entrance kiosk I bought my ticket and a guide book, which unequivocally starts the history of the place in the first century AD, within living memory of Christ. Close by the kiosk you pass the Glastonbury thorn. A native of Syria, the thorn flowers each Christmas time, and each Christmas a sprig is sent to the reigning monarch, the head of the Church of England (whose ancestor Henry VIII destroyed Glastonbury). According to a famous medieval legend, when Joseph of Arimathea arrived by boat at Wearyall hill, he stuck his staff in the ground and it took root. (As the tourist soon discovers, Joseph is a key figure in the Glastonbury legends, which also say that he visited Glastonbury with the boy Jesus: this is the tale behind Blake's 'Jerusalem'.) The thorn story is first recorded in the later Middle Ages; the tree itself was chopped down by a zealous Puritan in Elizabeth I's day, but it had plenty of offshoots by then, and this is evidently the offspring of one of them.

Walking from the thorn up to the abbey ruins, you come first to a great cross made of oak which was given by the Queen in 1965. It is inscribed: A CHRISTIAN SANCTUARY SO ANCIENT THAT ONLY LEGEND CAN RECORD ITS ORIGIN. Beyond, rising sheer from neat green grass sprinkled with daisies, are two great broken piers of the central crossing arch. After the Dissolution of the Monasteries under Henry VIII, the abbey buildings were sold off, demolished and quarried for building stone. Now these piers, the nave walls and the lovely, roofless Lady Chapel are all that remain of what many see as the birthplace of Christianity in England. The Church of England bought the site in 1907, and since then religious life here has been revived. Pilgrimages started again after the First World War, and now each summer 20,000 people come in late June for a festival, where the Catholic and Anglican Archbishops happily rub shoulders with representatives from Orthodox Churches, along with more way-out devotees, including druids and pagan mystics.

In the centre of the nave, a knot of visitors stood silently round the grave of King Arthur, on which a six-year-old laid a daisy chain, putting her hands together in prayer for the once-and-future king. On the plaque are the words: '*Hic iacet sepultus inclitus rex Arthurius in insula Avalonia*' ('Here lies buried the famous King Arthur, in the Isle of Avalon').

The landscape around Glastonbury, with its ancient and mysterious names, has always lent itself to fancy etymologizing. For the medievals, the Old English shire of Sumorsaete was the 'Summer land', a land of eternal summer, an Elysium. (Indeed, from its natural features, some modern New Agers claim to have been able to determine the dimensions of Paradise, no less.) And where the town is something of a disappointment, the surrounding landscape is still undeniably soaked in atmosphere. Even now, as you look from the long ridge towards Shepton, with the sun setting across the drained fields of the old Levels; or when black thunderheads gather over the 'isle', gusting in from the Bristol Channel, and the dark mass of the Tor stands out with its dramatic tower sticking up like a white finger, then you can easily imagine yourself back in that medieval world. Below the 'island' this was all shallow marshy flats in ancient times, flooded in winter, always susceptible to high tides. Writing eleven hundred years ago, in the days of the Vikings, Bishop Asser talks of the great tracts of marshy swamps, *permaxima gronna paludosissima*, through which you could only move by punt. Back in the Iron Age and in Roman times, indeed, Glastonbury seems to have been reachable by sea up the River Brue from the Bristol Channel. Food for thought for those who wish to imagine Joseph and the boy Jesus landing their galley here.

This old marsh landscape of the Somerset Levels was drained by the abbey's estate managers between the tenth and fourteenth century, producing the sort of country you see today: criss-crossed with narrow cuts and drains (called rhines in Somerset dialect), fringed with stumpy pollarded osiers, and surrounded by broad rich pastures beyond, with turf moors and cider orchards. The 'island of Glastonbury' with its dramatic pyramidal hill, the Tor, still rears up over these ancient waterlands – visible from twenty miles on a clear day, crowned with its lonely tower, what remains of the medieval church of St Michael. On its steep sides, which are still grazed by sheep, are strange striations which seem to be strip lynchets made by medieval farmers, though some scholars are prepared to believe they are the remains of a prehistoric maze: part of the 'womb hill' of the pagan Celtic Great Goddess.

That, then, is the setting of Glastonbury. In early mornings in winter, when mist surrounds the Tor and the other hills – Panborough, or the rocky outcrop of Godney – then they rise like real islands in a transparent sea of mist, recalling Bishop Asser's Saxon landscape of swamps and lagoons. Then for a moment the neat lines of modern housing estates vanish, and in one's fancy this becomes the spectral landscape in which Tennyson pictured the 'dusky barge dark as a funeral scarf from stem to stern', in which Arthur was borne by the veiled queen after his sword Excalibur had been thrown into the turbid water. The place becomes again, as the road signs say, the Isle of Avalon.

Avalon? The name first appears in Geoffrey of Monmouth's *History of the Kings of the Britons*, written in the late 1130s. A Welshman in Oxford at the time of Welsh independence movements against the Norman kings of England, Geoffrey concocted a fabulous historical pedigree for the Celts, in which Lear, Cymbeline, Merlin, and of course Arthur all make their appearance, some for the first time. Geoffrey's book was one of the best-sellers of the Middle Ages, a brilliantly fictionalized British history setting out to torpedo smug Anglocentricity with its revelation of the unimaginable antiquity of the Celts. More often than not, Geoffrey's source was his own fertile imagination, and where he got the name Avalon from is anyone's guess. In any case, Avalon is not identified with Glastonbury until long after Geoffrey's day, in a romance of the early thirteenth century. The name is assumed to mean the 'Isle of Apples', deriving from the Welsh *abala*, 'apple', but this is by no means certain. An alternative, meaning 'pointed rock' or 'hill', may possibly have existed in medieval Celtic, as it does in modern Welsh: it would be a rather good name for the Tor. A similar name, though, is attested in a Roman inscription from Burgh-by-Sands, Cumberland, near Hadrian's Wall, which refers to a Frisian unit of the Roman army based at a place called *Aballava*. This must come from the Celtic word *aballa*, which appears as 'apple' in medieval glossaries, and which has come down to modern Welsh where *afall* means 'apple tree', and *afal* means 'apple'. It seems most likely that the Avalon of Arthurian legend is of the same origin. Unfortunately, the association of the name with Glastonbury is only made rather late in the day, after the so-called 'discovery' of Arthur's grave there in 1191. Only after this is Glastonbury turned into *Ynys Afallon*: 'The Isle of Apples', perhaps with an echo of the classical Greek myth of the Garden of the Hesperides. With Avalon, then, as with so much in the Glastonbury story, there is no hard evidence, but it *could* just be.

Humans have lived in the Glastonbury region for a long time, since the retreat of the ice after the last Ice Age. *Homo sapiens* is now known to have used the caves at Cheddar from around 11,000 BC. (In an amazing recent discovery, the DNA profile of a living Somerset man proved him to be a direct descendent of a prehistoric cave-dweller from the Cheddar Gorges whose bones had been discovered in Wookey Hole!) The first definite evidence of settled occupation of the Glastonbury area comes from around 4,000 BC, with a remarkable series of wooden trackways crossing the marshes linking the islands with the higher ground of the Polden Hills. The Sweet Track is the oldest, dated by tree rings to the winter of 3,807–6 BC (what uncanny precision from so long ago, when much more recent history is so impossible to pin down!). From late prehistory come the Glastonbury Iron Age lake villages of around 300 BC. In the Roman period, Somerset was a part of the province of Britain, its wealth suggested by the rich finds made in the recent excavation of the king's bath in the Roman city of Bath, and the adjacent temple of Sulis Minerva, a Celtic goddess whose cult was adopted by the Romans. So modern archaeology has begun to fill in some of the detail of the vast gap in time between the Iron Age and the Old English period when the first documents appear, from the seventh century onwards, when Glastonbury first emerges in the record as a religious site. Archaeology has now shown us something about the survival of ancient cults and their transformation into Christian places of worship. That Glastonbury was one of these is asserted in all New Age literature. Of course there's no reason *per se* why a Celtic holy site could not survive through the English invasions, but unfortunately there is not the slightest evidence of this from Glastonbury itself. Indeed it has yielded only the meagrest indications of Iron Age or Roman use: just a few fragments of Samian ware, not enough to say whether someone had been living there, or whether a traveller had simply dropped a wine bottle on the way to a Saturday-night symposium in Bath.

It is during the collapse of the Roman empire that archaeology finally lifts the veil on Glastonbury. The finds, however, were made on the Tor, not at the abbey site. Excavations in the mid 1960s (made under difficult conditions, humping gear up precipitous slopes in howling gales) revealed a few scattered flints going back to Palaeolithic times, but the first settlement dated from the fifth to the seventh century AD, and no earlier. There were traces of wooden buildings on top of the Tor in which were found sherds of imported Mediterranean pottery, and Roman tile fragments. There was also evidence of metalworking – slag and ash pits – in the immediate post-Roman period. Finally, a large number of animal bones were found on the site. Putting these clues together, the excavator suggested that the settlement on the Tor was not religious, but was a small stronghold belonging to a Dark Age chieftain. Be that as it may, at some time during the seventh century, the time when the Anglo-Saxon invaders were penetrating the West Country, the Tor site was abandoned.

Our next clear information about the area comes from the *Anglo-Saxon Chronicle*, which was written down in the late ninth century. In 577 the West Saxons captured the former Roman city of Bath after a battle at Dyrham in Gloucestershire. The region of Glastonbury must have fallen to them around that time, or soon after.

At some point in the seventh century, the territory of Glastonbury –
which had perhaps once centred on the Tor settlement – became
part of the royal estates of the kings of Wessex.

As for the origins of Glastonbury Abbey itself, we have no reliable
early source. The earliest claimed document in the abbey archive
purports to be from 601, a grant of land from a Celtic King of
Dumnonia (the West Country) at *Inesuuitrin*. Much later, this was
interpreted by the abbey monks as a gift to a British predecessor of
their house at Glastonbury. However, the Latin of the fragment
has no Celtic features and it cannot be what it claims; quite possibly
it is a forgery in its entirety. Glastonbury became notorious for faking
documents in the Middle Ages, a 'factory of fraud' as Ferdinand Lot
described it. No medieval house has been more often convicted –
on better evidence – of fakery, from Arthur's tomb to holy relics
to the abbey's foundation charter. In this light, therefore, it is
interesting and significant that the great early historian of England,
Bede, doesn't mention Glastonbury anywhere in his *History of the
English Church*, completed in 731. This would be, to say the least,
somewhat surprising if Glastonbury's history was what it later
claimed. Bede, we can be sure, would not have omitted to discuss
the 'birthplace of Christianity in England', had it really been so.
The first reliable dated evidence for the existence of the church at
Glastonbury, in fact, is a short and sober mention in a letter of the
Devonian saint Boniface in the mid eighth century, in whose
day, we learn, a monastery existed at Glastonbury. The first royal
benefactor cited in later documents is King Cenwalh of Wessex,
who died in 672, and this may be so, but surviving texts of land
grants start with King Ine's 'Great Privilege' in the early eighth
century. As it stands, this document is also a forgery, but most
scholars think it has a genuine core. Looking favourably on these
scraps of evidence, it is probable that Ine founded a small monastery
at Glastonbury, where a church already existed which had received
royal patronage. All we can say for sure is that the documentary
history for Glastonbury begins some time either side of A D 700,
and that the place was then of some, though not unusual, sanctity
in the south-west.

There is some archaeological evidence to back up this picture. The ditched precinct enclosing the site of the early church at Glastonbury was excavated in several archaeological digs between the 1920s and the 1950s. Unfortunately, as with every step of the Glastonbury tale, the excavations are dogged by fiction and fantasy. The digs were not, on the whole, scientifically conducted and recorded, and to this day none of the results has been properly published. The extensive dig in the 1920s was compromised when it was revealed that the excavator, Bligh Bond, had regularly used seances and automatic writing to ask the medieval monks to tell him where to dig! (Unfortunately, Bond's medium and her contact in the other world were only able to speak modern English – an attempt to talk to an Anglo-Saxon spirit was thwarted when they were told: 'he knows not thy speech'!)

Until the site of Glastonbury is properly excavated, all we can safely say is that a small English church existed there in the late seventh century and that by the mid eighth century there was a monastery. One feature, though, is enigmatic: the strange hypogeum or crypt, a sunken stepped chamber of uncertain date. This was excavated under part of the tenth-century church, and is possibly early Saxon or even late Roman, which could suggest that the first Saxon church was placed next to an important person's grave. Though there are no known Roman buildings at Glastonbury, the most likely analogy is the late Roman mausoleum found recently under Wells Cathedral. Perhaps, then, Glastonbury was the centre of a late- or sub-Roman estate (based on the Tor?), and the Saxon church was built by a late Roman tomb or in a late Roman cemetery. As always with Glastonbury, the hints are tantalizing, but unprovable.

From the eighth century, perhaps earlier, Glastonbury owned a cluster of estates which provided the monks with their staples of life: food, wood, animals and fodder. They can still be traced today: the 'islands' of Meare, Beckery, Godney, Marchey and Andersey (Nyland) were the core estates of the abbey. The 1930s mystical writer Katherine Maltwood mapped them as a star map, the so-called Glastonbury Zodiac, and her 'temple of the stars' is now recorded

as fact in New Age books such as John Michell's engagingly readable
View over Atlantis and *The Dimensions of Paradise*. The reality was
perhaps more prosaic, though I would venture no less interesting. Meare, for example, part in the marsh and part on the hills,
had a vineyard and arable and pastoral land, but also fisheries and
eel weirs in the surrounding swamps. Only a few miles west of
Glastonbury, it probably provided the monastic community with
its main diet of fish and eels from the Dark Ages to the Dissolution.
A glimpse of this older world can be seen in the first photographs
taken in the Levels in the mid nineteenth century, where old-
timers set their rows of wicker eel traps from punts in the last of
the marsh.

During the eighth and ninth centuries, more people seem to
have settled here to follow the religious life. A circle of chapels can
be traced on the outlying hills of Godney, Nyland, Beckery and
Marchey, which were once islands in the swamp. Beckery was
scientifically excavated during the 1960s and, in contrast to the
secular site on the Tor, has given us a clear picture of a tiny religious
community during the eighth century. Only a mile from the
Tor, Beckery was a Middle Saxon settlement with simple timber
buildings, a stone preaching cross, and what excavators thought to
be a monastic cemetery. The chapel seems to have been later
dedicated to St Bridgit, and in the High Middle Ages the area bore
the name 'Little Ireland'. (Bridgit died in the sixth century and was
buried in Kildare, where her tomb is still a place of pilgrimage, but
it is not certain how early her association with Glastonbury begins.)

The other outlying chapel sites mentioned in the Anglo-Saxon
documents have never been examined. But at one of them, Marchey
Farm, which is a short hike out into the flatland beyond Panborough,
there is a low hill surrounded by traces of ditches, which resembles
a small Dark Age monastic enclosure. The farmstead is now ruined
and overgrown, but Middle Saxon pottery and Roman coins have
been discovered under the kitchen floor. The site has never been
excavated, but these chance finds suggest that this little 'island'
outpost of Glastonbury was occupied as far back as Roman times.
Taken with the evidence from Beckery, we can perhaps assume

that little monastic communities existed on several of these outlying sites in the eighth century.

So to sum up this first stage of our search for the early history of Glastonbury, it is safe to say that a church here belonged to the West Saxon kings from the late seventh century. In the eighth century there was a monastery here which was gifted a number of estates, and on these, at Beckery, and perhaps at Marchey and other sites, there existed clusters of primitive huts where people lived the monastic life. But there is no narrative source which throws any light on this shadowy period. The truth is that there is nothing definite to suggest that Glastonbury was viewed differently from any other Dark Age religious house until the tenth century. Only then does Glastonbury emerge into the light of history. The text is the *Life of Saint Dunstan*, written in the 990s by an Englishman known simply as 'B.'.

Dunstan used to be seen as one of the makers of England. That was in the days when the historians of England tended to be bishops and Oxford dons, who naturally thought the nation's makers should be people like them. These days, things are a little more complicated, but Dunstan remains a fascinating and problematic figure whose character and motivations still await elucidation. A Somerset man, related to the royal kin, Dunstan was born at Baltonsborough near Glastonbury in the early years of the tenth century and rose to be Archbishop of Canterbury. I always imagine him as a big, clumsy, strange man with the build of a Bath rugby prop forward, but I have to confess this picture is in no way warranted by the sources! In an age of miracles and visions, he was apparently subject more than most to visions and dreams, and he seems to have antagonized people at every stage of his career. Emotional and volatile, he was quite prepared to manhandle the king if he felt the king was doing wrong. At times of acute stress, as a friend relates, he would talk to invisible people, argue with the dead, and physically fight the devil, whom he sometimes saw in the form of a dog, bear or fox. In Wells Cathedral, a small piece of medieval glass shows the mitred saint (in character, one imagines) tweaking the devil's nose with a pair of vicious-looking coal tongs! Not your conventional churchman of the monastic age, he played and composed music, and read Ovid's *Art of Love* and other books which more orthodox church-men perhaps would have left unopened. He dabbled in the works of pagan *phylosophantes* and he may even have composed a treatise on alchemy and the philosopher's stone. (At one point, as a young man, these kinds of interests got him ejected from court.)

According to his biographer, Dunstan conversed with Irish scholars at Glastonbury and read their books; he may also have known some Welsh (his classbook which survives has some of the earliest dated examples of Welsh script, certainly confirming contacts between Glastonbury and Celtic Britain). He was attracted, and attractive, to holy women and religious widows, who gave him lavish patronage. A man of interestingly eclectic learning, he was devout, holy and exuded an aura of intense, if eccentric, sanctity. Now B. claims to have known Dunstan in his adult life, but only as far as the mid century. In particular, he records many stories of Dunstan's childhood and adolescence in the 910s and 920s, stories which he says were told him by the saint himself. These include very intimate accounts of some of his dreams. And it is Dunstan's dreams, as we shall see, which are crucial to weighing up the antiquity of the Glastonbury legends.

Surprisingly, the *Life of Saint Dunstan*, though one of the key texts of early English history, has never been fully translated. I have translated the passage below about early Glastonbury from the Latin text published by William Stubbs in 1874, which remains the standard edition and is still the only detailed discussion of this work. (The text, by the way, comes from a contemporary manuscript and there is no reason to think that it is not an accurate version of what the author wrote.) The author sets the scene in the very early years of the tenth century in a remarkable passage, in which Glastonbury emerges from darkness into the light of history:

There was within the kingdom of King Athelstan a certain royal island known to the locals from ancient times as Glaestonia. It was of wide extent, with numerous inlets, surrounded by lakes full of fish, and fed by slow-running streams suitable for human use. And what is more important, it was endowed by God with sacred gifts. For in that place directed by God, the first neophytes of the Catholic law discovered an ancient church built by no human skill, they say, but prepared by heaven for the salvation of mankind. This church, as God himself, the architect of heaven, has clearly revealed by many performances of miracles and by many virtutibus of mysteries, was consecrated to Christ and the holy Mary his mother. To this church they added another, an oratory built of stone, which they dedicated to Christ and to St Peter. Henceforth crowds of the faithful came from all around to worship and humbly dwelt in that precious place on the island . . .'

It is a haunting passage. Across 1,000 years it has had an influence, either directly or indirectly, on writers from Geoffrey of Monmouth and Thomas Mallory to Blake, Tennyson, Yeats and John Cowper Powys, and even the rock musician Van Morrison. Its brief description of the Somerset marshlands has suggested to some modern readers a sense of the English landscape as haunting as Graham Swift's evocation of the fens on the other side of England in his novel *Waterland*. And as far as we know, this text is the beginning of the Glastonbury myth. In the line about 'no human skill' we can see the origin of the tale that comes down to Blake's 'Jerusalem', the legend that Jesus himself had set foot in Britain. It has always been assumed that by 'the first neophytes of the Catholic law', B. means the missionaries sent to Britain by Pope Eleutherius in AD 166, whom an educated English person of Dunstan's day could have read about in the *Anglo-Saxon Chronicle*. These would have been considered the first preachers of Christianity in Britain, and according to B. it was they who found the ancient church which had been consecrated and built 'by no human skill'. This of course means by Christ himself. And did those feet . . . ?

B.'s text marks the beginning of the Glastonbury legends: the story of the old church and the stone oratory of apostolic origins. There is nothing earlier save the archaeological traces and the forged land grants. But this is not mere literary fantasy, like the Vision of Merlin, Geoffrey of Monmouth, or the High History of the Grail. Though it has fantasy in it, of course, this is none the less a real historical description written by someone who knew Glastonbury. With B.'s text we are in a real place in the 910s and 920s. He gives us vivid details about the life of the monastery, which he populates with real people – kings, monks, old Somerset families, noble ladies, and of course the Irish pilgrims, who, says B., 'as well as other crowds of the faithful, had a special veneration for Glastonbury, especially in order to honour the then blessed Patrick the Younger who was said most happily to rest in the Lord there'. The *Life of Saint Dunstan* is one of the few Dark Age texts which gives us, however briefly, a delightful picture of royals off duty, relaxing with friends and family, chatting and drinking mead. B. singles out a lady called Aethelflaed, a noblewoman related to the royals, who was living in rather civilized retirement with her servants in a cottage adjacent to the monastery. Another lady, Aethelwynn, with the help of her needlewomen, embroiders a beautiful stole, one imagines rather like the one given to St Cuthbert's shrine at just this time, which can still be seen in Durham Cathedral's treasury. In another tale from Dunstan's childhood, B. describes him coming with his father from his village to the shrine on the occasion of a special festival, and sleeping in a primitive dormitory block, staying overnight for the purpose of prayer: *causa orationis pernocterent*. This recalls the present-day custom of 'incubation' among Orthodox and Catholic faithful in the Mediterranean, or the summer pilgrimages on the Greek islands, where whole families head to a sacred area with food and sleeping mats on an important saint's day, cooking and eating out of doors, and sleeping in simple hostel huts. B.'s Glastonbury of Dunstan's childhood is surely a real place, drawn from real reminiscence.

What early-tenth-century Glastonbury would have looked like is also given us by B.: a cluster of shrines, the small eighth-century church of King Ine, the monks' cemetery, a cloister, a small scriptorium and dormitories for pilgrims. Visitors could also have seen the ancient building referred to in B.'s account as 'built by no human skill'. This was the famous *vetusta ecclesia*, the 'old church', a wattle-and-daub structure with a thatched roof which was destroyed in the fire of 1184, whose dimensions are apparently preserved by the beautiful Lady Chapel which survives today. The claim by excavators in the 1950s that they had found traces of the old church, and that it was a Roman building, are now discounted. The most we can safely say is that the building was in existence before the tenth century, by which time it had become a pilgrim attraction. The 'old church' remains one of Glastonbury's more intriguing mysteries.

In the mid tenth century, Glastonbury experienced a dramatic transformation. In around 940, with strong royal backing, Dunstan reformed Glastonbury under the Benedictine rule as the first house of the English monastic revival. At the same time, the place was physically reshaped. The little wattle chapel and the small stone church were incorporated into a much larger and grander complex of buildings. Glastonbury now becomes the intellectual power-house of the reform movement, the main production house for manuscripts. An overtly political think-tank was trained here by Dunstan, technicians of the sacred, practitioners of the official new script which was developed and standardized here as an arm of government ideology. In little more than a generation, Glastonbury received a massive increase in landed wealth from the kings who created the tenth-century kingdom of England. It was, of course, not the only old English house to benefit from the tenth-century reformation, for at this time other regional saints and shrines were also being built up as focuses of a national cult – Cuthbert in the north, for example, or Edmund in East Anglia. In this way the spiritual world was co-opted in the creation of an English state. But Glastonbury does best of all out of the new movement led by Dunstan. It becomes a national shrine and the centre of a royal cult. And it is precisely at this moment that the Glastonbury legend appears.

Dunstan himself would make it to the very top, as bishop, then archbishop, and as chief adviser of the young kings of the mid century; a man so strong-willed that when the deeply unpleasant young king, Eadwig the 'All-fair', was consorting 'lasciviously' with his teenage wife *and* her mother in the royal bower during their coronation feast, Dunstan burst in in full ecclesiastical garb and hauled him out on his ear back to the banquet. Not surprisingly, the king did not forget this slight, and Dunstan soon found himself in exile in Flanders. With Eadwig out of the way, though, Dunstan finally got the see of Canterbury, and in old age became an admired figure on the Continent, where the ideals of monasticism were sweeping the European elites. By the time Dunstan died in 988, England can only be described as a nation state, and Glastonbury had been reshaped as its chief shrine, the greatest and richest English church. Essentially, that is the tale told by B.

Now there are some questions to be asked of the curve of this story – questions which I think are of crucial relevance to the origin of the Glastonbury legends. The first thing to remember is that Dunstan is a Glastonbury man, and B.'s tale of early Glastonbury derives from conversations between the author and Dunstan himself. So the story which begins the Glastonbury myth has one source: Dunstan. And the crucial part – the 'inciting incident', in Hollywood script-writer's parlance – is the tale of the little boy going to sleep next to his father with the other pilgrims on that festival night in Glastonbury, his impressionable mind full of the sights and sounds of the night office he had just attended in the crumbling old church. That night, says B. (and you can imagine Dunstan telling the tale), the boy Dunstan dreamed of a venerable old man in a gleaming white alb, who led him round and showed him a new monastery there with 'beautiful chapels and cells . . .'

Whether the grown-up Dunstan simply invented this tale, or whether the child really did dream it, hardly matters. The dream is to be understood as god-sent. The old man in the dream is clearly the tutelar spirit of the monastery, who calls on the boy to restore and rebuild the place. Dunstan, remember, is not from any old Somerset clan: he belongs to the royal kin. His family may even in some sense 'own' the abbey. We later discover that his older brother is the reeve or administrator of the 'royal island', one of the most powerful and wealthy thegns of the time. Reading between the lines, Glastonbury is the family shrine and Dunstan as biased as a brahmin telling the founding legend of his temple. This, I think, is the significance of Dunstan's childhood dream. When he achieved power, he carried out the injunctions of the venerable old man.

With royal backing – and prompted by a convenient miracle – he lavished vast wealth on beautifying, expanding and refurbishing his abbey. He erected a grand new church incorporating the ancient buildings, which were so venerable they had to be preserved. In the middle of the reshaped precinct, covered in protective sheets of lead, the 'old church' would remain to remind all visitors of the unrivalled antiquity of this sacred place. As its abbot, Dunstan was able to reshape not only the physical layout of the monastery, but also its historiography and its mental topography. And of course he has controlled the way the story was handed down: B.'s biography is Dunstan's testament.

So was Dunstan himself the real source of the Glastonbury legends? Or at least, of the first and most potent one – the tale which became Blake's 'Jerusalem'? That is my hunch. It may be, of course, that he reworked stories which already existed in local legend, or which he had been told by his father, spicing them with his own hopes and dreams, to add to the allure of his church. But Dunstan's radical reshaping of his church's fabric, and its 'origin tales' were a blueprint for a new age of miracles, and they also brought him the patronage of the young kings to whom he would become mentor. So long ago, of course, such things are beyond proof, but the supposition must surely be that the main source of the first and greatest of the Glastonbury legends was none other than Dunstan himself.

The Glastonbury legends, then, are really *English*. The creation and enlargement of the house and the spread of its legends were political acts. The reinvention of Glastonbury and the reshaping of its traditions took place in the tenth century. This regional Wessex shrine with Celtic connections now became a national cult centre with a mythology attached going back to the very beginning of Christianity. In Bede's *History* – the founding text of the English nation – all the most resonant Christian holy places lay outside Wessex. Now, with the West Saxon kings claiming to be rulers of all England, this inconvenient lacuna had been filled. Wessex could, after all, claim the primordial centre of British sanctity. Soon its status was such that kings were buried there. By 1066, Glastonbury was the wealthiest abbey in Britain. The creation of a kingdom of England and the elevation of Glastonbury to national shrine had gone hand in hand. The rise of Glastonbury, then, is to be sought not so much in the 'soul powers of Albion' as in the power politics of the Old English State.

As for the later fame of Glastonbury, the legends told in all the guide books today – about King Arthur, Joseph of Arimathea, the Holy Grail – are all, alas, post twelfth century, the creation of monks and scholars working for the Anglo-Norman kings after 1066. We know this for sure because the legends and claims of Glastonbury Abbey were summarized by William of Malmesbury in a book written in the 1120s on the antiquity of the church. William knew Glastonbury well, and had scrutinized its library and archives thoroughly over many research visits. In fact, when they read the finished article, the monks were irritated by William's scepticism about their claims, and would later produce their own 'augmented' edition of his work which gave the 'true story'. But as William does not mention any of these tales, we have to assume that they were invented after his day. The association of King Arthur with Glastonbury begins with the 'discovery' of his tomb in 1191. The Grail first arrives in the 1220s. Joseph of Arimathea comes later still: this wonderful tale is first mentioned in an interpolation into a manuscript of William of Malmesbury in the thirteenth century. Despite this, modern historians have not stopped discussing the workings of the tin trade, which might have brought a first-century Roman merchant like Joseph of Arimathea into the Parret Estuary.

This second great phase of invention of myth and tradition at Glastonbury had its political and economic motives, just as the first did. Not least, huge funds had to be found to make good the devastating damage of the 1184 fire, which had wrecked Dunstan's buildings and obliterated the 'old church'. A vast romantic and pseudo-historical literature now developed, embellishing the tales of the house, whose fame now spread abroad in the hands of courtly poets and romancers. Kings and queens came in person to pay homage at Arthur's grave. For all of these pilgrims, nobles and paupers alike, the monks' identification of Glastonbury with the ancient British past and with the very beginnings of Christianity had an intense emotional appeal in the twelfth and thirteenth centuries. From there, it was only a short step to fabricating not merely land documents but entire histories:

The Latin from whence this history was drawn into Romance was taken in the Isle of Avalon, in a holy house of religion that standeth at the head of the Moors Adventurous, there where King Arthur and Queen Guinivere lie, according to the witness of the good men religious that are therein, that have the whole history thereof, true from the beginning even to the end. (Perlesvaus, *The High History of the Holy Graal, c.* 1200–1225)

At the end of the Middle Ages comes the great divide of the Reformation and the Dissolution of the Monasteries, the plundering of the old houses by Henry VIII. The story of the end of Glastonbury is particularly affecting. The abbot, Richard Whiting, was hanged on 15 November 1539. One imagines a typical bleak late-autumn day, with a bitter wind scouring round the slopes of the Tor and buffeting the tower of St Michael's chapel on its summit. Whiting was now old, frail, sick and weakened by his long interrogation at the Tower. He and two loyal monks were dragged on hurdles up to the Tor; they were hanged, beheaded, and their heads were stuck on the abbey gate. The epic description by Dom David Knowles, the great modern historian of the monasteries, shows how even the most sober scholar can become swept up with the Glastonbury story:

The old man's eyes, as he stood beneath the gallows, would have travelled for the last time along the slopes of the clouded hills to Brent Knoll and Steep Holm; over the grey expanse of mere to the sharp outline of the Quantocks and the darker Poldens; over the distant ridges to the south where the Glastonbury manors near Domerham had been white with sheep, and over those to the north once hallowed, so the story ran, by the footsteps of the 'beauteous lamb of God'. No other landscape in all England carried so great a weight of legend. To the island valley at his feet the dying Arthur had been ferried. Through sedges from the Parret had come Joseph of Arimathea bearing the Grail. On the pleasant pastures of Mendip had shone the countenance of the Child Jesus. Below whom lay the now majestic pile of his abbey, desolate, solitary, and about to crumble into ruins.

The remaining forty monks were driven out, and any items of value were torn down and auctioned off from this 'most ostentatious of all monuments to Papal superstition'.

Only ten years later, in a last flicker of the tale, four former monks attempted a restoration of Catholic monastic life under Mary Tudor when they petitioned to get the ruins back. It is a touching document:

If there have been any flagitiouse deed since the creation of the world punyshed with the plague of God, in our opinion the overthrow of Glassenbury may be compared to the same . . . Wee ask nothing in gift to the foundation, but only the house and scite, in that with our labour and husbandrye we may live here a few of us in our religious habbitts till the charitie of good people may suffice a greater number . . .

They were refused. In Elizabeth's reign the site was sold off as real estate, and became a quarry. The stones of the abbey were used to rebuild the town and the causeway to Wells. Even among hardened Protestants, the abbey's fate elicited a strong response. The Elizabethan magus John Dee, for example, observed 'O Glastonbury, Glastonbury . . . How lamentable is thy case now? How hath Hypocrisie and Pride wrought thy Desolation?'

Michael Drayton, the Warwickshire friend of Shakespeare, in a book on the glories of Britain, reflected on the abbey's fate with more of a sense of history:

O three times famous Ile, where is that place that might
Be with thy self compar'd for glorie and delight,
Whilst Glastenbury stood? Exalted to that pride
Whose Monasterie seem'd all other to deride?

O who thy ruine sees, whom wonder doth not fill
With our great fathers' pompe, devotion, and their skill?
(*Poly-Olbion*, 1622)

Over generations, the site served as the local quarry, and by the early eighteenth century the monastic buildings had mostly disappeared. In 1723, the antiquarian William Stukeley described the Lady Chapel with a sense of irreparable loss: 'the roof beat down by violence and a sorry wooden one in its place, thatched with stubble to make it serve as a stable, the manger lies upon the altar and niche where they put the holy water'.

The last major quarrying of the ruins took place early in the nineteenth century to build the turnpike from Glastonbury to Street. To all intents and purposes, that was the final demolition of the great church. Only fragments have been left to modern times: the shattered arcades of the nave, the abbot's kitchen and the Lady Chapel. Privately owned, the site became a wasteland for grazing sheep. And that, you might have thought, should have been that. There the story should have ended, as it did for so many English Catholic shrines. But then a strange thing happened.

In the early Victorian period, there came a growing perception in British public culture of the ebbing of religious faith. Among the elite there was a corresponding search for alternative and older modes of spirituality. At the same time, the Victorians were increasingly fascinated by the idea of the Anglo-Saxon past being the true root of English identity. These preoccupations naturally led them back to the Dark Ages and to intense speculation, both popular and scholarly, about Celtic and Anglo-Saxon origins. These themes are articulated everywhere in Victorian culture – most obviously in the pre-Raphaelite movement, for example – and are found even in the statues and reliefs of the royal mausoleum at Frogmore, where Prince Albert and his courtiers appear dressed as Anglo-Saxon nobles. In Victorian art and literature, these ideas resulted in an extraordinary late flowering of Arthurian legends which had long lain dormant, and which now became seen specifically as tales of spiritual quest. All this led inevitably back to Glastonbury itself, and in this charged cultural climate the third great phase of Glastonbury myth-making was initiated, the one in which we still live today.

The Chalice Well, which was now owned by a Catholic religious group, was consecrated as a shrine on the basis of a legend which said that Joseph of Arimathea had been buried there with two cruets of the holy blood. The abbey site itself was bought by the Church of England in 1907 and reconsecrated. Before long, the pilgrimages were restarted, and soon a knot of 'believers' in the sacred power of the place settled in the town. In the 1920s came the 'New Avalonians': a group of poets, artists and mystics. With the help of Bernard Shaw, the esoteric theosophist Annie Besant and the socialist composer Rutland Boughton set up an annual religious and artistic festival. The Christian socialist Alice Buckton bought land round the Chalice Well and started an arts, crafts and drama centre there, and her colleague the architect Frederick Bligh Bond, the leader of the Avalonians, sought out psychics and spirit mediums. Bligh Bond (whom we have already met excavating the abbey site) subsequently published *Rose Miraculous, The Story of the Sangreal*, in which he published messages received through automatic writing supporting the medieval account of the first Christian mission to Glastonbury. Celtic revivalists jumped on the bandwagon, including W. B. Yeats, who wrote on the Celtic mystical tradition, the novelist John Cowper Powys, and musicians like Vaughan Williams and John Ireland. They were of differing temperaments – Katherine Maltwood, who mapped the Glaston-bury Zodiac and Powys, were frankly occultist, even pagan, hoping explicitly to tap into 'the Ancient Wisdom'. Others, like Bond and Tudor Pole, were more or less Christian, wanting to revive a Christian mythology. All, though, agreed with John Cowper Powys's *Glastonbury Romance*:

There are only about a dozen reservoirs of world magic on the whole surface of the globe . . . Jerusalem . . . Rome . . . Mecca . . . Lhassa . . . and of these Glastonbury has the largest residue of unused power. Generations of mankind, aeons of past races, have by their concentrated will made Glastonbury miraculous.

With that, the modern Glastonbury phenomenon was upon us. The reasons for its development are many and complex. One immediate context is, perhaps, the deeply nostalgic strain of English culture following the ordeal of the First World War, and also a growing sense of doom in the outside world as a whole – as Carl Jung said, a 'smell of burning on the air'. In the air, too, after the Great War was an intensified sense of spiritual crisis. This comes out strongly in the plentiful literature on England and Englishness written between the wars: H. V. Morton's *In Search of England*, for example, uses Glastonbury itself, 'the birthplace of English Christianity', to pose questions about the loss of tradition and how to get it back. But the underlying roots of the phenomenon were perhaps longer term. Looking back now from our standpoint, we can see that the Avalonians and their like were, in one sense, still attempting to deal with the psychic trauma of the sixteenth-century Reformation. The Catholic tradition had been submerged in English culture and history, and the loss of the old religion was beginning to be seen as a severance from the deep past of England on which, even after 400 years, the dust was only now settling. And for them, just as for the tenth-century myth makers, Glastonbury had a very special role to play. The point about Glastonbury was that in the legends of Joseph and the Holy Grail, it was holy *before the Catholic Church*. It had been a chthonic repository of British sanctity before the Church of Rome, and therefore it could be more than a Catholic shrine created by that Church and its agents. It was the primordial British shrine, free of sectarian taint. Where better to begin, then, as Dion Fortune put it, to 'mend the soul of Albion'?

Of course, all this tells us less about the early history of Glastonbury than about ourselves and our need to have a tangible connection with the past, as it recedes from us at an ever-faster rate, and as our links with our ancestors are more and more tenuously conceived and maintained. Pioneers like Buckton and Bond had little to go on after the sixteenth-century destruction, the death and dispersal of the monastic personnel and the ruin of the church and its books. Faced with the unreliability of surviving medieval records and the lack of scientific analysis of sources and scientific archaeology, they tried to reach back, as far as they could, to retrieve something of the ancient spirit and live by it in an increasingly secular and disenchanted world. It was not an ignoble aim, although their works were, by and large, discounted by their contemporaries. But their efforts did not lead to a dead end. The New Avalonians were the precursors of another movement, from the 1960s on, to reimagine Glastonbury: the New Agers. Today, many different strands sit together in Glastonbury. At first part of the counter-culture, the modern Glastonbury experience has now entered the mainstream. Following on from the hippies who claimed Glaston-bury as a power place, and those who claimed it was the intersection point of ley lines, or of dragon paths along which UFOs flew, there are the pop festivals, alternative-healing centres and church events which have become a fixed part of the Glastonbury scene. Alternative lifestyles, playfulness and religious pilgrimage are all part of the life of twenty-first-century Albion. Not so long ago, even the Prince of Wales came to take the waters of the Chalice Well after he had broken an arm in a polo accident.

Some, though, like Robert the businessman, with whom I began this story, are of more serious intent, driven by the idea that sacred time is more important than historical time, and that the essential truth of myth is more valid, more useful and more beautiful than mere historical fact. For them there is an 'Avalon of the heart'. As the doyen of Glastonbury watchers, Geoffrey Ashe, wrote in the 'hippy' magazine *Gandalf's Garden*:

Britain will begin to be reborn when Glastonbury is. The Giant Albion will begin to wake when his sons and daughters gather inside the enchanted boundary, and summon him with the right words, the right actions, a different life . . . an enduring community of Avalon. The time to found that community is drawing near.

To sum up – the Glastonbury legends have been created by the English to meet English needs. There were three main phases in their creation: the first in the tenth century; the second in the twelfth and thirteenth centuries; the third roughly between the

1860s and the 1960s. The psycho-historian might wonder whether embracing the Matter of Britain was one way in which the rulers of the English state could try to co-opt the Celtic, to appropriate parts of Celtic mythology and to reimagine Britannia and Albion. And the Celts (or at least the littérateurs among them!) were all too willing to help, from the Irish and Welsh visitors who lent St Dunstan books, to Geoffrey of Monmouth in Oxford, Yeats, Cowper Powys, through to Van Morrison today. In this way, Anglo-Saxons and Normans and their descendants have assimilated Celtic myths and culture. The Glastonbury library was at first a transmission point, a place of interaction between the Matter of Britain and the Matter of England. Later it became a great generator of tales in its own right. But its products were more than mere pieces of state propaganda or monkish fiction. However fantastic, such literary products were reflections of a real process by which Celtic Britain became, in part, England, and England became part of Britain; the long and continuing interaction of Celtic and English culture which started in the fifth century and which still continues. In that tale, the myths create their own reality. They help make us what we are. They become part of history, too.

On a deeper level, then, I think Robert was right. History, the investigation of historical fact, can only take you so far, as the story of Glastonbury shows all too clearly. (And in any case, as we have seen, not all historical questions about Glastonbury, by any means, can be neatly answered.) Early cultures made a distinction between sacred time, which existed at the moment of creation, and profane time, into which humanity had fallen since. Early religion, by use of myth and ritual, was an attempt to transcend profane time and rediscover sacred time. In the absence of any real spiritual tradition or mainstream English church now, in the failure of the old religious language, that is the goal of the seekers like Robert who still congregate in Glastonbury.

Like most of history, the Glastonbury legends reveal as much about ourselves as about the past. One may suspect that virtually all 'historical' texts which claim to talk about pre-tenth-century Glastonbury are fictitious. As Ferdinand Lot said, the monks ran a factory of fraud, a 'laboratory of forgeries'. But that is not to say that the idea of Glastonbury does not exist as a metaphor in English culture which, in its way, is as valuable as real history. Glastonbury stands for English history in its myths and its ideals: for its Christian spiritual tradition, for its imagined golden ages 'builded here in England's green and pleasant land'. Scholars can show the sources for the tale, but they cannot impinge on its life, which is richer by far than mere fact. For believers, the ancient church of Glastonbury is an inner church, an inner temple, and that is still intact, still beckoning to those who can see.

The builders of Stonehenge have perished; but there are those who worship its stones still. The builders of Glastonbury have perished; but there are people, yet living among us, whose eyes have seen the Grail! (Powys, *A Glastonbury Romance*)

4. Merrie Englande:
the Legend of Robin Hood

Lythe and listin, gentilmen,
That be of frebore blode,
I shall you tel of a gode yeoman,
His name was Robyn Hode

The Gest of Robin Hood, c. 1420.

Few English legends have been so popular, or so long lasting, as the tale of Robin Hood. There is a famous scene in *As You Like It* in which Shakespeare conjures up the image of an English golden age: 'They say he is already in the forest of Arden, and a many merry men with him; and there they live like the old Robin Hood of England: they say many young gentlemen flock to him every day, and fleet the time carelessly as they did in the golden world.' The tale crops up again in Shakespeare's most elegiac vision of England: Shallow's Gloucestershire, where Justice Silence tries to sing of 'Robin Hood, Scarlet and John' after his drunken feast with the fat knight Falstaff and his cronies. Put the two together and you have the essential ingredients of the legend of Robin Hood: drinking, revelry, ballads, male bonding. Season it with a little cozening and coney catching, a buffeting or two, a little harmless robbery, and there's Olde Englande for you.

Even in the sixteenth century the myth was already rooted in the folk memory. Today's Christmas pantomimes had their antecedents in the May revels of Shakespeare's time, when revellers dressed up as Robin's merry band, Tuck, Little John and the rest, like Morris-men grotesques. And it wasn't just the common people. This was the fantasy of the May-revels pageant acted out, for example, before Henry VIII in 1515 when the court, ladies and all, went out to Shooters Hill. There they were met by a company of yeomen clothed in green and with bows, whose leader Robin 'desired the king and queen to come into the green wood to see how the outlaws live'. The royals were then feasted out of doors in a gigantic fairy bower made of timber, 'covered with flowers and sweet herbs'. Even further back in time this sense of play had already touched the tale, as we can see in this strange tableau staged in 1357 for the captive king of France by the Black Prince. As they travelled together towards London, five hundred men 'clad in tunics and cloaks of green, with bows and arrows' sprang out of the bushes 'as if they were a band of robbers'. The king of France was taken aback, thinking his life to be in danger. The Black Prince reassured him: 'the Prince said they were Englishmen, living rough in the forest by choice, and that it was their habit to array themselves so every day'. We are clearly already in the presence of an English myth.

The tale of a forest world existing outside the law can be found in many cultures. Such legends surround famous bandits and primitive rebels throughout history, from the Chinese tale of the robber Zu to Bonnie and Clyde. Most of them are good hearted and always a 'friend to the poor', as it says in the ballad of Jesse James. (Printed by Robert Graves in 'The English Ballad' these lines were reworked by Bob Dylan in his song about John Wesley Harding, who was 'a friend to the poor . . . and never known to hurt an honest man'.) So it was in *The Gest of Robin Hood*, the earliest cycle of ballads about our hero, printed in Tudor times but composed in the early 1400s: 'For he was a good outlawe/And dyde pore men moch god.'

The basic elements of the Robin Hood story are shared by all versions: the greenwood itself, the English longbow, the clothes of Lincoln green, robbing the rich to help the poor. The key characters are Friar Tuck, Little John, Will Scarlet and Maid Marion. It is an Eden in the forest, but one edged with danger as paradises must be if they are not to lack all life. The snakes in the forest are the wicked Sheriff, the sadistic Guy of Gisborne, and, of course, Prince John himself. They provide the ever-present threat of dungeons and gruesome medieval punishments, though they are always – or nearly always – outwitted by the quicksilver Robin. These key elements are kept by all the movie versions – featuring Errol Flynn, Richard Todd, Sean Connery, Kevin Costner, not to mention Monty Python.

Not all these elements are medieval, however. The movies carry more recent accretions which really began only in the 1820s with Walter Scott's *Ivanhoe* and Thomas Love Peacock's *Maid Marion*, not forgetting the first version of the tale which was specifically for children, *Robin Hood and Little John* by Pierce Egan (1840): perhaps the most influential Robin story. It is these which have really defined the modern version, as, for example, in a myth curiously perpetuated by Hollywood, that the story is about Normans and Saxons. In *The Adventures of Robin Hood* (1936 – one of the best swashbucklers of its kind), when Prince John (Claude Rains) sneers: 'Any objections to the new tax from our Saxon friends?' or when good Robin (Errol Flynn) stiffens his upper lip in reply: 'It's injustice I hate, not the Normans!' we encounter a modern myth: good solid Saxons, salt of the earth, against effete Normans who are sometimes played to extremes – as with the effeminate Prince John in the Disney version, a foil to Peter Finch's intense and introverted Sheriff. This idea is still there in the 1990s Hollywood version, in which the psychopathic sheriff is played by Alan Rickman as an alarmingly camp but hetero rapist. Though now reduced to a cardboard cut-out, played by the Californian Kevin Costner, with a Muslim friend who knows about the properties of lenses, Robin is still a Saxon rooted in the land: Robin of Locksley. His father is played by the stalwart English actor Brian Blessed, with a bushy beard and foghorn northern voice, in the small castle which is always the Hollywood Englishman's home. Actually, this tale of Normans and Saxons seems to have been invented only in the nineteenth century. There certainly was great anti-French feeling in the thirteenth century, when Robin is assumed to have lived, and a parallel growth of English consciousness; some people may still have harped on about the Norman Conquest. But there is no evidence to show that outlaws of the thirteenth century identified themselves as Saxons. More to the point, the ballads show no trace of such animosity, which surely would have been in there had such things mattered to their audience. As it first appears in Scott's *Ivanhoe*, it is safest to assume that the tale is a fiction. A salutary warning to all who pursue the historicity of myths.

While Arthur is the central figure in English medieval literature, no English folk story has had such currency as Robin Hood. Thomas Becket was a great saint, a goal of pilgrimage and a worker of miracles; Simon De Montfort was the subject of ballads, and of miracles too; Harold, the last Saxon king, has a Norse Saga to his name; Hereward the Wake made the balladeers' repertoire long before Lord Lytton's nineteenth-century best-seller. But good Robin has easily outstripped them all. The roots of the tale go far back in time. The story of Robin Hood was already well known by the 1370s, when William Langland in his *Piers Ploughman* speaks of the ballads of Robin. The largest collection of stories, *The Gest of Robin Hood*, probably originated soon after Langland's time. But the newest research suggests we must go even further back to find the roots of the legend.

The key discovery has been made only in the 1990s: research in local court records has found the nickname Robin Hood attached to criminals between the 1260s and 1290s. This discovery suggests that he was already a legend then, and it also takes a possible real-life Robin back into the time legend says: the reigns of Richard the Lionheart and John. Of course, there is no need to look for a historical figure. As we have seen already in this book, it is entirely possible for legends to arise with no basis in historical fact. Indeed, until not so long ago, Robin tended to be dismissed as a folk myth more akin to a fairy tale. His appearance in May Day revels, when Tudor people dressed up as Robin Hood and the merry men, led many folklorists to think his roots lay in popular paganism, and even in witch cults. Robin was a woodland sprite like Puck or Robin Goodfellow. But the ballads are so full of references to the realities of thirteenth- to fourteenth-century life that this seems unlikely. The social context of the story in the early versions is particularly rich: in particular, the details in *The Gest of Robin Hood* (*c.* 1420) strongly suggest a real background in the thirteenth century, with their stress on sheriffs, royal forests, usury of the Church and so on. Such stories must come from before the time when local administration was in the hands of the gentry and justice was administered by JPs; a time when the forests were still royal. There is also, as we shall see, an unusual specificity about the settings of the ballads. This has recently led many to search for a real man behind the story, a medieval outlaw in the forests of Nottinghamshire and South Yorkshire whose deeds were extraordinary enough to have gathered a great body of legend. Over the last few years in particular, Robin has lent himself to much historical speculation, and a huge amount of energy has been spent trying to locate the 'real' Robin. Especially in the era required by the legend: the times of Good King Richard and Bad King John. So was there a real Robin?

Back in the 1850s, the Yorkshire scholar Joseph Hunter was ploughing through the fourteenth-century court rolls of the medieval manor of Wakefield. Hunter had noticed that the original location of the Robin Hood story was not in Sherwood in Nottinghamshire, where the Larder Oak and the rest are today landmarks on the Sherwood heritage trail, but in Barnsdale, thirty miles to the north of Sherwood: on the Great North Road between Wakefield and Doncaster. This is not to say that any outlaw worth his salt couldn't have roamed between the Wharfe and the Trent, but Barnsdale is where the early ballads of Robin place him. Joseph Hunter was the first to reject the idea of a mythical Robin and to offer a real model in a real historical setting. He suggested Robin was active in the time of Edward II (1307–27), and was perhaps one of the disgruntled supporters of the rebellion of Thomas, Earl of Lancaster in 1322. Hunter even connected the ballad's tale of the king's visit to Robin in the greenwood with the royal visit to the North in 1323. To cap it all, Hunter noticed that the king's wardrobe accounts recorded a payment to one Robert Hood. Unfortunately, this man was a porter, not an outlaw. Nor, on inspection, do the Robin Hood ballads refer anywhere to Thomas of Lancaster and his rebellion. Hunter's researches, however, provided later sleuths with plenty of ammunition to take his case further. For he also found a Wakefield family called Hood or Hod.

It is not clear whether the Hoods were several families or one large extended kin with many branches. Most likely there was more than one family. They certainly used the Christian name Robert several times between the 1270s and the 1340s. The family, though, was much older: they were long-established tenants on the Manor of Wakefield and have now been traced in other documents back to 1202. More on them may yet come to light from the vast quantity of medieval court records yet to be sifted. The main cases involving the Hoods are in the Wakefield court rolls, which are conveniently published now in translation from the thirteenth to the sixteenth century by the Yorkshire Record Society. Some of these cases focus on the area of Sowerby, some way north-west of Wakefield. None of these Hoods was an outlaw, but they were involved in a staggering amount of casual violence which seems to have been usual in the society of their time. Especially interesting are the cases which tie them in with foresters. One branch of the family seems to have been in constant aggravation with the foresters of Sowerby and they are variously fined for violence, attacks, trespass, and stealing animals. Among the Wakefield Hoods is a particularly pugnacious Robert, whose many fines include three in one day in December 1308 for 'drawing blood from the wife of Henry Archer . . . And from Juliana Horsse . . . And for making his haystack in the common way'. Thirteenth-century Neighbours from Hell.

It was a violent time, of course: death and extreme physical cruelty were inescapable in everyday life. Any crossroads you passed on a journey might be marked by a gallows hung with the corpses of criminals; the city gates were festooned with severed heads and the quartered bodies of traitors; horrific punishments were meted out in full view of the populace in any busy market-place. The court records are full of day-to-day quarrels which led to violence and bloodshed. And all this intensified in times of social conflict: lords beat and hanged rebellious peasants; peasants got their own back if the chance arose.

One imagines that this was Robin's world: especially if the legend that he was an outlaw and a bandit is true. Highway robbery was a major crime in the thirteenth century and highway robbers like Robin were common figures on the social scene, their deeds described in fantastic detail in the court records. Medieval crime figures, of course, have to be interpreted as carefully as crime figures do today, and with as much scepticism, but some local archives, such as those of Northamptonshire or Buckingham, are so rich and full that modern scholars have been tempted to extrapolate figures from them and build up a tentative picture of the nation's crime over 700 years ago. It is a picture which casts an interesting light on the legend of Robin Hood.

First, a few background facts. In the thirteenth century, 40 per cent of all crime which came to court was larceny: this involved any kind of carrying off, but mostly consisted of the removal of farm stock, with gangs often rustling big herds. As one would expect in a society where the ordinary person's personal possessions were few, only a quarter of all these larcenies involved household goods. Nearly 20 per cent of recorded crime was burglary (forcible breaking and entering of a house or other structure, often breaking through the wattle-and-daub walls to do so). Ten per cent of recorded crime was robbery (nearly half of which was on the highways or streets). Homicide accounted for nearly 20 per cent, and of the remainder, 6 per cent was handling stolen goods; there were small percentages also for counterfeiting, arson, rape and treason.

What leaps out in these figures is the homicide rate: a very high percentage by any modern standard. Even in today's USA – which with its widespread possession of guns is considered a notably violent society – usually only about half a per cent of crimes are homicides. Obviously, we have to take into account here the problem of the nature of crime records and what is actually reported: modern crime figures report far more minor crime than do medieval court rolls. But a useful insight into the thirteenth-century homicide figures is the modern estimate that London in the thirteenth century had five murders a year per 10,000 people, with a population estimated at some 200,000. In comparison, Miami today, the self-proclaimed murder capital of the USA, has 1.5 homicides per 10,000 people per year; Britain is off the chart with a tiny 0.05 homicides per 10,000 people per year. For what it is worth, one scholar guesses that the threat of murder or serious wounding in thirteenth-century London was nearly twenty times higher than now.

Many robbers in the court rolls were loners. In one case in the Bedford Coroner's Rolls the weapon was a bow in the hands of a real-life Robin:

At twilight on 25 April an unknown felon was standing among the blackthorns below Putnoe by the king's highway in the parish of Golding-ton, when brother Ralph Carpenter, a woodseller, came with Henry Hayward, a serving boy. They were heading for their lodging at Putnoe, but the felon stole a good coat of 'blanket' and four pence in coin from Ralph and a coat of 'rosset' from the hayward and ordered them to go home. They went to their lodging and immediately raised the hue and cry . . .

This robber was unlucky: caught below Putnoe Wood, he resisted arrest and was killed. His worldly goods were pathetic: no money, a bow and arrows worth 3d. (with which he had threatened his victims); a poor coat worth 6d., a horn worth 4d., and two knives worth three and a half pence. None of the jury or witnesses knew him. Where he had come from, whether he had a wife and children, and if so, what happened to them, is not known.

Gangs like the Merry Men are very prominent in the records: large, powerful gangs as well known in their day as the Capones and the Krays today. Well organized and armed, such bands might go so far as to hold ports, towns and city gates, and rob the people inside. With no police force, markets and fairs were good targets for robber gangs, just as the Robin Hood legend has it. Most robbery, though, just as today, was on the streets or highways. Crimes were more usual between Monday and Thursday, a lot less frequent from Friday to Sunday – medieval robbers clearly liked to keep their weekends free – and twilight was the best time, as is faithfully reported in the court books: 'towards vespers . . . at twilight on the first of September'.

The level of gang violence was at times terrifying. Gangs could take on a whole community, crashing through the walls of every house in a village; carefully planning when and where to make their move. On 17 November 1269, the small Bedfordshire village of Roxton was attacked. According to the Bedfordshire coroner, the gang first of all burst through the walls of the house of Ralph Bovetoun, where two girls, Margaret and Alice, were staying. The girls escaped, though the house was robbed. The occupants of the next house were not so lucky. The brigands broke down the wall to find two women, Maude del Forde and Alice Pressade. Maude was killed in bed by axe blows to her head; Alice too was struck down, and their house was stripped. Then John Cobbler's house was assaulted on two sides – perhaps because the gang knew that a man was inside. They broke the east door and the shutters on the west window, hit him with an axe, dragged him outside and killed him. John's wife Alma and their daughter Agnes were then subjected to a frenzied attack; both sustained head wounds from an axe and knife wounds in their chests and arms, and were left near to death; another terrified daughter hid between a basket and a chest. It is the savagery of the attack which horrifies: the coroner's account spares no detail of the horrific wounds to Maude, 'whose brain issued out', and Alice, who died without regaining her speech. Alma, though, was able to identify the criminals before she died. She testified that the gang comprised a servant of the Prior of Newham, 'certain men who had collected tithes for the Prior of Cauldwell in Roxton the previous harvest', and some glovers from Bedford. So the criminals were on the fringe of the legitimate money-gathering rackets of the thirteenth century – the legalized extortion of big ecclesiastical landowners; a bunch of semi-legal debt collectors who decided to go private in pursuit of bigger profits. One would like to think that a 'real' Robin would have been against these sort of people, but that would not be a conclusion justified by the broad evidence of the day. Study of the copious records of the medieval courts explodes the balladeers' myth of

Robin Hood as representing a real-life situation. Almost always, far from robbing the rich to feed the poor, outlaw gangs robbed the poor and kept the takings for themselves.

Some crimes were big stings, as well planned as the famous escapades of the Merry Men. On occasion, gangs gambled on the kidnap and ransom of a high-profile public figure – just as Richard Todd's Robin abducts Peter Finch's sheriff in the 1950s film version. A famous case in the early fourteenth century was the daring seizure of Sir Richard de Wylloughby, a king's bench justice. Getting him returned safely involved the cooperation of important local families and dignitories and the criminal fraternity: the Folvilles and Coterels and several lesser gangs in the West Midlands. For the criminals, it was a huge risk which paid off: they got away with 1,300 marks – enough to live in retirement on the south coast, if not quite with the flamboyance of a Great Train Robber.

The penalties were severe. Among them was outlawry; this was a terrible sentence in Anglo-Saxon and Norman England. Your property was confiscated, you were pronounced outside the law; and thenceforth 'bore the wolf's head'. In other words, anyone could kill you; you could be hunted down like a vicious animal. Something of that idea survives in the traditional tale of Robin Hood's outlawry, though in fact it had become a less serious punishment by the thirteenth century, when crime had become so prevalent that it had lost its force as a threat. Increasingly, it became a sanction used to make people attend court: it took four successive failures to appear before you were outlawed, rather like the repeat-offender legislation in today's United States. By the thirteenth century, when Robin's tale took its first shape, outlawry no longer allowed the lawful killing of an offender, though he still forfeited land and goods. Nor did one necessarily have to be guilty of homicide to be made an outlaw – or indeed guilty of anything: even victims of oppression might be framed in this way, especially when the legal system could be swung by powerful local interests. Then, as a fourteenth-century poem says, if a man was unjustly accused and feared the outcome, 'the only remedy is go to the forests'. And perhaps that was the kind of person Robin was, unjustly accused, taking off to the woods, as in most modern film versions. But unfortunately that tale first appears only in the 1630s.

Whatever the exact historical background, then, it would certainly have been nothing like life for the merry men in the greenwood, where the worst that can happen is a good-humoured cudgelling; a world of quick-witted courteous yeomen living carefree outside the law. The world of a possible real-life Robin was brutal in the extreme. Even the ballads revel in a kind of primitive ferocity. In *The Gest of Robin Hood*, when Robin fights to the death with Guy of Gisborne, he cuts off Guy's head and impales it on the end of his bow so he can mutilate the face with his knife (a scene faithfully rendered in Victorian children's books). In another tale, 'Robin Hood and the Monk', when Little John traps the monk who betrayed Robin, he not only cuts off his head, but kills his 'little page' too, so that no witness survives. The early versions of the tale are fierce and often macabre, none more so than the account of Robin's own death at the hands of the Prioress of Kirklees, who bleeds our unsuspecting hero to death – a tale told by the poet with ghoulish glee:

> At first it bled the thick thick blood
> And afterwards the thin
> And well then wist good Robin Hood
> Treason was there within.

So let's sum up our findings so far: the legend, as far as we can tell, was already taking shape in the thirteenth century, and was full blown by the fourteenth. In the absence of hard evidence for its origins, the Wakefield Hoods remain quite plausible as a starting-point: especially as the locus of the tale is not Sherwood but close-by Wakefield in Barnsdale. The Hoods remained in that area for centuries (there are still Hoods in Sowerby), and on their land in Tudor times we find 'Robinhood strete', so either the family gave Robin to the world or, perhaps more likely, came to associate Robin with their family traditions. In later days, perhaps, a lurid thirteenth-century criminal record might have become a matter for patriotic pride among the Tudor Hoods of Barnsdale; rather as in South Muscombe in Nottinghamshire my wife's family treasured the tale that they had victualled Dick Turpin one night in the Lord Nelson Inn.

But was there a specific, a real Robin? The first really suggestive clue was discovered in the 1930s in a court roll of the Archbishop of York. On 25 July 1225, the royal justices held their assizes in York, adjudicating cases of wrongdoing in Yorkshire over the previous months. The penalities were recorded in an Exchequer Pipe Roll dated Michaelmas 1226. In this document, 32s. 6d. was levied from the chattels of *Robert Hood* (or *Hod*), *fugitive*. This was a fairly large sum of money: a villein's annual income might only be a couple of pounds, so Robert was not a poor man. His name occurs again the next year, but this time in an apparently colloquial version or nickname: he is now *Hobbehod* ('that devil-Hood' – or a mistake for Robbehood?). Interestingly enough, 'Hobbe the robber' is a well-known bogeyman in later folk stories. This suggests either that our Robert has already been identified with some legendary robber figure, a 'Hobbe the robber', or that this is the very start of the legend unfolding before our eyes. Hood's deeds took place on the demesne of the Archbishop, so he was a tenant of the Church of York, whose nearest estate to Barnsdale, incidentally, was at Sherburn, ten miles or so to the north. But that's all we know about him: unfortunately, the full deposition records are lost. Otherwise we might have had his native place, and specific details of his crimes and his family background. Nothing more is known – except the crucial fact that Robert Hod (or Hood) had fled the jurisdiction of the court: he was an outlaw.

This Robert Hood of 1225–6 is so far the earliest model for Robin who can be proved to be an outlaw. And his fame may just have spread. We now know that by the late thirteenth century, the nickname 'Robehod' had already become a criminal *nom de plume*: one man actually calls himself that, even though we know his real name was leFevre-Smith. So the name had passed into the language as a pseudonym. By the fourteenth century, the nickname appears in its modern form: *Robynhood*, and thieves and rogues are sometimes pejoratively called 'Robert's men'. A 1331 Act of Parliament, for example, refers to 'robberies homicides and felonies done in these times by people called Roberdesmen, Wastours and Draghlacche' [drag-latches]. In *Piers Ploughman*, Langland calls robbers 'Robert's knaves', and a ballad of the same time talks of the 'Robertes Men who . . . raken aboute at feires and at ful ales and fyllen the cuppe'.

So Robin/Robert and his men, 'robbehoods' and 'hobbe the robbers' had now entered the language – and the imagination – of the English. During the Peasants' Revolt of 1381, the radical priest John Ball wrote his famous letter to the rebels:

John Schep greets well John the Nameless and John the Miller and John Carter and bids them that they beware of guile in the towns, and stand together in God's name, and bids Piers Ploughman go to his work and chastise wel Hobbe the Robbere . . .

This is obviously an instruction to curb wanton plunder and indiscipline: and Hobbe is a catch-all. Not only is 'Hobbe the robber' a folk name by 1381, but as Ball mentions Piers in the same breath, we might guess that the allusion is literary. What happens to the tale of Robin Hood after that time is a matter for literary, rather than historical, detection.

So as it stands, the only serious candidate so far for a real-life Robin is the northern outlaw Robert Hood in 1225. This date might also agree with the other protagonist of the tale, the wicked sheriff, for at this time the sheriffs were the chief local representatives of the king, his local financial agents, and were often notorious as masters in the art of extortion. Sheriffs were also responsible for mobilizing forces to compel tenants to pay rents, and to perform services or to dispel and arrest rioters. Several real-life thirteenth-century sheriffs of Nottingham would fit the bill offered by the Robert Hood case. Most attractive, perhaps, is Eustace of Lowdham, who was sheriff of Yorkshire in 1225–6, and deputy-sheriff in late 1226; he became sheriff of Nottinghamshire in 1232–3, just at the time of the northern risings; but it was Eustace who in Michaelmas 1226 had to collect and account at Michaelmas 1226 for the penalties imposed on Robert Hood/Hode, and would have supervised the sale of his goods and chattels. A tenuous chain, perhaps, but Eustace is the only known sheriff with a link to the only known outlaw bearing the name Robert Hood – and he later became sheriff of Nottingham.

Then the setting: the identification of Barnsdale as the real centre of Robin's activities adds some specific local colour and plausibility to this hypothesis. Barnsdale, the 'merry Barnisdale' of the Robin Hood ballads, is first mentioned in connection with the tale around 1420. It's a small shallow valley in the parish of North Elmshall, an old mining village south of Ferrybridge and east of Wakefield. Today the traveller heading north on the Great North Road, the A1, passes over it a few miles beyond Doncaster, at the point where the old Roman ridge, now the A639 to Pontefract, splits off to the left. Next door in Campsall parish the place names Barnsdale Bar and Barnsdale Wood also appear on modern maps. But these are not ancient: the wood was called Oak Wood as late as 1841; one suspects the intervention of local antiquarians here, as one does with Little John's Well nearby at Hampole. However, Robin Hood's Well, which is recorded in the 1620s a mile south of Barnsdale, may be a different story, for here the 'stone of Robert Hode' is mentioned in a deed as early as 1422. Barnsdale, then, has more than a whiff of medieval reality about it.

The Roman road from Doncaster which crossed Barnsdale was the most important highway into Yorkshire from the Midlands in the Middle Ages. Today its successor the A1 sweeps over the River Went on a new viaduct to the east of the Roman crossing; the medieval road, though, curved down into the wooded valley of the Went: here's the old crossing at Wentbridge, with a church and a little group of inns, now left with little trade by the new motorway. This was once an important overnight stopping place for travellers, especially the king's agents. North and south of here was wild open land between the Don and the Aire, with no major settlements. It was important for travellers to reach the inns of Wentbridge by nightfall: this was not countryside to negotiate in darkness unless one was travelling in large armed groups (as had long been recommended in travellers' tales). Tucked away in a wooded fold of the valley, this was an ideal spot for bandits, a place so famous for robbers that by 1306 it was said, 'on account of Barnsdale . . . places so dangerous with outlaws wandering by day and by night . . . so many homicides and robberies were done that no one small company could pass through those parts without being taken killed and spoiled . . .'

This is precisely where the earliest stories place Robin Hood. So the facts fit together very well, even if the historian is not permitted on the available evidence to make them do so. But it does give us a possible scenario for our Robert Hood. Let us speculate: the time he was active is in the minority of Henry III, but may be back into the time of John and Richard Lionheart. He is a tenant of the Liberty of St Peter's, York. For unknown reasons, he is made an outlaw in 1226–7, and all his goods and chattels are seized. These were unstable and edgy times, at the end of the 1220s and the early thirties. In the winter of 1231–2, when our Robert Hod or Hood was active, there were risings in the north against foreign clergy with English benefices. A situation then arose with some striking similarities to the later Robin Hood ballads. Among those is the anti-clericalism. Papal messengers were attacked on the roads of Yorkshire, their bulls destroyed; one was killed. Some went into hiding, some were captured and ransomed. Armed bands attacked and pillaged the foreigners' estates and took their stored corn. Some bands went around with their 'heads hooded'. (So is Hood or Hobbehood perhaps a pseudonym? A badge like the Luddite Captain Swing?) And now there comes a very interesting detail from an absolutely contemporary observer, the St Albans chronicler Matthew Paris: when the rebel bands seized the clerics' barns, they sold the grain at low prices 'for the benefit of the many' – or even gave it away to the poor. This sounds uncannily familiar.

The official view was that all this was the work of only one company which moved from county to county, led by a disaffected knight with the pseudonym 'William Wither'. They no doubt exaggerated the organization of the rebels, but there certainly was at least one real William Wither: Sir Robert Thwing, a Yorkshire knight who had been deprived by the Church of his rights in an estate at Kirk Leatham. This man's chief lands were up in the North Riding, around Thwing, but he had friends. Could our 'Hobbehod' perhaps have been a member of his company, or leader of another group of rebellious northerners stalking the highways in the troubled winter of 1231? He was at any rate an outlaw, he lived just at the time the later Gests point to; and he may have been of the minor landowning class whose troubles are echoed in the ballads. Within five years of his appearance in the courts as an outlaw, there is an outburst of Robin Hood-like activities by men of his class. It is not hard to imagine how stories and songs might have come into existence around such a tale, at such a time, later to gather accretions and detail till no one outlaw or time can be discerned in the developed tale.

Whoever was the original focus, the legend spread fast, reaching the Sussex coast within two generations. At this early stage, Hood was a criminal hero pure and simple, with none of the jolly pro-social values of the modern version. Perhaps sung by bards, the tale swiftly fed back into the criminal fraternity; soon to be a 'Robinhood' would become the goal of any self-respecting outlaw. In a fascinating case in Berkshire in 1261, William, son of Robert leFevre, was indicted for robbery; his name is changed in the records to William 'Robehod': either this is a pseudonym or the name had already become a catch-all nickname for robbers: a 'robbehod'.

The transformation and embellishment of the legend continued over two centuries, from the 1260s to the 1450s. During that time the outlaws' area of action spreads from Barnsdale to Sherwood; Lincoln green is their dress and their weapon is the English longbow. As Chaucer says in *The Knight's Tale*, Robin's most endearing qualities in the eyes of the medieval audience were robbery and the killing of landowners, especially Church landowners: he and his men maintain a low-level guerrilla warfare against established authority represented by the sheriff. In today's parlance, they are terrorists. The ballads also have a notably anti-clerical slant, and it is interesting that the token priest in Robin's band, Friar Tuck, is wittily unspiritual: a hard-drinking, fighting man who always gives as good as he gets. It is quite likely that during this period other sensational real-life cases were incorporated into the tale: like the story of Roger Godberd, a 'leader and captain of malefactors' in Leicestershire and the Sherwood area in the aftermath of the Barons' Revolt in the late 1260s. Here, possibly is the inspiration for another important element in the later story of Robin Hood, for like Robin with Sir Richard of the Lea, Godberd (it was alleged after his capture) had been protected by a good knight, Sir Richard Foliot, whose lands, incidentally, touched both Sherwood and Barnsdale.

As for the band of Merry Men – it didn't take long for the legendary highwayman to gather a gang. It is in a Kent homicide case of 1313, for example, that we first encounter one of Robin's best-loved companions, when a real-life criminal John of Shorne is introduced to the court with an intriguing alias: 'also known as Johannes Petit' – Little John.

For Friar Tuck's first appearance, we must wait till the early fifteenth century in Kent, at just the time that the ballads of Robin were at the height of their popularity. Then we meet one Richard Stafford, 'alias Frere Tuk', who in Henry V's time was robbing the king's lieges, poaching venison and burning foresters' houses in the woods of Surrey and Sussex. Worth a social history all of his own, Stafford was evidently just the kind of forest bandit portrayed in the ballads, and again the fact that a real person takes a fictional name known from ballads and literature suggests that Tuck was already current as a popular character.

For others among the Merry Men, though, historians have had less luck. We have yet to meet prototypes, if indeed they exist at all, for Will Scarlet, Mutch the Miller's son, or the minstrel Alan à Dale. And as for Maid Marion, she, alas, came very late into Robin's tale. The first known connection of the two is by the poet Alexander Barclay in the early sixteenth century, though there were much older pastoral tales and summer revels which depicted the love affair of the shepherdess Marion and her lover Robin. So the delightful Marion is, sadly, the character with the least firm hold on history.

As the ballads developed, so did the theme which the tale shares with many famous robber stories in other cultures: namely that Robin robbed the rich to feed the poor. By the early fifteenth century, Robin is now a 'Good outlaw that did the poor much good.' In a famous passage Robin tells his men:

> But loke ye do no husbonde harme
> That tilleth with his plough.
>
> No more ye shall no gode yeman
> That walketh by grene wode shawe
> Ne no knyght ne no squyer
> That wol be gode felawe.
>
> These bishoppes and these archebishoppes
> Ye shall them bete and bynde;
> The hye sherif of Notyngham
> Hym holde ye in your mynde.

Robin's social class changed through time, as no doubt did his audience and readers. His invention as a dispossessed noble, Robin of Loxley, the son of the Earl of Huntingdon, came much later, in the seventeenth century in Martin Parker's *True Tale of Robin Hood*. This is now writ in stone as the accepted version in Hollywood. The earlier medieval version, though, sees him as a *yeoman*, in those days a poor freeman under the rank of knight, gentleman or squire. It's an interesting word: one of the earliest sources for it is in a text of the twelfth century on forest law (once mistakenly attributed to King Cnut). In this, it is stated that foresters are drawn from the class of 'middling sort of men [*mediocribus hominibus*], whom the English call lesser thegns [*laessthegenes*] but the Danes [i.e., in the East Midlands and Yorkshire] call yeomen [*yongermen*].' So the yeomen of England were originally the middling sort of free peasantry, and the word actually came from the old lands of the Danelaw, where, as far as we can tell, the tale originated. In the earliest layers of the story, that, perhaps, was perceived to be Robin's status. And as for his emblems: bows and arrows were the badge of foresters – they are shown on their tombs. Killing deer, too, was their *métier:* '*we lyve by our kynges dere*'.

And the king? Robin's real enemies in the stories are the sheriff, the abbot and the baleful Guy of Gisborne. King Richard, on the other hand is always 'comely', brave, strong, merciful and generous, as Sean Connery plays him in Kevin Costner's film. In reality, of course, the king would have been implacably against such people, and would have done all he could to strengthen the sheriff's hand. But medieval peasants, yeomen and lesser gentry all saw the king as the font of justice – justice which to them meant protection from oppressors, landlords and grasping local officials, and the reaffirmation of the 'good old law' which had operated in the past. The illusion that the king was on their side, which we see reflected in the ballads, shows their protest was not against the English state, but against the immediate hardship and unfairness of the system as it worked in the hands of greedy landowners and partial judges. The idea that the king was their protector ironically would lead to their downfall in the Peasants' Revolt of 1381.

Looking through just a part of this vast collection of records, stories and songs, it is easy to see why historians have been tempted to suggest a real Robin. But in the end it all comes down to what sources do and do not say. It is probably fair to assume that the Robin Hood tales arose some time around the end of the twelfth or the beginning of the thirteenth century, the time of Richard the Lionheart and King John, or the minority of Henry III. It is an attractive hypothesis – but no more than that – that the Yorkshire risings of 1231–2 played some part in the construction of the tale, though we cannot prove it. Other real-life tales, like that of Gosberd, may have entered the mix later. It is possible that the Hood name comes from the family around Wakefield, close to the Barnsdale robbers' hideout by the River Went on the Great North Road. The legend grew in the late thirteenth century, and by the mid fourteenth was the subject of many ballads which are crystallized in the full-length *Gest of Robin Hood*, written down soon after 1400.

That is to outline a tentative history for the growth of the legend. That Robin himself was a historical person is still a long way short of proof. Indeed, we would hardly expect it ever to be provable, due to the very nature of the literary sources for Robin, and the historical sources for his time. Even the Robin Hod or Hood of 1226, the outlaw with the mysterious nickname Hobbehod, sounds as if he is already caught up in a process of myth-making. What is clear, though, is that the story arose from historical situations. But as always, the appeal of such tales goes beyond historical fact. As Shakespeare's *As You Like It* shows, Robin's is a Golden Age myth about Merrie England; a golden time of good-hearted bandits living outside the law. In a society which since the tenth century had had a strong sense of national law, harshly enforced after 1066, it is not unnatural that such a balancing imaginative world should have been created by the bards. It's a tale which finds an echo in many cultures. It is a little one-dimensional, perhaps. Where the lays of Arthur enter real tragedy with a dark strain of betrayal and sexual jealousy, Robin's world is uncomplicated: good King Richard will return; Robin can marry Marion and go back to Loxley; Guy of Gisborne gets his grisly come-uppance without ever upsetting the children. That's why it still works so well, even for Hollywood in the 1990s. But as it says in Monty Python's version of the story: 'this redistribution of wealth is a lot more complicated than it first appears'. The simple historian can only agree.

5. When was England England?

The English are having a hard time of it these days, if you believe the Press. Derided abroad either as a yob culture or a heritage theme park; at home, on the verge of divorce from their partners in the United Kingdom of Great Britain and Northern Ireland. For the English, 1997 was what the medievals would have called an *annus mirabilis*. In the year in which we celebrated the 1,400th anniversary of the Roman mission to our island, the New Labour Government launched an ambitious attempt to clear away the baggage of history, to untangle the relations of the English with the Welsh, Scots and Irish, the legacies of 1922, 1707, 1603, and further back still. It has all left the English feeling understandably nervous. With European union already on the horizon, along comes the break-up of Britain.

We became Britons in the eighteenth century, recast for our new imperial role in the world, and a new history was created for us. But with the pulling down of the Union flag over Hong Kong, that history has finally been put to bed. And suddenly the eighteenth-century settlement is being questioned. Older allegiances are reasserting themselves with Scottish and Welsh devolution. With shock we begin to see that Great Britain is not a solid unchanging entity at all; indeed the Act of Union of 1707 might be a temporary blip in an older continuum. And so, just as we adjust ourselves to being part of the global culture, and prepare to be good Europeans too, we have been forced to look back into our past. For the English, this is proving a strangely painful exercise. No nation, it would appear, manages self-criticism with such intensity. (What other nation so willingly accepts, and publicly expresses, imperfection and failure as a national characteristic?) Commentators as diverse as the TV anchorman Jeremy Paxman and the novelist

Julian Barnes have voiced the fear that all the English have left is a heritage industry. 'England no longer has a defining identity,' said the Northern Irish poet Tom Paulin recently on the BBC. 'It has no shape: you can't define it.'

It's an extraordinary turnabout, for England was never questioned by earlier generations. After all, when Nelson ran up his signal flags at Trafalgar, it was England, not Great Britain, which expected. Queen Victoria had to lie back and think of England (or so we were told before we discovered how much she enjoyed sex!). And in the old song from the First World War, it was in England that the Poor Bloody Infantryman at Wipers would rather be, 'to fornicate my bleeding life away'. From Edward Thomas and Stanley Baldwin to George Orwell and even John Major, in that speech about warm beer and cricket, we all thought we knew what England was about. And now, we are told, the English find themselves to be a lump whose outline can no longer be drawn, either literally or figuratively.

Part of the problem lies, perhaps, in our habit of defining England sentimentally, by moods and images: by red pillar-boxes and cricket, by Adelstrop or Baldwin's harvest home. Such things may or may not tell us about national character, but the best England watchers have always seen something altogether different. Alexis de Toqueville, for example, that most acute of observers, has a lot to say about the funny way the English do things, but the key to what made them tick, he thought, lay deeper than that. He thought English identity was crucially to do with our regime; essentially our non-existent Constitution. The genius of the English lay first and foremost in the way we organized ourselves. And to him it was the deep past which explained the uniqueness of England. Such ideas are unfashionable now. But I wonder? Let's go back first to a politician's speech from a thousand years ago, to a time when they had no cricket, but more than likely some kind of football, and, no doubt, alehouses and warm beer.

In 1014, Archbishop Wulfstan of York gave a 'Sermon of the Wolf to the English' (his pen name was *Lupus*, 'Wolf'). After more than twenty years of war, the land had been overrun by the

Vikings. By Christmas 1013, the government had collapsed and the incompetent Ethelred the Unready had gone into exile in Normandy. Wolf was a powerful figure, a lawmaker, and his sermon appears in a manuscript in the British Library with material in his own hand (including his own corrections and changes to the text). It's a catalogue of terrible stories about the breakdown of law and order, of violence, slaving, gang rape and murder. The core message is the disintegration of group feeling: the failure of the law. For Wolf, there definitely was such a thing as society:

The devil has led this people too far astray . . . the people have betrayed their own country [literally their 'earth']. And the harm will become common to this entire people [*eallre thyse theode*]. There was a historian in the time of the Britons called Gildas, who wrote about their misdeeds; how their sins angered God so much that finally He allowed the army of the English to conquer their land. Let us take warning from this . . . we all know there are worse things going on now than we have heard of among the ancients. Let us turn to the right and leave wrongdoing . . . Let us love God and follow God's laws.

What is so interesting about this speech is Wolf's stress on the state of the nation: literally, 'this people', 'this nation'. (*Theod* means 'people' or 'nation'; he also uses *theodscipe*, 'nation', and *theod scathas*, 'crimes against the public good'.) Wolf seems to accept unquestioningly that through his sermon he can address *the whole nation*: that the English were one people, with defined customs and laws, and that allegiance to this entity was a generally recognized fact. The problem now for him was the collapse of 'group feeling'. And if we look in Wolf's speech for key words, as modern commentators might, for example, examine a Tony Blair speech ('new', 'challenge', 'fresh', etc.), there is one word which stands out above all others: *law*.

In modern terms, Wolf was a think-tank member. No ordinary bishop, he was responsible for key policy statements, he wrote law codes, and a manifesto of rulership, the Institutes of Polity. This sermon was preached in the darkest hour of Ethelred's England to

the highest in the land. And it assumes an English state under
English law.

We take the state for granted today; we grumble about it, resent
its 'nannyism' or whatever. But we can't live without it. Literally
– for to be stateless is just about the worst fate that can befall
someone today. It wasn't always so. There were times – and not
so long ago, as historians measure things – when states didn't exist;
when protection by a powerful lord or kin group was the only
guarantee against being enslaved, robbed or coerced. The idea of
organizing human society under law to make the best use of its
human and natural resources, to protect people from violence and
war, to codify our obligations to one another – this is not a given
in history. Most of the world's 180 states today are recent – and
unstable – formations, but among the stayers there is no question
that one of the oldest, most effective and indeed most successful
has been England. In these last days of the British state, it is interesting
to ask why.

The continuity of the English and British states is one of those
great myths of England: perhaps *the* great myth, much employed
by conservatives and railed against by radicals. Since the 1950s, it
has been somewhat unfashionable to trace English roots very far
back in time. The Tudor revolution in government tends these
days to be seen as the starting-point of the modern State; the Union
in 1707 the formation of British identity. The idea that certain key
aspects of English culture – local organization, the law, the English
state itself – were firmly in place by 1200 has not been taken
seriously for quite some time now. The trend in political and
historical thinking during the past thirty years has been against this
idea of real continuities. Post-modernist critiques of the fantasy of
the British past – in polemics like those of Tom Nairn, Patrick
Wright and Anthony Barnett – and also in imaginative literature –
have focused on reactionary England and the triumph of the past
as heritage. There are several reasons for this. Part of it is an
unwillingness to engage with what is felt to be a historical anachronism, now we know so well how much of our 'tradition' has actually
been invented in modern times, since the advent of mass newspapers,

radio and TV. Even the 1953 Coronation so breathlessly larded with archaisms by Richard Dimbleby, actually followed an order that had been re-created from the Anglo-Saxon coronation order only in 1901! In part, too, I suspect, there has been a natural reluctance to appear to embrace what sounds like a Victorian racialist myth in multicultural modern Britain. But recently, Old English historians have begun to reformulate the idea that many of the key elements which make up Englishness – and the English State itself – go back before 1200, or indeed before the Conquest.

Unbroken continuity was the great theme of nineteenth-century historians like Kemble, Greene, Stubbs and Freeman. As they expressed it, the theme carried a dangerous layer of racism: the idea of the superiority of the 'Teutonic race'. The greatest twentieth-century Anglo-Saxon historian, Sir Frank Stenton, was free of such taint, but inevitably, writing in the early years of the war (in *Anglo-Saxon England*, published in 1943), he couldn't help give his interpretation of the rise of England a teleological slant, a sense of destiny even. He traced the germ of English unity back to the wars of the seventh and eighth centuries, which he saw as 'steps towards an ultimate unity of all England'.

The key to this unity, Stenton thought, was to be found in Bede's idea of an *imperium* ('overlordship') over all the English peoples south of the Humber, which he ascribed to seven early kings. Then in the 890s, the *Anglo-Saxon Chronicle* adds an eighth king to this list, describing them with a vernacular term, *bretwalda*, which was interpreted then as 'Britain ruler' but originally meant 'wide ruler' (*brytenwalda*). This evidence is perhaps vaguer than Stenton thought, but it allows us to believe that the Anglo-Saxons did have a notion of a hegemony over England, and perhaps over 'Britain' – that is, the British mainland. Some scholars have compared this with Roman ideas, and with what the Welsh later called the *unbeinyaeth Prydein*, which sounds something like the high kingship of Ireland. One Welsh poem has Edwin of Northumbria and Cadwallon of Gwynedd fighting it out for the 'rulership of Britain'.

A poetic idea of the unity of Britain is one thing, but a state of

England is quite another. Nor should we think, because England exists now, that the move towards it was inevitable, although history shows recurrent examples of smaller kingdoms eaten up by larger ones. It is true that some minor entities vanish before the Vikings: the East and South Saxons, for example. But some of the early English kingdoms, Mercia and Northumbria in particular, were powerful state-sized groupings with strong regional identities, which in different circumstances could have lasted. Whether English political unity would have come about without the intervention of the Vikings, though, is impossible to say, delightful as it is to imagine archaic units of Mercia – the autonomous county of the Hwicce, say, or the special development zone of Wrocset – surviving today in the EEC in a Mercian republic!

But the Vikings changed everything – or at least, the English experience of the Vikings did. Though revisionists have recently played down their impact, most scholars still do not find the idea convincing that Viking numbers were small, that the rape and pillage were greatly exaggerated, and that the dreaded long-haired Northmen were more into trading and origami than war. The Vikings had a tremendous impact on Britain, and changed for ever the political landscape of England. Out of the fire of the Viking invasions, the West Saxon dynasty under Alfred the Great emerged as the one clan with the power, clout, nerve and ruthlessness to dominate lowland Britain. Alfred's victories set the marker. As so often in history, an external threat strongly focused ideas of identity and accelerated administrative change. By the end of his reign, Alfred in some sense had come to see himself as 'king of all Englishmen'. There is no evidence that people beyond Wessex would have agreed with him. East Anglians, East Midlanders and Northumbrians had all made their own terms with the Vikings. Some (especially in Northumbria) would come to see Viking kings as best representing the interests of their region, class – or even Church – against the southern English ('to whom we have never been subject', as one northerner remarked bitterly). It was the military conquest of the Midlands and East Anglia by Alfred's son Edward Elder (a 'reconquest' in all the historiography until only recently) which set up a West Saxon kingdom of all England, which was finally achieved by Athelstan after 927. This is the real foundation of the English state. By 973, Athelstan's descendant Edgar could celebrate his coronation in Bath with unmistakable imperial overtones, in a former Roman city whose buildings around the hot springs recalled Charlemagne's Aachen. Edgar was 'king of the English', but legislated within that for a 'nation of Englishmen, Danes and Britons': one kingdom, but one whose language and customs varied. Speaking the English language was a help, but not essential. From the start, England was ethnically diverse; the key was allegiance to the English king and his law.

Two crucial elements aided England's longevity from the very start, and they are two of the most important features of the early English state. In fact, historians now see them as more important by far than the ambiguous evidence of tendencies to political unity. First is the *idea* of the unity of the English people, an idea that goes back to Bede, writing in the 720s. In the very title of his *Ecclesiastical History of the English Nation* he speaks of *one* English people. If Bede is to be believed, back in the 590s the name of one of the Anglo-Saxon peoples, the Angles, captured the attention of Pope Gregory the Great, who saw some of their women and children in an Italian slave market. They were, he said, 'not Angles but angels'. The happy pun stuck. Organizing the mission of 597, Gregory habitually referred to them as Angles. As a result, Christians in Britain of Germanic speech, the children of the Church of the English at Canterbury, were ever after Angli, Angelcynn, of English race. This was a crucial unifying idea. And it was fixed long before political union was achieved by the West Saxons: if it had not been already present, we would perhaps be Saxons today, speaking the Saxon language across the Saxon-speaking world. Instead, Alfred's people were 'English', even though he was a Saxon. From the seventh century onwards, the *gens Anglorum* was a given. In the tenth century, when the English nation included Danes, Norsemen, Britons, Saxons and Angles, the kings who created the kingdom of England still saw their task as the fulfilment of the promise implied in Bede: an English people under one king.

As politicians forever remind us, political consensus resides ultimately in a shared sense of history: this is at the core of allegiance (and is why, for example, revolutions must rewrite history). Bede gave the English a history which all could share, an interpretation which made sense of their past – and their future. They had been a pagan people ('out on the edge of the world, worshipping sticks and stones' as Pope Gregory famously put it); they had been given by God a beautiful island, a land of milk and honey; the Gregorian mission had given them Roman Christian civilization. From then on they were a chosen people, for whom loyalty to God's law became a condition of survival in the future. So the English became a people of the Covenant, like the Israelites, their destiny indissolubly bound up with duty to the divine law. Allegiance to that kingship and its law therefore becomes a pre-condition of being English in later times – and in a sense still is.

The role played by the English language in this is interesting. Several languages were spoken within the boundaries of tenth-century England. And the English language was as responsive to new trends then as it is today to, say, West Indian dialect or American English. The monastic reformers in the tenth century – a tight-knit group of politically motivated men, if ever there was one – tried to standardize the official language based on West Saxon. Their efforts can be read in literary works sponsored by the ruling elite such as St Aethelwold's translation of the Rule of St Benedict. However, the English we speak today is not descended from this southern upper-class official language, but, surprisingly enough, from the common speech of the East Midlands, which was a dialect strongly influenced by Scandinavian. Like German today, Old English in its sentence structure is what linguists call a subject-object-verb language (I have the cup broken). But today's spoken English is a subject-verb-object language (I have broken the cup), as was the speech of the Scandinavian Viking settlers, and this had already become English common speech before Chaucer's day. There is much argument among scholars over how this creole came about: but the best bet is that today's spoken English is descended from a language which developed naturally as a result of contact between people along the Watling Street frontier which divided Danish and English England. In Alfred's day, this was a new border which cut across very old connections and contacts. Within two generations access was free again, and speech rapidly altered in response: a fascinating illustration of the process by which England became England.

So in the tenth century, the idea of one English people was given political reality. And the interests of the ruling elite were unquestionably national rather than local. Hence in the law codes the rich are enjoined to 'feed poor Englishmen'; homilists make sermons to 'all this nation', and the *Chronicle* in Ethelred's day talks of the 'good of the country', 'this nation', 'all the people of England', 'all the flower of the English nation'. The regions still had their own sensibilities, especially the northerners, the Northumbrians, but after the eleventh century Northumbria never seriously threatened the integrity of the English State. In the northern rebellion of 1065 when the thegns marched south, they were not asking for a separate state in the north; they simply wanted rid of a bad earl. The king agreed with them. In 1052, Godwin's revolt was forestalled because they didn't want the slaughter of so many Englishmen, because there was 'hardly anyone on either side who was not a good Englishman'.

There can hardly be room for doubt, then, that the sense of belonging to an English State as Englishmen and Englishwomen, under English law, was created before 1066. Of course, it was in part driven by the agenda of the Church: at few times in our history did legislators have a stronger sense of creating a society with a moral order, however unpalatable it may seem to us now. But they would have rebutted in no uncertain terms the idea that they did not have a national perspective on things, a sense of Englishness and a conception of an English State, a *res publica*. Some of the ancient regional divisions no doubt still mattered: the Mercians and Northumbrians had to be handled carefully by the West Saxon kings, and the most successful of them – Alfred, Athelstan and Edgar – had strong Mercian connections and friendships. North of the Humber, the tacit acknowledgement of a distinct identity continued until well into early modern times. The result of rubbing northerners up the wrong way was as violent in Tudor times as in the eleventh century. But from the eleventh century, there is no evidence anyone thought in political terms other than of membership of the English people under a king of the English.

This sense of Englishness, along with the State itself, survived the cataclysm of 1066, even though the ruling class of Anglo-Saxon England was wiped out by the Normans. This remarkable fact was rapidly understood by the Normans themselves. In the historical writing of the twelfth century, both by Normans and by half-Englishmen like William of Malmesbury, we find an English *res publica*, not a French or Norman State. A long French poem, 'Lestoire Des Engles', was even compiled by Geoffrey Gaimar for his Norman patrons to help them understand their English identity. So Englishness was the creation of the Anglo-Saxons, and it was they who made England.

Of course, it is one thing to create a state, quite another for it to be long-lasting. Plenty of states in the modern world are recent creations with no real historical identity, and hence command no deep loyalties. (As a result, they may not all last long: states founded on an idea, one suspects, are particularly vulnerable.) To be long-lasting, a state needs not only ideologies, but institutional structures, which in English history in the long run have tended towards allowing citizens certain freedoms to pursue their own work and happiness while protecting them from oppression. If the first great state-building factor was ideological, the second was practical: the creation of institutions which were durable and adaptable.

The formidable powers which accrued to the West Saxon dynasty in the Viking Age enabled them to do this. They organized society for war, with heavy burdens on landowners and peasantry. They had seen the Carolingian kingdom in Europe and learned fast, creating a network of shires, hundreds and parishes, a society bound by common oath to its lord. Many of these arrangements were continental in inspiration: the hundreds, for example, were a Frankish system, imposed on southern and Midland England between the 890s and 940. But in part they were based on older units: the Wessex shires are very ancient, some based on Roman or British territorial groupings.

Throughout the Middle Ages, outside the boroughs, the hundreds and their courts were crucial for taxation, justice, policing, law, military defence, and for the administration of the oaths which bound individuals and kin groups to king and community. Above the level of the hundred, the Old English sheriff, which is still an office in the USA, of course – administered the shire through bailiffs, who held office in each hundred (originally the bailiff was the king's justicer employed in the hundred for the detection of crime). But the hundred was the key unit of local administration: the records of land tenure and tax obligation, for example, were held centrally by the government's clerks under hundred headings. This was the way the Domesday Survey of 1086 was organized, on the sworn testimony of local juries; and by the time of the great surveys of the thirteenth century, the Hundred Rolls, we have a picture of the grass-roots functioning of a medieval government which is unrivalled anywhere in the world. (The Hundred Rolls are still kept in the Public Record Office, the great bundles of parchment rolls with the jurors' seals hanging from them on tags, the bundles of exchequer tallies notched to denote pounds, shillings and pence.)

And these arrangements proved very long-lasting. These characteristics of the 'premature' Dark Age State came through to modern times in England, just as de Toqueville saw. The shires were still working institutions into the twentieth century, to which the reforms of the nineteenth and twentieth centuries gave a new lease of life, until the reorganization of 1974.

In 1886, when the Victorians celebrated the 800th anniversary of Domesday Book, they had no doubts about the continuity of their institutions from the distant past; it was clearly something they felt much more directly than we do. At that time, many old lesser institutions survived, if only residually. Superseded in the nineteenth century by the Poor Law Union and the Urban and Rural District, the hundred faded so swiftly that it now sounds like a completely archaic institution from remotest antiquity. But though the Old

English hundred courts were abolished in the 1860s, it was only in 1886 that the last legal significance of the hundred (in the case of making good damages occasioned by rioters) was finally done away with. Borough councils and manor courts continued to exist for a while longer yet: an example of the tenacity of primitive representative institutions at grass roots (rather like the village and cantonal assemblies which still function in Switzerland). The great nineteenth-century constitutional expert William Stubbs gave a striking example from his native town, Knaresborough in Yorkshire, where he traced his ancestry for sixteen generations to a tenant of the forest in 1359. In the forest courts of Stubbs's day, each of the townships from the manor of the forest was represented by a constable and four men, from whom the local jurors of the leet were chosen. This arrangement had come down directly from the Old English custom where the representation of the vill or manor was by a reeve and four men; this is described in Domesday Book in 1086, and was evidently old by then.

What was true of the hundred and the shire is also true of the boroughs, as can be seen in the voluminous records of the old town councils, which in their way are as impressive testimony as the Hundred Rolls to the cooperative maintenance of order which is the mark of English history. I remember seeing this for myself as a fledgling journalist in Yorkshire in 1974, covering the end of the old boroughs under Edward Heath's government: Batley, Dewsbury and the like. There was great dismay felt locally, and old councillors were seen breaking down in tears. What lay behind this dismay was the strong feeling that local government is one of the key props in the peculiar non-parliamentary democratic system of England.

As imperialists, the Victorians were more susceptible to racial myths than we are in multicultural Britain at the end of the twentieth century. But one imagines that it was also easier for the Victorians to feel continuities. They were not only nearer in time to the medieval world, but the sweeping changes of the last century – and the accelerated pace of change – have made it less easy for us to see ourselves in relation to our history. Parliament is one obvious case. Parliamentary elections in the mid nineteenth century, after all, were not so very different from what they had been hundreds of years before. In Stubbs's famous *Constitutional History*, he looked at a document which says that 494 freeholders voted in the Hunting-donshire election of 1450. Stubbs pointed out that in 1852 Hunting-don still only had 2,892 registered voters, and amazingly, until 1872 they voted in public and met to do so, as the ancient Germanic assemblies did, in the open air! The point here is not whether England was democratic in the Middle Ages – obviously it was not – but whether it had developed mechanisms of government which allowed discussion and negotiation between localities and the centres of power.

These days, it is fashionable to dismiss the representative role of medieval parliaments and see them as feudal instruments. But by the fourteenth century, limited though it was in composition and representation, Parliament unquestionably had a political role. In Edward II's reign, a calendar was compiled on what Parliament did, the *Modus Tenendi Parliamentum*. Under the first heading of parliamentary business, it lists matters of foreign policy, war and questions concerning the king's family; under the second heading: 'matters of common concern to the kingdom, so that laws shall be implemented against defects of customary law'. Clearly, this was in some sense a political assembly, as is underlined by the importance the document attaches to the knights representing each shire: 'it must be understood that the two knights who come to parliament from each shire have a greater say in granting and denying than the greatest earl in England'. And it was fourteenth-century parliament-arians, after all, who came up with the idea of the impeachment of the king's ministers. Here there is an absolute continuity between medieval and modern constitutionalism. When Richard Nixon left the White House Lawn by helicopter in 1974, or when Bill Clinton became mired in the Lewinsky scandal in 1999, what they faced was the medieval sanction of impeachment: a constitutional pro-cedure for 'high crimes and misdemeanours' developed in the fourteenth century for bringing corrupt or unjust ministers to justice, like Michael de la Pole, Chancellor of England in 1386.

Such institutions gave the medieval state a structural solidity even where it was politically volatile. In this respect, the fledgling Anglo-Saxon state is particularly interesting. The king and his court were itinerant, but had strong centralizing powers none the less. The coinage is the most fascinating example: a coinage so efficient that by Edgar's day the coins could be recalled every few years, and recoined to a new design, their weight and silver content adjusted in a way that some scholars interpret as a response to inflationary or deflationary pressures in the economy! From Athelstan's time onwards, the coinage was centralized in the sense that only the king's name was allowed on the money, but regional designs were permitted to appease regional sentiment: something, we are told, even today's devisers of the euro do not feel able to permit.

The kingdom of Athelstan or Edgar might appear to us to have been worryingly unstable: certainly it needed energy on the part of the ruler to make it work well. But its system proved to be very long-lasting. Many modern observers have wondered about the peculiar mix of archaic and modern in the English system, most brilliantly de Toqueville. He was surely right. England's old regime came down to modern times.

'The Making of England' is a very old-fashioned idea these days, something that seems to belong in the books of Winston Churchill and Arthur Bryant. But it is worth a fresh look, especially now that the Scots and Welsh are poised to go their own way, and the English find themselves in need of a new history, not as Britons but as English. When was England? What was distinctive about the English? The answers are not John Major's cricket and warm beer, or Orwell's red pillar-boxes. In some sense, they are surprising answers too.

The modern English state was not created in one go. It is the product of a long – and continuing – process, but its roots lie in the Anglo-Saxon period, just as the Victorians thought. But from the beginning, it was not about race, or blood, as some Victorian racial theorists liked to say. It was rather about acceptance of common language and authority, about 'group feeling', about allegiance to the state and its way of doing things. That's the core of the English story, recalling Fernand Braudel's great passage on the identity of France:

As if prehistory and history were not one and the same process . . . which still constitutes across hundreds and hundreds of years, a living feature of the present-day world . . . as if our beliefs and languages did not come down to us from the dark ages of the more distant past . . . an obscure history, running along under the surface, refusing to die.

Is that still true? Whether such ideas are still alive now, after the dramatic changes of the last half-century, I, for one, am not sure. Old institutions have outlasted their usefulness; Europe beckons; modern Britons must take their place in that wider society which was so courted and admired by the Old English. And global culture is now rapidly breaking down those insular characteristics which once persisted, as Braudel observed, across centuries. In the twenty-first century, surely, we will finally leave that past behind, even though its residue will still persist in our ways of speech, thinking and doing things. We will be living After England.

In conclusion, what we can say is this. The Anglo-Saxons created England; the Normans and their successors attempted to create Great Britain, not succeeding half so well, despite their long attempts to dominate the cultures and societies of Ireland, Wales and Scotland. By the late tenth century, the rulers of the English had already come to a *modus vivendi* with their Celtic neighbours: marking the limits of England almost exactly as it is today – that shape of England which Tom Paulin could not visualize. It was the Normans who tried to subdue the whole island, and their failure has finally been acknowledged in the late twentieth century. England, on the other hand, is the creation of the Old English. It is something real to go back to, unlike so many modern countries whose attempts to build such allegiances have had to be fabricated. This is not to say that it doesn't need reform now: not least the system of democracy itself – for who now would claim the English are better off than, say, the Germans? But it has a long and distinguished pedigree, which, contrary to the modern critiques, is more the product of history than myth. It goes back to Gregory the Great, Bede, and the Old English and Norman lawmakers, and for a country on a small island off the shores of Europe, its practical achievements in history have been considerable. At root was a grand idea – the sense of a chosen people – but also something very practical: a workable conception of society, of order and of mutual obligations. The latter is still in place and still working; and even the former has taken a long time to fade away.

PART TWO

Manuscripts and Mysteries

'This Is Your Life': King Athelstan gifts St Cuthbert with Bede's
version of the saint's life, c. 934.

6. Heritages and Destructions:
The Troublesome Journey and Laborious
Search of John Leland

> When it was proclaimed that the Library contained all books, the
> first impression was of extravagant happiness. All men felt themselves to
> be the masters of an intact and secret treasure . . . At that time it was
> also hoped that a clarification of humanity's basic mysteries – the origin
> of the Library and of time – might be found . . .

> Jorge Luis Borges, *The Library of Babel*

No one knows precisely where within the abbey precinct the lost
library stood. Perhaps it lay south of the nave, the footings of its
buildings unidentified now under the grassy hummocks dotted
with daisies which visitors pass over each day. We must imagine it
in the mid 1530s, when it was intact, before the Dissolution. The
great church was then 'the most ancient and famous monastery in
our whole island'; it had a vast array of chapels, cloisters, dormitories
and refectories; there were still fifty monks at that time (it was the
largest house in Britain). But its crowning glory was the library.
Here we have to speculate. The library of Glastonbury has never
been found; nor has the scriptorium, the writing house, which
must have been next to it; though there are those who have not
quite given up hope that one day a secret hole, bricked up in a
wall, might reveal treasured books hidden by the monks at the final
fateful moment when the library was destroyed and the abbot and
his last faithful companions were hanged by King Henry's agents
on a bleak November afternoon in 1539.

At the end, the library may have had two or even three thousand
books; other treasured volumes were kept separately in reliquaries
in the sacristy, liturgical books in the main church; some of them
were chained, like the *Textus of St Dunstan*: gilded and jewelled

heirlooms which had been treasured for centuries. The room was locked and guarded, and visitors needed the abbot's permission to enter; for, as we know from the fictions of Borges and Eco, libraries are secret worlds, containing arcane knowledge which is not open to all. It would have had a wooden door, and inside, rather as a Durham source tells us, great cupboards

of waynscott all full of bookes (with great store of antient Manuscript to help them [the monks] in ther studdy), wherin dyd lye as well the old auncyent written Docters of the church as other prophane authors, with dyuerse other holie mens wourk, so that eueryone dyd studye what Docter pleased them best, hauing the librarie at all tymes to go studie in besydes there Carrell.

The lock turned with a big iron key. You would have noticed the smell first; for ancient libraries smell of old leather, calf skin, vellum. Along the walls there would have been book cupboards, as there are in the surviving medieval library rooms in Merton College and Duke Humfrey's Library in the Bodleian, Oxford, and at Hereford Cathedral. To the south, perhaps, were tall glazed leaded windows which looked out over the ancient cemetery of the monks and through which shafts of light fell on the desks. Here, then, the monks kept their books, and in the old days copied and illuminated manuscripts with all the paraphernalia of the scribe: goose quills, specially prepared inks of different colours, soot, and lamp black, purple dye, gold leaf and powdered lapis, scrapers and pumice for smoothing the vellum, styluses for pricking, folding and lining the quires (always arranged with the hairy side of the sheets outwards, as was the custom in insular monasteries).

In Leland's father's day, all this had become old technology almost overnight. In the last couple of generations, writing by hand had been superseded by print. The Gutenburg Bible of Mainz in the 1450s had pointed the way to the future, and the next few decades had seen a tremendous boom in printing. From that moment, the art of writing was doomed, although it is only in our own time that it has finally vanished in the face of electronic technology and the Internet. In the monasteries, for a little while longer writing continued to be used. There were those old-fashioned scholars and scribes who pronounced themselves ashamed to receive a printed work into a library. There were those who still, in a futile gesture, extolled the copying of books by hand as an essential monastic occupation in itself, a kind of Zen act, like meditation, prayer or chant. But this, one imagines, soon became an eccentricity, rather like persisting with a typewriter in the age of computers. The twilight of the manuscript book had come after a millennium and a half. But at this moment, in the 1540s, although writing was now on the way out, the library at Glastonbury still possessed the greatest collection of handwritten books in the British Isles.

These books had been accumulated over nearly ten centuries. Like all religious houses, Glastonbury had endured its destructions. The library had been badly damaged in the fire of 1184; then many precious texts had been rescued by the monks, 'when they had in the confusion saved relics treasure and books in *pannis sericis*', silken bags perhaps improvised from church vestments, chasubles or copes. Only sixty years on, however, the library had been reconstituted, for the catalogue of 1247/8 names about 500 texts bound in 340 or so volumes, excluding run-of-the-mill liturgical works. This list included many ancient texts. No less than ninety volumes are described as *vetustus*, 'very old': Augustines, Bedes, Gregory the Great. Eight books, intriguingly, were *vetustissimus*, 'extremely old': of these, three were ninth-century authors; but others were Early Christian fathers from the Late Roman period: three Jeromes and an Origen, which, for all we know, may have been older, even considerably older. (Late-Roman books were available in early England: the fourth-century fragment of Cyprian's letters found not so long ago in the binding of a Gloucester parish register was written in Hippo in North Africa during the lifetime of St Augustine!) At least some of these old books in the 1248 catalogue must have come from the monastery's collection before the 1184 fire. The library grew further over time, especially in the fourteenth century, when several bibliophile abbots expanded the collection with their gifts. By Leland's day it possessed perhaps two or three thousand manuscripts, which would have taken an expert several days to inspect even cursorily.

Leland was certainly an expert. Now in his mid thirties, he had taken holy orders in the new Protestant Church of England, and was a man confident in his scholarship. He knew Latin, French, Italian and Spanish, and enough Greek to recognize the contents of a book. A quick, alert, difficult man, almost mystically driven, he had a nose for manuscripts and a yearning for the magical learning they contained. He was, for example, fascinated by the mystical fringe of Glastonbury texts; he believed passionately in the authenticity of Geoffrey of Monmouth's tale of King Arthur; he took the 'Prophecies of Merlin' perfectly seriously. In that, he was a man of his time. But his interests were very wide and, fortunately for us, he recorded his impressions. By a great stroke of luck, Leland's diary of his visit to the library survives, in notebooks written in Latin, as was the custom of the day. This was his first visit: he had evidently not gone there in the first place to record books; and at this point he cannot have known the terrible fate awaiting the library – or its last abbot, Whiting. In fact, on this first visit it was no matter of urgency to him to record the texts. Leland had come for solace and intellectual feeding, as he tells us:

I had intended, by the goodwill of the abbot Richard Whiting, to refresh my mind, then weary after a long course of studies, when the passion burning desire to read and discover inflamed me afresh. So I straightaway went to the library, which is not freely open to all, in order to examine with great care all the remains of most sacred antiquity, of which there is here so great a number that it is not easily paralleled anywhere else in Britain. Scarcely had I crossed the threshold when the mere sight of the most ancient books took over my mind with an awe or stupor of some kind, and for a while literally stopped me in my tracks. Then, having paid my respects to the deity of the place, I examined all the book cases for several days with the greatest interest.

We can imagine him, accompanied by a monk attached by the abbot, perhaps by the librarian himself, opening the cupboards one

1 & 2. The drama of English history: two Victorian views. The Vikings descend on the Northumbrian coast (above); the tragedy of Hastings, 1066 (right). Both themes were popular among the Victorians, whose historians, like Edward Freeman, sought English roots in the Anglo-Saxon past.

At six o'clock that afternoon, King Harold's army halted – *for the first rest in all that nightmare march southwards.*

THERE LIE THE ENEMY, SIRE! NEVER IN ALL MY LIFE HAVE I SEEN SUCH A MIGHTY ARRAY! AND LOOK AT OUR POOR FELLOWS! HALF OF THEM WERE TILLING THE SOIL LAST WEEK—AND ALL OF THEM ARE DROPPING WITH FATIGUE AND STARVATION!

HAVE NO FEAR, EDRIC! TONIGHT, MY WARRIORS WILL EAT AND SLEEP THEIR FILL— AND, WHEN TOMORROW'S SUN RISES, THEY WILL LEAP TO THEIR FEET WITH BRAVE HEARTS AND STRONG ARMS TO STRIKE A GREAT BLOW FOR ENGLAND!

The long night passed. At five o'clock in the morning, there came to the straining ears of the Saxon army the sound of the Normans preparing for battle. *At nine o'clock on Saturday, 14th October, 1066, the mist cleared away – and the morning sunlight shone on the mail of fifty thousand Norman soldiers.*

STAND READY, O WARRIORS OF ENGLAND! AND WHEN THE MOMENT COMES —*STRIKE HARD AND TRUE!*

Then William of Normandy's voice boomed out!

FOOT SOLDIERS, CHARGE!

And so the Battle of Hastings began! The Norman foot-soldiers threw themselves long at the wall of stakes – but King Harold and his gallant men stood firm!

DO NOT EXPOSE YOURSELF, SIRE! IF AN ARROW STRIKES YOU, ENGLAND WILL DIE WITH YOU!

WHAT DO I CARE FOR ARROWS? STRIKE, WARRIORS OF ENGLAND! *STRIKE!*

3. 'The Last of the Saxon Kings' from the boys' comic *The Eagle*, 1961. Still essentially the Victorian view; but after Hastings and the Norman Yoke, the strip concludes, 'a greater England would arise'.

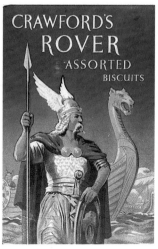

& **5.** A Danish raid on East Anglia, from a late-Victorian children's book (above). Englishness itself is at stake, even though the Vikings are still part of the English story, and the 'sea rovers' would be used to sell everything from cars to biscuits (right).

Alfred the Great inciting the Saxons against the Danes – and inspiring the House of Commons. In the mid 1840s the rebuilt Parliament was decorated with the key themes of English history.

"*Well, perhaps they are a SHADE overcooked, but what does that matter in war-time?*"

7, 8 & 9. Famou[s]
English defeats,
from Hastings t[o]
Dunkirk, have a
peculiar place i[n]
the mythology.
Alfred and the
cakes is one of
the earliest: Dav[id]
Wilkie's paintin[g]
(top), 1806,
cigarette card
(middle), 1924,
Punch cartoon
(bottom), 1941.

An Edwardian painting showing Alfred the Great presenting a cloak and sword to his
grandson Athelstan *c.* 899.

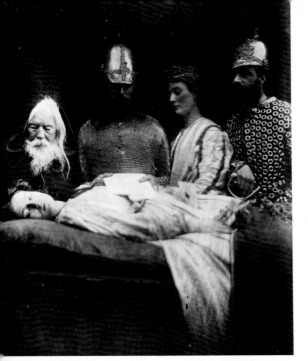

11 & 12. Photography opens up new ways of looking not only at the present, but at the past. This photograph (left) to illustrate Tennyson's Arthurian epic, *Idyll of the King*, offers a graphic insight into Victorian doom-laden imaginings which influenced all later versions of the Arthurian myth. *Le Morte d'Arthur* (below), by James Archer, was bought by the history-conscious Manchester City Council.

13 & 14. Daniel Maclise's classic mid–nineteenth-century version of the myth of Robin Hood (above): a constant theme in the English pastoral tradition from the fourteenth-century ballads through Shakespeare right down to Errol Flynn (left) – and beyond.

15. The continuity of English history: this British Empire Exhibition poster (1924) offers a vision from the last period of empire.

16. World War Two poster: the popular idea of England was changed by the cataclysm of the Great War and the social and economic changes which accompanied it. Where First World War posters emphasized duty and social order, Second World War artists emphasized the unchanging rural England of the imagination.

after another. The books were still organized under the same main headings as in the medieval catalogue, the basic division being between sacred and secular learning. In the former were the works of the Church fathers; letters; history; lives of saints; passionals; homilies and so on. In the latter were scientific, philosophical and grammatical texts, what the medievals called *Physica*, *Logica* and *Grammatica*; also books of the Greek and Roman writers, the pagan *phylosophantes* which St Dunstan had studied here as a young man back in the 920s. Of these thousands of texts, only a handful survives today. But by cross-checking the survivors with Leland's notebooks and with the old catalogues and book lists, the ghost of the lost library can at least be fleetingly glimpsed, if not brought back to life.

Leland describes in detail some forty-four manuscripts: at least thirty of these could be pre-Conquest; all but four of them are in the 1248 catalogue. Here then, courtesy of Leland's notebooks and the older catalogues, is a fascinating snapshot of the shelves of the lost library, the greatest in early Britain. It is a compendium of the learning which was the basis of English culture before the Reformation. Contrary to the expectations of many today, there is almost nothing here from the mystical fringe; no secrets of the occult (unless we believe there was a secret catalogue to which even the librarian did not have access!). There is no mention here of the Zodiac, the Maze, the Glastonbury star map, the realm of the Great Goddess; no visions of Albion or hermetic keys to the magical landscape of Avalon. As one would expect, these are practical texts, works of mainstream orthodoxy serving the personnel of a Benedictine monastery. Some books evidently still survived from the vast collection of books which existed before the fire of 1184, and among them perhaps one or two very old books, going back to the early days of Christianity: as Leland says, 'examples of extraordinarily wonderful antiquity'.

Among the manuscripts Leland examined, he tells us, was the manuscript now known as 'St Dunstan's Classbook': a strange miscellany including a Breton grammar, and Ovid's *Art of Love* (the book survives today in Oxford; and bears Dunstan's characteristic handwriting caught in the act of annotating and correcting texts). There were works of the great age of English missions: a *Life of Saint Wilfrid* by Eddius Stephanus; the eighth-century Life of the Fenland saint Guthlac. There were numerous works of Bede, of course: his *History of Jarrow* among them. There was the tenth-century *Life of Saint Wilfrid* by the continental scholar Frithegode. Here, too, were works of the scholars of Charlemagne's court circle who had been the 'think-tank' behind the first European Renaissance. Among these were many works by the English scholar Alcuin, literary eccentricities like Hucbald of St Amand's *On Baldness*, and devotional classics like Hrabanus Maurus's famous work, *On the Cross*. Interestingly enough, a fine copy of this last book survives, a de luxe illustrated manuscript from the 930s which looks very much like a royal commission, its pages adorned with magical word patterns; this was perhaps picked up nearby in Wells after the break-up of the library at the Dissolution and is now safely in Trinity College Library in Cambridge. There were also books from later Anglo-Saxon England, such as the *History of Orosius* in the Old English translation by Alfred the Great. Classical works were represented too: Hegessipus's *History*, for example (written in the second century AD), and Aristotle's *Categories*. There were, of course, standard monastic works like the Rule of Saint Benedict; an eleventh-century fragment of this text now in Wells Cathedral may come from this book. But we should not gather too austere a picture of monastic reading tastes in the Dark Ages; the library was not all heavy scholarship. Among the books noted by Leland were old favourites like the Riddles of Aldhelm Tatwine and Eusebius, which were used for teaching grammar and metre and whose gentle bawdy tickled monkish fancies everywhere:

I have a long thick root with a big knob at the end: and when women get their hands on me I make their eyes water: What am I???

The answer is an onion! Perhaps this book survives as the British Library manuscript Royal 12 C 23, which is from the late tenth century.

Others Leland could not find. In his notebooks we can see him thinking aloud: 'Nothing as yet of the books of Gildas,' he notes (though this text, one of the most fundamental works in British history, which is discussed in Chapter Two, was in the 1248 catalogue). 'I have searched for him with the utmost diligence,' Leland says, his disappointment plain to see. 'I felt it an almost certain hope that I would find something at Glastonbury, but not a single page . . .' Perhaps by his day it was bound up with another volume and he missed it. There was enough there, though, to fill notebook – and a mind.

What an experience! Imagine standing in Leland's shoes – one might almost feel a hot flush of panic. But that is hindsight. We know the end of the story. As I have said, it is likely that at this moment, on his first visit to the library, Leland did not yet know the likely fate of most of these volumes. When he returned on subsequent visits it was a different matter: then it was a case of how many he could save. Without a special warrant from the king, the likelihood was only a handful. But even on this first visit, as one may well imagine, Leland understood the importance of this moment. The thought, he says in telling words, induced 'an awe or stupor of some kind', as if the scale of the task was beyond him, and he feared he could only record a few selected texts: 'for that reason I was stopped in my tracks for a while'.

It's a moment worthy of the bibliophile parables of Borges, or Umberto Eco, with all the connotations of lost libraries from Alexandria to Vivarium to the mysterious fictional temple library described by a tenth-century historian (clearly a precursor of Jorge Luis Borges): 'a treasury of books in which are preserved all the sciences of Earth and heaven, and the chronology of times past and times future . . . a place barred to all save those of highest wisdom . . .'

What would we not give to be there with Leland, and to make our own notes on the books destined to be burned? Leland was standing on the dividing line between old and new: at the beginning, symbolically, of the severance between the medieval and modern worlds, when the monasteries were dissolved and their treasures

dispersed, their libraries broken up. In the age of print and Protestantism, such works almost overnight ceased to be valuable. A
manuscript text of Augustine or Jerome, no matter how old, was
soon of little value, especially if the text already existed in print.
Too late they realized that a manuscript carries its life history with
it; that in the story of a manuscript book and its successive additions
and glosses, in the evidence of its ownership, of the changing
patterns in the way it was studied, there are rich insights to be
gained into cultural history (see Chapter Nine). No doubt there
had been many earlier losses, during Viking invasions and the
Norman Conquest, but the greatest destruction of the heritage of
these islands occurred in the 1530s and 1540s; this is the threshold
over which we must pass in any attempt to get to our early roots
through the texts; to recover the lost history of English culture in
the thousand years before the Reformation.

Today, only 1,000 manuscripts and fragments of manuscripts
survive anywhere in the world which were owned by English
monasteries between the sixth century and the Norman Conquest.
These are often the sole testimony not only to our early literature, but
also to history, law, liturgy, medicine and science. From Glastonbury
only forty survive; from Malmesbury thirty; from Bath even less;
from little Horton, now a field off the Blandford road, just one.
The number would be even less but for the efforts of Tudor and
Stuart antiquarians and collectors who saved books during and after
the destruction. Of these, Leland was the first.

Leland was born in around 1503/5 and died, while only in his
late forties, in 1552, five years after he went mad. He was probably
of a Lancashire family. Leyland, as all Lancastrians will know, is on
the M6 south of Preston. The area was the heartland of Catholicism,
as it still is; still the home of old Tudor Catholic families like the
Heskeths and the Hoghtons. On his journeys, Leland mentions
visits to a Sir William Leland at Morley near Leigh, who was perhaps
a kinsman at the family home. In his notebooks, Leland also gives
a wealth of local detail around Morley, singling out Leylandshire
and its eight parish churches, 'whereof Leland paroche is one'. Here
were probably his roots. Orphaned at an early age, he was adopted

and educated by a London mercer, Thomas Myles. At St Paul's School in London, he was one of the first generation of scholars trained under the English humanist regime established by John Colet with a curriculum shaped by Erasmus himself. From St Paul's, he went to Cambridge where he got his BA in 1521–2. After a short spell at All Souls, Oxford, he took holy orders, and then spent several years in Paris, to study languages and to perfect his knowledge of Belles Lettres: 'to visit excellent luminaries', as he said, so he could 'travel through fluent Italy and mix Latin words with Greek wit . . .'

In France, Leland immersed himself in European humanism; and it was there that he became seriously interested in the study of manuscripts, one of the key branches of study in the great act of retrieval of the ancient world which we call the Renaissance. 'Moreover,' he wrote home, 'I am searching for, investigating and digging out from the deep shadows many manuscripts of the ancients.' During those years in Paris, Leland came to know some of the best European scholars of his time: the royal librarian Guillaume Bude, the greatest scholar of his age; the humanist and translator of Aristotle, Jacques leFèvre; the Greek scholar Lascaris. Leland wrote flattering poems to them all, in particular to Lascaris, who rescued old manuscripts for Lorenzo de Medici, and who helped form the royal library at Fontainebleau. The poetry Leland wrote in Paris (which was published after his death by the Cheshire poet Thomas Newton) is a gushing memoir of those exciting days in the company of 'men of perfected education . . . whose names are worthy of immortality!'

> Most celebrated Cambridge taught me the seven arts,
> And the school which takes its famous name from the Isis.
> But it was Paris which taught me to honour the Muses:
> And from then on I sang songs composed in differing modes.

Leland's story, then, is part of the tale by which the European Renaissance percolated into English culture. These foreign scholars gave him, for example, the glimmerings of the idea to set up a royal library for Henry VIII with the best of the treasures of the monastic libraries. During these Paris days, Leland developed his special interest in manuscripts, and no doubt his continental perspective helped develop his remarkable overview of the story of English culture.

But Leland is also an important figure because of his contribution to British topography. Soon after his return from France in 1529, he began a programme of systematic travel in Britain which eventually bore fruit in his *Itinerary*: the first detailed exploration of England, and one of the greatest physical descriptions of the country. There had been a solitary trailblazer, William of Worcester in the late fifteenth century, whose work was known to Leland. But Leland's vast work goes far beyond William's. It is nothing short of a discovery of England: a land seemingly waiting to be explored and described; a land also undergoing great changes. Leland left an unrivalled description of the whole country, from Hadrian's Wall to Land's End; he was the forerunner of every travel writer on the subject of England from Defoe and Cobbett to H. V. Morton, Arthur Mee and Pevsner. Leland was the first great physical explorer of English antiquity, as he wrote to the king himself (translated from the Latin):

I was totally inflamed with a love to see thoroughly all those parts of your opulent and ample realm that I had read of . . . insomuch that I had travelled in your dominions both by the sea coasts and the middle parts, sparing neither labour nor costs, by the space of these six years past, that there is almost neither cape nor bay, haven, creek or pier, river or confluence of rivers, beaches, washes, lakes, meres, fenny waters, mountains, valleys, moors, heaths, forests, woods, cities, boroughs, castles, principal manor places, monasteries and colleges, but I have seen them; and noted in so doing a whole world of things very memorable.

The travel diaries were private jottings and never intended for publication. But here, for example, in his own prose, is Leland riding on horseback into the small Lancashire town which later became the hub of the Industrial Revolution:

I pasid over the Medlok river, and so within lesse than a mile to Manchestre.

Manchestre on the south side of Irwel River stondith in Salfordshire, and is the fairest, best buildid, quikkest, and most populus tounne of al Lancastreshire; yet is in hit but one paroch chirch, but is a college and almost thoroughowt doble ilyd ex quadrato lapide durissimo [ashlar masonry], wherof a goodly quarre is hard by the towne. Ther be divers stone bridgis in the toune, but the best of iii. arches is over Irwel, cawllid Salford bridge. This bridge dividith Manchestre from Salford, the wich is as a large suburbe to Manchestre. On this bridge is a praty litle chapel. The next is the bridge that is over Hirke river [the Irk], on the wich the fair builded college standith as in the veri point of the mouth of hit [this is Chetham's College, which still stands today]. On Hirk river be divers fair milles that serve the toune. In the towne be ii. fair market placys. And almost ii. flyte shottes [bow shots] withowt the towne beneth on the same syde of Irwel yet be seene the dikes and fundations of Old Man Castel yn a ground now inclosid [the ruins of the Roman fort at Castlefield].

Here, on the other hand, is Leland as antiquarian, pursuing one of his favourite themes: his almost fanatical belief in the historicity of King Arthur. He is in Somerset now, approaching the great Iron Age hill-fort of South Cadbury:

I rode from the bridg up a stony hille to a very fair and fruteful champain [open farming country], and so passid forth a v miles by litle wood; at the 4. miles ende of this way I passid over a broke by a stone bridge, and so cam strayt to North-Cadbyri a village, and about a mile farther to South-Cadbyri . . .

At the very south ende of the chirch of South-Cadbyri standith Camallate, sumtyme a famose toun or castelle, apon a very torre or hille, wunderfully enstrengtheid of nature, to the which be 2. enteringes up by a very stepe way: one by north est, and another by south west. The very roote of the hille wheron this forteres stode is more than a mile in cumpace [compass, i.e., circumference].

In the upper parte of the coppe of the hille be 4. ditches or trenches,

and a balky waulle of yerth betwixt every one of them. In the very toppe
of the hille above al the trenchis is magna area or campus of a 20. acres
or more by estimation, wher yn dyverse places men may se fundacions
of walles . . . This top withyn the upper waulle is xx. acres of ground
and more, and hath bene often plowid and borne very good corne. Much
gold, sylver and coper of the Romaine coynes hath be found ther in
plouing: and lykewise in the feldes in the rootes of this hille, with many
other antique thinges . . . The people can telle nothing ther but that they
have hard that Arture much resortid to Camalat.

Even today this would be a good description of this great Iron
Age site which we know now was reoccupied in the Late-Roman
period, the so-called Arthurian epoch. The passage is typical of
Leland's interests – and of his exceptional eye for detail. He visited
the Roman Wall and discussed it with local antiquaries; he examined
Roman sites like Caerleon and Richborough and recorded Roman
discoveries in many other places. He made a list of the Romano-
British sculptures he saw in Bath, and always made a point of
recording Roman coin finds. He knew Watling Street had been
used by the Romans; he recognized Offa's Dyke at several points
in its course; he was interested in hill-forts and realized that some,
like Cadbury Castle, were pre-Roman: he even noted the remains
of carved stone crosses from the Anglo-Saxon period. And all
this, remember, was outside his chief aim, which was to make a
contemporary portrait of Henry VIII's England.

So the story of John Leland's life has a metaphorical quality: it
is a series of physical and intellectual journeys, and a series of acts
of discovery. Through exploring both topography and texts –
exterior and interior landscapes – he presents us with a map of what
we can no longer see. Two key strands in the exploration of the
British past therefore come together in his work. His description
of England's landscape is the predecessor of all modern attempts.
His notes on manuscripts, on the other hand, constitute a kind of
mental topography, mapped through the lost libraries. And here,
perhaps, lies the most valuable part of his 'laborious search'.

As early as 1533, Leland received some sort of commission from

Henry VIII 'to make a search after England's antiquities, and peruse the libraries of all cathedrals, abbeys, priories, colleges etc, as also all places wherein records, writings and secrets of antiquity were reposed'. The aim was simply that these forgotten 'monuments of ancient writers' might be brought 'out of deadly darkness to lively light'. During his travels, much time was devoted to an examination of the monastic and collegial libraries. It was in his capacity as the king's antiquary that it fell to Leland to be the last person, perhaps the only person, to see the monastic libraries on the eve of their destruction. Some, like Glastonbury, he examined and recorded before the end; at others, like Bury, he saw only selected books already saved by the king's agents.

There are vignettes of the destruction of the libraries by many Tudor authors. At New College, Oxford, shreds of books were seen showering through the air; at Malmesbury, according to the later diarist John Aubrey, ruined pages were blowing in the streets and used to stop bung-holes. Of the thousands of books at Glastonbury, as we have seen, only forty survive, and Leland's host on the memorable visit recorded in his diaries, Abbot Whiting, was condemned in a trumped-up show trial and hanged on the Tor.

Leland was an ardent Protestant (so far as we can tell in an age when dissimulation was a necessary part of the game), but the havoc caused among the monastic libraries at the Dissolution caused him profound distress. All his life had been dedicated to the past, to humanistic learning, to a love of manuscripts and the history they encode, and he was shaken by the deliberate and wanton physical destruction. In 1536, as the Dissolution was under way, he wrote in desperation to Thomas Cromwell, the chief minister of Henry VIII, asking him to extend Leland's commission to allow him to take any manuscripts for the royal collections to save them . . . which would be of 'great profit to students and succour to this realm', he said, with an eye on posterity.

After his grand tour of the libraries was finally completed – and by then it was a race against time – Leland presented Henry in 1545 with a 'New Year's Gift' describing the aims and method of his researches. His ultimate plan was to pull all these diverse strands together into a gigantic work in fifty books on 'The History and Antiquities of this Nation'. Six more volumes were to cover the islands around the coasts, and there would be further books on the history of the English aristocracy. Not surprisingly, this vast project was never accomplished, though some of the great works of seventeenth-century antiquarian scholarship, like Camden's *Britannia*, or the massive and still invaluable study of British religious houses by Dugdale, seem to be inspired by Leland's vision.

But Leland's mental health was now fragile. He got himself a Church preferment at the rectory of Haseley in Oxfordshire. But most of his time was spent in his house in St Michael le Querne in London, arranging his notes. He had not endeared himself to everyone. Some said he was a vain and arrogant man, and he was certainly a fierce and tendentious controversialist. His earlier feud with the Italian court historian Polydore Vergil is a case in point. Vergil had denied the existence of King Arthur and accused the twelfth-century historian Geoffrey of Monmouth of 'most impudent lyeing', indeed, of 'concocting the great fable'. This reduced Leland to paroxysms of rage. Firing off polemical pamphlets, he accused his adversary of monstrous conceit and ignorance. A case of the pot calling the kettle black, some might say, but to Leland such meddling with our history was 'a greate and greevouse crime, not only worthy of stripes, but also of all kinde of punishment, if any man should derogate from her the glory due to his Cuntrie . . .' He perhaps felt things too hard. He certainly pushed himself beyond what was humanly possible for one man before the age of computers and research teams.

An engraving of a now-lost bust of Leland shows a long face with an aquiline nose. His hair is cut in a bob halfway down his ears, his eyes are large and piercing, heavily lidded, under a quizzically raised brow. A sardonic downturn at the corners of his mouth hints at the withering scorn which could be directed at those who crossed him. In his defence, one might say that single-minded, driven people like him are often described as arrogant, and indeed it would be surprising if a man like Leland had not rubbed people up the wrong way. With his broad scholarship, his fluency in

European languages and his European perspective, he may well have made enemies in the inward-looking Tudor society of the 1540s, when Europhiles were not always welcomed with open arms. But clearly Leland's problems towards the end were no longer just a matter of cliques and patronage.

At this stage the magnitude of the grand design, the great act of restitution, took over his mind. The sheer volume of his notes, one imagines, was too much to put in order. However that may be, 'the intensity of his researches overtaxed his brain' and he became incurably insane. On 21 March 1550, the Privy Council gave him into the custody of his brother. He died on 18 April 1552, still not quite fifty years old, and was buried in St Michael le Querne at the west end of Cheapside: the church was destroyed in the Great Fire and was not rebuilt. His bones must lie today somewhere under the Bank of England.

His story was told by his friend John Bale, the great bibliophile, in his preface to Leland's 'New Year's Gift' in *The Laboryouse Journey and Serche for Englandes Antiquitees*, London 1549, in famous and affecting words which perhaps throw light on the reasons for Leland's own illness:

to destroye all without consyderacyon, is and wyll be unto England for ever, a most horrible infamy among the grave senyours of other nacyons. A great nombre of them which purchased those superstycyouse mansions [i.e., the monasteries], reserved of those lybrarye bokes, some to serve theyr iakes [i.e., as lavatory paper], some to scoure theyr candelstyckes, & some they sent over see to the bokebynders, not in small nombre, but at tymes whole shyppes full, to the wonderynge of the foren nacyons . . .

Today's scholars attempting to recover the intellectual history of early England must follow in Leland's footsteps; poring over every scribble in his notebooks, sifting the wreckage for clues. The interpretation of England's past through the texts is an act of recovery from fragments; a process which began in earnest with Leland and the Tudor antiquarians in the generation after him who first began to print the Old English sources. And the process continues now, as manuscripts are identified and examined for clues, as new discoveries are made in country houses and local record offices, precious fragments in which no scrap is insignificant.

When he was young, Leland's fondest desire had been for literary immortality. In Paris he had hoped that his poetry would generate his greatest fame, as he wrote in a youthful poem from the Left Bank: 'One day Britain will celebrate my Muses.' But ironically, Leland's fame and importance today come from his private jottings. His memorial is the volumes of notes by which he recorded the libraries on the eve of their destruction; he provided the link between the medieval world and ourselves. He had seen the lost library. And as a tenth-century story tells:

Anyone permitted to behold it is seized with violent emotion in which impatience, sadness and an attraction that captivates the heart mingle with a fear lest this temple and its library may be destroyed or ruined for ever.

This, I imagine, is what drove Leland mad. Like an inhabitant of Borges' Babel, he had stood inside the library, and been permitted to see its contents.

7. Alfred the Great: the Case of the Fenland Forger

A single jail, in Alfred's golden reign,
Could half the nation's criminals contain . . .
No spies were paid, no special juries known,
Blest age! but ah! how diff'rent from our own!

Samuel Johnson, *London*, 1738

Walking through that Gothic fantasia on English history, the Houses of Parliament, reveals a lot about the way we have constructed our past. Heading for the Commons public gallery, for example, you pass an extraordinary series of historical paintings. Among them is a huge canvas showing Viking galleys with dragon prows and striped sails grappling off the coast of Kent. It is entitled 'King Alfred's Longships Defeat the Danes'. The painting was part of a historical cycle commissioned in the 1920s on topical themes (in this case, Alfred as the founder of the British Navy). It is not the only celebration of Alfred on the walls of the Mother of Parliaments. In the Lords there is G. F. Watts's stirring epic of 1846, 'Alfred Incites the Saxons to Prevent the Landing of the Danes'. Daniel Maclise's famous version (now in Newcastle) of the king disguised as a minstrel in the Danish camp was also planned for a cycle for the Mother of Parliaments. And all because at that time Alfred was viewed as the founder of English liberties.

The image of Alfred as the quintessential English hero was part of the currency of education in Victorian and Edwardian times. My father, for example, who was born before the First World War, learned his first British history from a children's book illustrated by just the kind of paintings which adorn Parliament. There was the morning of Agincourt; Drake's fireships and the Armada; the Thin

Red Line, Rorke's Drift. But most striking were the paintings of Alfred: the Burning of the Cakes, the Baptism of Guthrum. Best of all, in my eyes, was a picture of Alfred's enemies, the Vikings. The scene is the deep fens, somewhere near Ely (or so I have always imagined). On a damp autumnal day, the trees turned golden brown, ornate prows glide through the reed beds; in the foreground trudge heavy-footed giants with improbably huge Gothic winged helmets, sombre and irresistible in their demeanour as they burn their way through the great fenland monastries, looting treasures and killing defenceless clerics. The image, I have to admit, stuck with me, as such things tend to in childhood. Alfred and the Vikings is one of those great English stories, encapsulating the Victorian idea of history: the Vikings as barbarians, Alfred as a great educator and civilizer, a pious and moral family man, practical and plucky, improvisor and inventor as well as fighter. When the Victorians celebrated the thousandth anniversary of his death in 1900, they erected a statue to Alfred in the centre of his capital, Winchester, saluting him as the 'Truthteller', 'England's darling'. But how did that come about?

Strangely enough, unlike Charlemagne or Alexander, Alfred was not 'the Great' till modern times. He was praised by the Plantagenets as a law-giver and a purveyor of wise saws, and there were popular ballads about him. But only in Tudor times was the seed sown of Alfred as English icon, with the publication of his laws and the ninth-century *Life of Alfred* by Bishop Asser. During the build-up to the English revolution, his tale provided exemplars for theorists on both sides: for Royalists, in Robert Powell's elaborate treatise on Charles I as a new Alfred (1634); for parliamentarians, who cited Alfred as defender of freeborn Englishmen and sponsor of an independent English Church. After the revolution, when Milton wrote his history of England, he was particularly impressed by 'the most renowned Alfred'.

But real interest in Alfred began in the eighteenth century. For reasons which are not entirely clear – it was Greeks and Romans who were 'in' during the Enlightenment – this ninth-century king of Wessex was turned into the 'founder of English liberties'. One polemicist of the day, Thomas Evans, went so far as to link Alfred, as the founder of an English agrarian commonwealth with tithings, hundreds and shires, with Moses and Christ: ancestor and model for the limited democracies of his age. Thomas Jefferson too went back to his Saxon predecessors for his conception of liberty. Others (Edmund Burke among them) argued Parliament itself had begun under Alfred, 'a prince of the most exalted merit that ever graced the English throne'.

The contemporary *Life of Alfred* by Asser was finally translated into English in 1848, and its picture of the king helped fuel the Victorians' interest in their Saxon roots. Some of the readings, it has to be said, stretched the evidence somewhat. Alfred was quoted by the campaign for shorter working hours because of his division of the day into three eight-hour periods – work, sleep and prayer – and he even attracted the attentions of the Lord's Day Observance Society, who cited him as 'founder of the English Sunday'. Such are the revenges of History!

Only in the twentieth century has Alfred begun to emerge from this extraordinary burden of anachronistic accretions. He was a man who lived in dark times. Faced with invading Viking armies which had destroyed most of the early English kingdoms (and threatened his own), he spent much of his life fighting, but he also tried to halt the distintegration of justice by recording English law. Though illiterate into middle age, he sponsored the translation of key books which he thought it was 'needful all men should know', in an effort to stem the decline of learning and literacy. In one of these is an astonishing geographical portrait of Scandinavia as far as the Arctic Circle, garnered from interviews with Norse merchants who visited Alfred's court and told him about the 'boundaries of Europe'. This provides a striking picture of the king's personal interest in a wider world than the one he inhabited. Stripped of fantasies, then, our image of the king is hard to grasp, indistinct in many places, but it is still impressive enough.

Since the 1960s, archaeology in particular has greatly enriched our picture of King Alfred, giving us concrete detail, for example, of the network of fortresses constructed by him, and demonstrating the wholesale replanning of towns as centres of trade and population, with new street-plans which survive even today – in the pattern of lanes in London between St Paul's and the Thames, for example. Whatever else he was, Alfred was clearly a man of great energy, tenacity, drive and vision.

But what was Alfred *like*? Despite the recent advances in archaeology, the key sources on Alfred are still what they have always been: a cluster of texts contained in several original manuscripts of the Old English period and some later ones. First in importance is the *Anglo-Saxon Chronicle*, which was sponsored in Alfred's reign and was probably written under his supervision. The king's laws survive, in which Alfred placed himself in a line linking Moses with the earlier English kings. There are also some charters (land grants) and a text on the fortification of towns. And Alfred's will has come down to us too: a revealing testimony to the way Dark Age royal families managed their patrimony and kept rival kinsmen at bay. In addition, there survive several manuscripts of the translations Alfred sponsored, some of which contain important additions in which (if this is not delusory) an impression of a real person comes over, wrestling with real problems: an intensely religious man, but a man interested in practical solutions, in how things work on all levels, who had learned well from hard experience and was good at applying it. His metaphors are down-to-earth ones: carpenter, woodsman, builder. He was the very opposite of a dreamer, as one would deduce from the evidence of the far-reaching social engineering in town and countryside with which southern English society was transformed during the Viking wars. On occasion, like any medieval king, he was prepared to be ruthless: to kill his hostages, for example, or to confiscate Church lands, for which he was attacked by one clerical writer as a latterday Judas. Alfred was clearly concerned about how other people saw him – there is an unusual amount of self-justification in his writings. But in his case, so far as we can see, this did not extend to fantasizing. He was evidently someone who called a spade a spade, a man who did not stand on ceremony. In one revealing anecdote, he is interrupted during his ablutions in the royal residence at Wardour and gives his judgment in a thorny legal case 'whilst washing his hands in the royal bower'. He was, as he put it, someone who used the tools of his day and dealt in the currency his friends – and enemies – expected: 'warriors and workers are what a king needs,' he said, 'and these are the things which are most useful to him . . . weapons, gifts, food and drink, hospitality.'

But that is as far as the hints in his own writings take us. On Alfred the man, the key source is Asser's biography. This purports to be by a Welsh bishop who was with Alfred during the late 880s and 90s and whom we know was part of his scholarly seminar: Alfred acknowledges Asser's help in the preface to the translation of Gregory the Great's *Pastoral Care*. On the face of it, Asser's work is one of the most remarkable sources in British history, because it is an insider's view: a warts-and-all picture of one of our greatest rulers by a man who knew him well; someone who spent years with Alfred, and who was party to his intimate thoughts and plans, doubts and fears.

Unfortunately, it is not as simple as that. The work known as Asser, in fact, has been a major problem ever since it was published in Elizabeth I's reign. The work had only survived in one manuscript which belonged to Archbishop Matthew Parker, who has become notorious for the 'doctoring' of his texts. The book later came into the collection of Sir Robert Cotton, in whose library at Ashburnham House it was totally burned in the fateful fire of 23 October 1731. Of many other books burned that night something remains, shrivelled, shrunken and blackened perhaps (Gildas among them, as we have seen). But of Asser no fragments survive, not a shred: not even one piece to give us a sample of the handwriting. So we are dependent on the editions published before the fire (Parker 1574, Camden 1602, Wise 1722) and on surviving transcripts made in Tudor times for Parker. As a result of Parker's questionable accuracy and honesty, however, the lost MS has proved – and is still proving – to be one of the trickiest customers in English history. Indeed – and here's the rub – since the last century a persistent minority of experts have dismissed Asser as a fake.

Now Alfred Smyth, in a new study (*King Alfred the Great*, 1996), has thrown the whole thing into the air. In a massive work of 700 pages, nearly 400,000 words, Smyth argues that Asser is a forgery of the late tenth century. Smyth's promise to turn the academic world upside down got him into the pages of the London *Evening Standard* and the *Daily Mail*, and has led to a furious scholarly debate, with Smyth accusing the Cambridge establishment in particular of a whitewash, a conspiracy to suppress open academic debate because of their desire to protect the Victorian vision of Alfred. Fair enough, one might think, but Smyth goes on to accuse the Cambridge school of closing ranks to protect the memory of the old Cambridge Professor of Anglo-Saxon Dorothy Whitelock and her mentor Sir Frank Stenton, the century's most revered Anglo-Saxonist. Whitelock and Stenton had staked their reputations on the genuineness of Asser. For Smyth it was an academic scandal which had to be lanced: a 'century of cover up and 1,000 years of deceit'.

Smyth thinks that Asser was forged around the year 1000 by an inmate of the Fenland monastery of Ramsay, a well-known (and very distinctive) author called Byrhtferth. The fake, he thinks, was modelled on a monkish life written in Cluny in the 930s, whose style Smyth thinks Asser displays. These stylistic arguments are complicated and hinge on whether Asser's Latin is really of the ninth century (most expert critics think it is) and whether Byrhtferth could have written Asser (most agree that he couldn't). On Asser's Latin, there is no question that Smyth lost the argument; even his most charitable critics think he looked to the wrong place and person for his forger. Smyth's biggest worries, though, centre on the nature of the biography itself. Like earlier doubters, he thinks Asser's biographical detail on Alfred is completely implausible as the portrait of a ninth-century king. Now even some 'believers' think there is something fishy about Asser: but all this was lost in the fog of scholarly battle as astonishingly intemperate language flew back and forth.

The exciting thing about all this is simply that it has happened at all: that it still matters. It also underlines how, in the late twentieth century, 1,100 years after Alfred's death and over 900 years after the Conquest, in terms of reconstructing Old English history the experts really are still at the stage of recovering basics: sifting the wreckage left after the ravages of time and the Reformation, and the accidental burnings of libraries like Cotton's. The basic tasks are still being done: identifying and cataloguing manuscripts, editing law codes, authenticating and editing charters, and so on. The huge amount of material preserved in later medieval manuscripts has hardly begun to be sifted. The collections and notebooks of later antiquarians are another untapped resource. And those are just the basic building blocks. Full-scale interpretation is still a long way off, and as for understanding the mind of a ninth-century king, many scholars would consider it a futile exercise.

Unless, that is, Asser is what it purports to be – a biography written by someone who knew Alfred intimately. So what is Asser and how has the text come down to us? It's a story with some remarkable twists and turns.

Sometime in the 1540s, at the time of the Dissolution, John Leland, Henry VIII's antiquarian, got hold of the unique manuscript of Asser's life of King Alfred, probably in Worcester. At some later point Matthew Parker obtained it from Leland; after the accession of Elizabeth I, Parker found himself archbishop, with the job of defending the newly constituted Protestant Church and steering a fine line between attacks by Papists and Puritans. Parker supported his Church's position by an appeal to history. To him it was the natural successor to the primitive Anglo-Saxon English Church. The sixteenth-century reformers had simply cleared away the accretions of the Church of Rome, and got back to the roots. In this search, the ancient manuscripts of Saxon England were key evidence: in 1568, the Privy Council issued a letter making clear the queen's interest in these 'auncient recordes' and her concern for 'such historicall matters and monuments of antiquitie, both for the state ecclesiasticall and ciuile gouernment'. Parker was given the special duty of seeking out manuscripts to help the cause. The next few years saw a flurry of publication of key texts: the early English laws, the vernacular New Testament. Parker was even able to find homilies which showed our Saxon ancestors were quite comfortable to conceive of the sacrament as symbolic only. All these works were arguments from history, part of a wider agenda, namely the debate over Protestantism and the character of the pre-Conquest English Church. This was of crucial importance to people in the charged atmosphere of Elizabeth's reign. Even William Shakespeare owned – and studied – a copy of Lambarde's edition of the Old English laws.

In this climate, Parker published the text of Asser from his unique manuscript in 1574, but with many interpolations which he added from other sources. Parker's purpose was political; this explains his wholesale – and to our eyes shameless – altering of the text, and the interpolation of another source, the *Annals of St Neots*, into Asser. He was not alone in this; many of the manuscripts in Cotton's library were broken up, rebound, items pasted into them from completely unrelated volumes. Even the most famous Old English book, the Beowulf manuscript, is now thought to have been rearranged in Parker's day. The problem is that the Asser manuscript doesn't survive. So far as we can tell, Parker left the book in a strange state, interleaved, with many additions, glosses and annotations, and whole pages added. Some earlier commentators called his fiddling with the text 'wicked' and 'fantastic'. Just how fantastic can be seen from one of Parker's most enduring additions, the story of the Burning of the Cakes, which he believed was by Asser:

Now it happened one day that a countrywoman was getting ready to bake bread, and the king, sitting by the fire, was busy preparing a bow and arrows and other weapons. And when the unhappy woman saw the loaves of bread burning on the fire she ran over quickly and pulled them out, scolding the unconquerable king, saying 'Look here my man, you are slow to turn the loaves when you see them burning, but you're quite happy to eat them when they come warm from the oven.' The unhappy woman did not in any way realize that he was King Alfred who fought so many battles against the Vikings and gained so many victories. (*Annals of St Neots*, twelfth century)

At least the story of the cakes is pre–Conquest in origin – it first appears in a late-tenth-century source. The same cannot be said of the famous tale of Alfred's founding of Oxford University, Camden's outrageous fraud interpolated into his Asser edition of 1602.

Considering that Asser is one of most important sources in British history, this was not a happy state of affairs. So the key to the search for the 'real' Alfred is to establish what was actually in the lost book, and when it was written. Fortunately, the contents of the Cotton library were listed before the fire by Thomas Smith in his Catalogue of 1696 and again by Humfrey Wanley in 1722. Like the contents of many medieval manuscripts, the book is a strange hotch-potch, but only the first two items concern us:

1. Asser's life of Alfred 'in an ancient script'.
2. 'Superstitious exorcisms against fevers', glossed in Old English (Wanley reveals there was also an exorcism or charm *against melancholy*; 'in addition to a lengthier one against chills and fevers').
3. The Old English poem on the Battle of Maldon.
4. and 5. Hagiographical works from Canterbury and Barking.

Items 3–5 were bound up with the Asser in the sixteenth century or later. So only the first two items are relevant to us. A witness of 1600 says the Asser made up the first fifty-five folios; the charms the next two. So the original manuscript consisted of fifty-seven folios; the rest of the contents were successive accretions of the eleventh, twelfth and seventeenth centuries. But what was the date of the Asser? All who saw the lost book agreed that the Asser section was Late Saxon. Luckily a more exact dating is possible, because among those who saw the book before the fire was one of the towering figures of early Old English studies, the palaeographer Humfrey Wanley.

A one-time draper's apprentice from Coventry, Humfrey Wanley is one of the most remarkable figures in the retrieval of the lost past of England. Like Leland, he was a cataloguer of what would otherwise have been lost. His rubicund face 'peppered with variolus indentations' looks down today from a portrait on the wall of the manuscript room in the British Library, like Squire Allworthy from

Tom Jones. Holding a manuscript in his hands, he looks the type to be happy with a side of beef and a glass of claret; a reassuringly plain English face, its 'want of spirituality', it has been observed, 'counterbalanced by evidence of saturnine strength'. In his work on Anglo-Saxon manuscripts, Wanley described Cotton's collection before the fire. Wanley was an expert for his day; he saw the Asser before it was destroyed, and he had no doubt it was genuine.

'The first and earliest hand' in this manuscript, he said, 'was from around 1000–1001 AD. . . My authority for adjusting the age of that exemplar is an original charter of King Aethelred, dated AD 1001, which as to the hand, agreeth very well with the first part of the Asser.' The other hands, he said, were from 'much the same time'. Now the charter to which Wanley refers still survives, and was also in Cotton's collection, so Wanley could have held the book against it: he was not even citing from memory. Behind Parker's text, then, whatever his interpolations, there was a genuine Late Saxon book.

So far so good! Our text of Asser comes from a manuscript written a century after Alfred's death; and possibly by a royal scribe at that. If that were all, then the Asser riddle could be closed. But again, things are not so simple. For even though Wanley's date for the book is accepted, Wanley of course is only giving us a date for the *original* hand: he is not giving an account of the whole book, nor making judgement on Parker's interpolations. And exactly what was written in the book before Parker got his hands on it has never been agreed. Indeed, it took over 300 years for a satisfactory text to be published. Only in 1904 did W. H. Stevenson attempt to untangle Asser's presumed text from Parker's additions. After that the main experts stated their faith in its authenticity. At last the king could be seen for the first time, or so it was thought, in the eyes of his ninth-century panegyricist, stripped of later myth. Or so we thought.

Asser claims that he wrote the book in the king's forty-fifth year, 893, six years before Alfred died. This is Asser's account of how they first met:

About this time I too was summoned by the king from the remote westernmost parts of Wales and I came to the Saxon land [England]. When I had taken the decision to travel across great expanses of land to meet him, accompanied by some English guides I arrived in the territory of the right hand [i.e., southern] Saxons, which in English is called Sussex. There I saw him [King Alfred] for the first time, at the royal estate called Dean. When I had been warmly welcomed by him, and we were engaged in conversation, he asked me earnestly to put myself in his service and to become a member of his household, and to give up for his sake all that I had on the left hand and western side of the Severn [i.e., in Wales].

Asser employs Welsh usages, and he talks about the English as 'those people'. His treatment of English place names is equally revealing, as if he is explaining them for a Welsh audience. For example, when Alfred rides to Egbert's stone in the eastern part of Selwood Forest, Asser describes the forest as '*sylva magna* in Latin and *Coit Maur* in Welsh'; Cirencester he says is '*Cairceri* in Welsh'. Some details are just dropped in in passing: at the battle of Ashdown, Alfred charges 'like a wild boar', a traditional simile in Welsh vernacular poetry. His sources are revealing too: for example, he uses the Old Latin Bible, favoured in Dark Age Wales, not the Vulgate used in England – even now, a forger would have to be very sharp to spot that.

All very suggestive, though not perhaps clinching evidence. It is when Asser comes to contemporary politics that he really convinces. His information on the leading Welsh rulers of his day is particularly persuasive; and their name forms, according to modern linguistic experts, are pure ninth century. This kind of detail is so good it would be almost impossible for a forger not to have been tripped up – unless he could lay his hands on a contemporary document. The Welshness of Asser adds up. Welsh scholarship was not dependent on English in the ninth century. It had its own life with direct connections to Francia, the powerhouse of European learning in the ninth century. Some of its bishops may have been more learned than their English counterparts in the 880s. Though one can see Asser was not a great mind, Welsh scholarship was not negligible and it was through scholars like him that some of the texts came into England which became standards in education in the tenth-century revival. With his Welsh latinisms and his use of Welsh sources, the case for our author being a late-ninth-century Welshman is seemingly overwhelming.

Professor Smyth, though, will have none of this. His biggest problem centres on the very form of the biography. To him, Asser just doesn't ring true as the work of a ninth-century royal watcher. Hypochondriac, neurotic, morbidly religious, obsessed with his bad health, stressed at work, suffering sexual problems, good at inventing – the portrait feels like some ridiculous monkish fiction. The broad biographical structure bothers him too (as it disturbed one or two good critics before him). He thinks it smacks of someone who had no information about the first twenty years of his subject's life and scraped something together from the *Anglo-Saxon Chronicle*. Asser gives details of Alfred's birth, genealogy, his father's and mother's families, then uses the *Chronicle* to lay out the pattern of years up to the king's accession: in this there is virtually nothing not available in the *Chronicle*. Surely a real contemporary biographer would have taken the chance to ask the king about his early life instead of just cobbling together a potted biography from the *Chronicle*? Wouldn't he surely give us one original fact?

This, perhaps, is to apply the preoccupations of twentieth-century biographers to the ninth century: when Asser and Alfred sat together in the royal chamber, one imagines they did not engage in idle chat about the king's repressed Freudian memories. That is not what biography in the ninth century was all about. A king, as poets of the time never ceased to reiterate, should be 'seated on a high watchtower, armed and vigilant . . .' The key interest in a king's early life was not childhood anecdote but the facts of his birth and his pedigree. Kings in the Early Middle Ages were expected to be strong, magnanimous, big souled, good at fighting – and legitimate. A contemporary of Alfred recoils with horror at the situation on the Continent: 'creating false kings out of their guts, raddled with arrogance'. If Alfred claimed to be king of the English, not to mention protector of the Welsh, then his pedigree was part of his credentials. And Alfred's pedigree was exemplary, second to none in fact, given a little tidying up here and there, some slight tweaking of the evidence (exactly how grandfather Egbert fits into his pedigree is still strangely unclear). But here was a family tree going back to the sixth century, and beyond, if so required, to Woden and the rest: as good, if not better, than that of any king in Europe. If any king could justify his claim to be head of the island of Britain, it was Alfred.

In recent years, royal biography has become a growth industry, no part of the royals' private lives being spared, especially their health and their sex lives. In this light, it is interesting to look at Asser's account of Alfred's possibly psychosexual illnesses, for on its detail the credibility of his portrait of the king's personality stands or falls. Professor Smyth is not the first to have found Asser's epidemiology incredible. Even some believers in Asser have been uncomfortable about his emphasis on Alfred's sex life: Stevenson found it repellent; Dorothy Whitelock, who was of the First World War generation and never married, admitted that she found it unpleasant and 'wearisome'.

Asser's account of Alfred's health is rather convoluted and incoherent, with hints dropped here and there, but clearly the subject was of great import to Asser as he comes back to it several times. The story goes something like this. When he was in his early teens, Alfred was unable to suppress his carnal desire (Asser doesn't go into details here). Tortured by guilt, the prince prayed to God for an illness to strengthen his resolve: 'for some illness which he would be able to bear – not though that God would make him unworthy and useless in worldly affairs'. Then 'after some time, through God's gift' he contracted *ficus* (probably piles, an agony for a Dark Age king who spent so much of life in the saddle on bad roads, but *ficus* is also sometimes explained as a 'weeping ulcer'). This he is said to have endured for some years to the point of despair. Then one day on a hunting expedition in Cornwall, he visited the ancient Cornish shrine of St Gueriir, where he prayed to God to 'substitute for the pangs of the present and agonizing infirmity some less severe illness'. His prayers were heard and for a while he was cured of the piles.

Then, at his wedding in 868 at the age of nineteen, he was struck suddenly by a new and unidentified illness, which lasted from his twentieth to his forty-fifth year, the year in which Asser was writing.

This is Asser on the illness:

Some thought it was due to the piles because he had suffered this kind of dreadfully painful irritation right from his youth but . . . it seized him at his wedding feast, and plagued him remorselessly, and if at any time through God's mercy that illness abated for the space of a day or a night or even an hour, his fear and loathing of that accursed pain would never desert him, and it seemed to him it rendered him virtually useless for heavenly and worldly affairs.

What on earth are we to make of this? Why did Asser think it worthy of mention? And why did he keep coming back to it? This is as excruciatingly intimate as some of Andrew Morton's more lurid passages on Princess Diana, and it sounds a lot more debilitating than the venereal infections which Seymour Hersch claims were not enough to take JFK's mind off the game during the Cuban Missile Crisis. If Asser is to be believed, it was touch and go whether Alfred could get out of bed and fight the battle of Edington.

Convinced the text is a forgery, Professor Smyth dismisses this picture of Alfred's health: he simply doesn't believe that this can be the leader who showed such grit, tenacity and stamina against the Vikings. The effort to picture Alfred as a suffering saintlike figure, he thinks, is 'nauseating and repellent' and clear evidence of a later monkish forgery. But there are a number of suggestive hints which seem to support Asser's story. The preface to Alfred's translation of Boethius's *Consolation of Philosophy*, for example, refers to 'the various and multifarious worldly distractions which frequently occupied him both in mind and body, preoccupations which beset him during his days on the throne which are virtually countless . . .' In the text of the same work, Alfred's translation talks of the *haefignes*, the 'heaviness' – the grossness or corporeality of the body – and the *untheawas* as of the flesh, 'which have the power utterly to take away righteousness from his mind'. This and other passages were translated euphemistically by the Victorians: *untheawas*, for example, as 'infirmities of the body'. But *untheawas* is a much stronger word than 'infirmity': it means evil practices, wicked habits, or vice, and is even glossed directly as *fornicatio*. Alfred is talking about carnal lust. He is concerned with its ability literally to make the mind oblivious and to lead it into a 'mist of delusion'. He continues in his own words: 'but nevertheless a grain of the seed of truth is ever dwelling in the soul . . . then shall one find righteousness hid there amid the "heaviness" of the body, and the distractions and afflictions of his mind'.

Early medieval penitentials are full of warnings about sex, which was basically only allowed between married people, and then only for procreation. This teaching of the Church placed an intolerable strain on people's lives, creating a fundamental dissonance between human nature and the law of God. In this era of teenage sex magazines and pornography on the Internet, we moderns may find the medieval attitude to sex inexplicably convoluted, but control over men and women's sex lives played a central part in the Church's teachings.

Could there, perhaps, be some connection between Alfred's sexual concerns and his mystery illness, which started on his wedding night? These concerns come out again in the king's translation of Boethius's chapter on fleshly vices (*flaesclican untheawas*). Here Alfred emphasizes the penalties of the delights of the flesh: 'a woman in labour suffers great pains and in childbirth, according as she has formerly enjoyed great delight'. Indeed, Asser tells us later of Alfred's decision, after fathering many children (an unknown number of whom died in infancy), to give up sex altogether.

The Church in the age of the Carolingian Renaissance asked a lot of its princes, and in our age of sexual freedom this passage is strangely moving. It sounds like an intelligent man trying to talk frankly about the pitfalls of the flesh from his own experience – with all the weight of Church teaching on his back. Alfred knows about the great delight of sex but still believes that unlawful sexual pleasure will be punished. At the end of this section, in Alfred's translation, Boethius says that unlawful lust (*unrihthaemedes*) disturbs the mind of almost every man that lives. In Old English, *haemed* is specifically the sex act, and to do it *unrihtlice* is to commit adultery, to have carnal intercourse, or even to rape. Having translated this last line of Boethius, Alfred adds his own conclusion: 'on the evil desire of lust . . . every soul must perish after unlawful sexual lust (*unrihthaemede*), except a man return to virtue'.

Buton se mon hweorfe to gode: except a man return to virtue. There, surely, is the key to Asser's picture of Alfred's health. This is not gossip to titillate his audience: illness and pain had a meaning. They too are God-given. Rising to exaltation through suffering is one of the keynotes of medieval hagiography. And not just medieval: this trajectory is, for example, central to the tabloid hagiography of Diana Princess of Wales. She overcame a broken marriage, bulimia, sickness, attempted suicide, utmost despair and self-abnegation before she rebuilt herself as a person of moral substance with her campaigns for just causes. The meaning of her rise to secular sainthood is the same. Out of illness and degradation – *humilitatio* in medieval terms – comes *exaltatio*. How medieval we still are!

Medieval kings, one imagines, were a very strange mixture, their lives 'forever mingled with the scent of blood and roses' as Johan Huizinga put it so memorably in *The Waning of the Middle Ages*. Superstitious, politicized by their dreams, limned by a spirit world where the unseen continually threatened to burst upon the everyday. Racked by bad health like the rest of the population, they were constantly reminded of the presence of death and judgement, nagged by the remembrance of private or public sin, especially with bishops around them who saw it as part of their job to prod the royal conscience. No wonder Alfred took his unknown illness so seriously – whatever its connection with his youthful sexual indiscretions. It is, to say the least, a far cry from the Christ-like Victorian family man portrayed on the walls of Parliament.

The picture would be clearer if only we knew what exactly it was that Alfred was suffering from. Asser's account is vague and confused, and he was no doctor. But as it happens he is not the only witness. At one point, Asser tells us that the Orthodox Patriarch of Jerusalem had sent letters to the king which he himself had seen. These included medical recipes. By a happy conicidence, a manuscript survives from an English doctor of Alfred's time, moreover a doctor with connections with the royal court: the so-called 'Leechbook' of a physician called Bald.

The Leechbook of Bald is a compendium of pre-Conquest medical practice; a vast and impressive range of herbs, spices and plant remedies were used, many of which were imported from abroad. One specifically deals with *ficus*. The relevant section heading (II 74) says this:

A medicine, scammony for constipation of the inwards, and gutamon for pain in the spleen and stitch, and spikenard for diarrhoea, and trugacanth for corrupt phlegms in men, and aloes for infirmities and galbanum for shortness of breath and balsam anointing for all infirmities and petroleum to drink alone for inward tenderness and to smear on outwards, and theriac is a good drink for inward tenderness . . .

Some of these could be remedies for piles, but Alfred's troubles sound more serious (perhaps Crohn's disease?). Unfortunately, the detailed exposition on use and dosage is missing from the manuscript, but at the end of this section of the Leechbook comes this:

All this the Lord Patriarch of Jerusalem Elias ordered to be told to King Alfred.

Even now, peering through the circumlocutions of official biographers is never easy, and Asser no doubt left a lot unsaid. Successful kings were usually robust: this was one aspect of the *fortuna* ('luck') which made a good king. A successful king had magical aura. Charlemagne's biographer Einhard portrays him as being as tough as old boots, an enthusiastic swimmer into old age, careful with his diet, capable of staying in his saddle all hours. Asser had read his Einhard, and there was much to learn from it. But

Alfred was a different character, and Asser's picture of him is nearer to other early medieval royal lives which stressed more saintly virtues.

So when we consider Asser's strange account of Alfred's health in detail – and what he leaves unsaid – it can be made to yield a convincing psychological picture. Asser's account was not the sort of thing the spin doctors of modern ruler cults would want put out. But a medieval biographer could turn such tribulations, even ones born of sin, to a higher message. Alfred had sinned when he was young, suffered for it, fought against his desires and in the end conquered them. And so to the biographer the will of God is always operating: driving worldly concerns on to a higher purpose.

Far from being ridiculous and unbelievable, Asser's story of the king's sex life is revealingly contemporary in its concerns. In the unlikeliest part of the book, the area which has least appealed to some modern readers, is corroboration of the genuineness of the text.

Such a pilgrim's progress was obviously of great interest to Asser as a bishop. The same goes for the other great maturation story he tells in the book – the tale of Alfred's ascent first to bare literacy and then to Christian wisdom. For Asser, this was perhaps the key message of the book; particularly as – if we can believe him – he himself was intimately involved in how it happened. And here again, as the authenticity of his text has been questioned, it is worth looking at precisely what he tells us.

The patronage of learning was a crucial aspect of a king's life and personality in the Viking Age. The Carolingian kings had set a shining example as patrons of learning and founders of court libraries. In comparison, the efforts of the English kings were small beer (at least it was thought so till only recently), but nevertheless, far-reaching efforts were made by the Church in the ninth century to make kings Christ's vicars on earth. And to read texts such as Asser is to glimpse something of the process by which they gradually constructed order: practical, moral and religious.

So Alfred's ascent to literacy is the key achievement in his biographer's eyes. To be truly a Christian king you needed to be able to read and write, for Christianity, after all, is predominantly the religion of the book. The story is told by Asser in touching detail, and as befits such a turning-point, Asser for once – and only once – gives a precise date. The day when, 'prompted by heaven', the king begins 'the rudiments of Holy Scripture' – that is, reads Latin for the first time – was St Martin's day, 11 November 887. A red-letter day, more significant to Asser than any battle. The king had been illiterate as a boy, only able to master poetry by hearing it and learning by rote. Now Asser helps him to read for the first time:

One day when we were sitting together in the royal chamber discussing all sorts of topics (as we usually did), it happened that I was reading aloud some passage to him from a certain book. As he was listening intently to this – all ears – and carefully mulling it over in the depth of his mind, he suddenly showed me a little book which he constantly carried on his person, and in which were written the day time offices [of the Church] and some psalms and certain prayers he had learned in his youth. He told me to copy the passage in question into the little book . . .

The moment has wide implications for kingship as a whole. How Alfred went on to attempt to restore learning (Asser writing in 893 has little on this, since the programme had only just started) we know from the preface of Alfred's translation of Pope Gregory's *Pastoral Care*, which survives in the actual manuscript sent to Worcester around 890.

It has very often come to my mind what men of learning there were formerly throughout England, both in religious and secular society . . . and how nowadays if we wished to acquire these things we would have to seek them abroad. Learning had declined so thoroughly in England that there were very few men on this side of the Humber who could understand their divine services in English, or even translate a single letter from Latin into English; and I suppose there were not many beyond the Humber either. There were so few of them that I cannot recollect even a single one south of the Thames when I came to the kingdom.

It sounds overwrought, a government making a special plea about the poor state of education left by the blunders of earlier administrations. But modern studies have been able to confirm Alfred's picture: the massive losses of books, the failure of literacy, even the decline in scribal competence, so that by the time of Alfred's youth the chief scribe at one of the main English houses was an old man who could no longer see properly. The situation had to be remedied, otherwise Christian kingship could not function. Alfred saw that clearly. So in the middle of his desperate struggles with the Vikings, Alfred took time off to try to translate the handful of key books he thought could form the basis of a core curriculum to revive literacy: 'I thought it best to turn into the language we all can understand certain books which are the most necessary for all men to know.'

To do this, Alfred gathered a team of scholars. Among them were several foreigners: a Frank, Grimbald from St Bertin; a German, John the Old Saxon; and of course the Welshman, Asser. None of them was an intellectual heavyweight (compared, say, with the stars of the Frankish Renaissance: Alcuin, for example, or the great Platonist, John Scotus). But needs must. The books they chose make an interesting selection, a kind of Dark Age Penguin Classics or Everyman's Library. There was, of course, Bede's *History*, the founding text of the English nation; Boethius's *Consolation of Philosophy* (a work with an astonishingly long life in English: among its later translators were Chaucer and Queen Elizabeth I); Gregory the Great's *Pastoral Care*, St Augustine's *Soliloquies* and *Dialogues*, Orosius's *History*, and the Psalms (a fundamental text not only for devotion but for learning Latin). They may even have made a start at the Gospels. A tiny pile of books; a shelfload only. But if the worst came to the worst, through flood, war, or other cataclysm, they must have reasoned, enough to pass on.

Asser names some of these helpers, and though a forger could have had genuine manuscripts of Alfredian translations, Asser nevertheless sounds strongly like an eyewitness here. That Werferth of Worcester translated the *Dialogues*, for example, is only stated in Asser, but we know there was indeed a Mercian priest of that name at Worcester at the time, and the dialect of the translation confirms it was done by a Mercian. But Asser is especially interesting when he talks about what went on between the scholars, how they actually worked. The text was read out in Latin and explained in English, with the help of commentaries to elucidate difficult readings. Then an English version was written down. Asser says Werferth translated *aliquando sensum ex sensu*: 'sense for sense'. The same phrase is used of Alfred in the preface to his Boethius: *Hwilum he sette word be worde, hwilum andgit of andgite*: In the *Pastoral Care*, Alfred himself says that he translated 'sometimes word for word, sometimes sense by sense as I learned it from . . . Archbishop Plegmund and Asser my bishop . . .' This phrase 'word for word' is from the great Christian translator Jerome, but it is hardly likely that Alfred himself got it from Jerome's Latin; probably he heard the expression in their seminars from Asser himself.

By an amazing chance (given how little survives), a text of Boethius dating from this time survives in the Vatican Library, written in a beautiful, Carolingian, miniscule hand from the Loire valley. During Alfred's reign or soon after, this book came to England where it was carefully annotated with a commentary of the kind used by the authors of the Alfredian translation; some pages are almost covered with neat black additions, marginal and interlinear. There are four annotating hands of various times, but most interesting for our purposes is the earliest layer of additions. The text has been covered with syntax marks, which are common in Welsh manuscripts, and the punctuation and abbreviations used in some of the marginal glosses is also found in Welsh texts. And the first glossing hand is ninth century – and Welsh.

Can we get any closer to identifying this first hand? There are clues in the content of the marginal notes. Take, for example, the commentary note on the 'sad pagan tale' of Orpheus, a story which was often interpreted by Christian commentators as a metaphor for the soul's journey. It is told briefly by Boethius, but was expanded by Alfred, who rarely missed a good story. Orpheus, a great harpist, was a figure easy to place in English heroic society. Alfred would have employed someone like him, some West Saxon scop to sing away the long winter nights at Cheddar or Athelney. So, with the help of a written commentary, Alfred and his team added details to the tale of Orpheus – on Charon, the 'frightening door keeper', and Cerberus, the 'monstrous guard dog' guarding the royal hall of the king of Hell. At this point, Boethius says simply that Orpheus 'also met other goddesses that punish men according to their deeds'. Boethius thought these were the Furies, but Alfred adds the explanation that these were 'the fell goddesses that men of the people call the Parcae, saying that they know no respect for any men but punish each according to his deeds, and they are said to rule each man's fate'.

Uniquely among surviving commentaries on Boethius, the Vatican manuscript agrees that these goddesses are called the Parcae, adding their names – 'these are Clotto, Lochesis and Atropos' – with a note that they 'are always full of anger and fury; and they punish souls'. This little detail, which our Welsh annotator took, incidentally, from the encyclopaedia of Isidore of Seville, is one of several which point to the same conclusion: the Vatican commentary is the set of glosses used by Asser to talk Alfred through the text in their oral sessions together, 'word for word and sense for sense'. And though we'll probably never know for sure, one might well wonder whether the careful black annotations are in the hand of Asser himself.

Whether faking Van Gogh's *Sunflowers* or Hitler's diaries, forgers have to be very clever, and technically extremely adept, to get away with it. They have to get the basic picture right, but also the detail, the background, the nuance. There was a famous case in the nineteenth century of *The Journal of a Spy during the Reign of Terror*, which was forged as a joke and taken seriously for a while before it was exposed in 1896. Even with all the resources libraries provide, the forger succumbed to anachronism and error. This the author of the Asser manuscript does not do. The detail in the end is unanswerable, and it is by engaging with the 'difficulties' that we actually get closer to the real life of the time. The marginal notes in the Vatican manuscript are merely one of several converging lines of investigation which together prove the genuineness of the Asser text.

But was the book ever finished, let alone published? Asser's text as we have it ends abruptly. The last line is this: 'I have explained this concern for learning how to read among the young and old in order to give some idea of the character of King Alfred.' This has suggested to some that the work is incomplete. But it is just as likely that Asser intended this to be the end. Possibly he took few pains to polish it up and had said all he wanted to say. He was writing in Alfred's forty-fifth year (893) and may have finished the book soon afterwards. We know he lived till 908, so he would have had plenty of opportunity to do more shaping, to add later events, had he wished. But evidently he did not. So there the book ends, with no sign of it having been reworked with later events in mind. Perhaps Asser simply turned to other things. It was never widely circulated, perhaps only in a couple of manuscripts, so it is a minor miracle that despite the fire of 1731 it has come down to us, albeit in a problematic state.

As for why Asser wrote the book, it follows the popular genre of a 'mirror of princes', a handbook on kingship, and one might speculate that it could have been written for Alfred's children. The king's first grandson was born around the time the book was being written. Conceivably it could even have been inspired by that fact, the grandfather Alfred unsure with his continuing ill health how much longer he had to live. Perhaps we should not underestimate Alfred's concern for the succession: maybe he was already toying with the idea of a grandson succeeding in due course.

But as we have seen, most speculation has centred on the Welsh-ness of the text: the fact of a Welsh cleric writing this favourable picture of an English king, representing him as the Solomon of his age. Coupled with the Welsh usages, and the translation of over a dozen place names into Welsh, this has convinced many that Asser was writing for a Welsh audience. Which is as we would expect from Asser's wordy justification of his decision to accept Alfred's offer, his long hesitation and his eventual agreement 'by the advice and permission of all our people, for the benefit of that holy place [St David's] and of all who live there . . . in order that England should benefit from the teachings of St David'. This may suggest

– though it does not prove – that the book was aimed at Welsh readers; an apologia for the benefit of critics who disapproved of a Welsh bishop leaving his own Church in Wales to enter the service of a foreign king, especially a king of the English, the old enemy. But it would make sense of Asser's choice of material: his insights into Alfred's Christian character and his ability to beat the Vikings, all to persuade the Welsh that Alfred was a good Christian king in whom they could place their trust.

If that was the case, the timing of the book was crucial. In the year Asser was writing, 'all the kings of Wales submitted to Alfred king of the English'. What the English wanted in the long run was to be acknowledged overlords of Britain, the Celtic kings their 'co-workers by land and sea'. This would happen in the tenth century when Hywel Dda allied with the English, and gave his son an English name, Edwin; when the Welsh kings bowed to Edgar at Bath and rowed him on the Dee – the real beginnings of Welsh *rapprochement* with the English inhabitants of mainland Britain which has seen dramatic new twists even in the late 1990s.

Asser's book is patchy, unpolished, uneven, but in its roughness and its vivid detail it gives us a remarkable portrait of a ninth-century king, warts and all, and in some of its detail – its treatment of the king's health problems, for example, and the king's ascent to literacy – it strikes this reader, at least, as compellingly realistic. Our reading of it, of course, is loaded with the preconceptions of our own time – though through the work of scholars over the past few decades we have come a long way from Victorian children's books and the paintings in the House of Commons. Alfred was his father's fifth son, and may never have expected to be king. With his piles, his pox and his hypochondria, he makes an unlikely hero, but hero he was – especially to his children, grandchildren and great-grandchildren, who took his blueprint, the family plan, and created the first English state and the first British empire. And in Asser's strange biography we have not only the most intimate portrait of Alfred, but a most revealing testimony to the continued working out of the Matter of Britain and Matter of England.

8. The Lost Life of King Athelstan

'This was the mature and manlie age of the Imperie then especiellie
flowringe in menne, in valiaunce, and vertewe.'

Polydore Vergil, *English History* (1534)

The medievalist's problem – the lack of material and its often poor
quality – is both the charm and frustration of studying the Dark
Ages and the early Middle Ages. 'Many an investigator will leave
his bones to bleach in that desert before it is accurately mapped,'
as F. W. Maitland wrote. With King Arthur, one can see how the
whole edifice of books, films and reconstructions of the Age of
Arthur is based on no more than three or four sources which don't
stand up to the light of day. Even with a historical figure like King
Alfred, whose life is well documented in contemporary sources,
we are still in danger of losing most of our biographical material
when a modern revision brands the key source as a forgery. The
problem is just as acute with another man who along with Alfred
and Edward Elder is one of the makers of England: Athelstan. With
Athelstan, the question is what the key source really is. The problem
is a lost life – and a lost *Life*.

Athelstan lived in the bleak early tenth century, the 'blackest
time in Europe', an age of pessimism and foreboding when it was
'by no means certain that Christianity will survive in these islands',
as one English cleric wrote. It was a time when a large portion of
the world lived on the threshold of starvation; when the lot of the
peasantry was to work to feed their betters – and if they were lucky,
then to feed themselves. Cycles of dearth, famine and disease were
endemic; war was a condition of life. On top of that, a succession

of freezing winters (especially severe in the 940s, for example) brought further misery. 'We live in a new Age of Iron,' pronounced a meeting of Frankish bishops in 909, and looking from this distance, it is hard to disagree. But periods of creation are almost more interesting than golden ages. The struggle to create from scratch, to build things up by going back to first principles, is as important to the historian as times of high achievement – and perhaps more revealing about what really made people in the past tick. As a great modern exponent of humanistic scholarship, Arnaldo Momigliano, wrote after the Second World War:

We, the members of the race of iron, have learnt to appreciate the lesser men – the men who tried to save what could be saved and who did not disdain the task of elementary teaching when elementary teaching was needed.

In this battle against hunger, want and disorder, kingship was the great institution created in the Dark Ages which laid the foundation of the States of modern Europe. Kings, of course, were also there to serve the interests of the ruling class and the Church, but as remodelled in the Carolingian renaissance, Christian kingship often had a high moral purpose, however unpalatable some of its methods may be to us today. It has gone now, save for the last ceremonial flickerings in Windsor or Madrid. But kingship was the key institution in European history for 1,500 years, conditioning art and literature as well as shaping society. And in its formative years of the early Middle Ages, kingship was subject to intense scrutiny and debate. As the Carolingians said, *quid sit proprium ministerium regis* ('what do we want a king to do?').

The West Saxons were among the most successful. Their ancestry, they claimed, went back – and perhaps it really did – to an adventurer of the sixth century called Cerdic, from whom the present English queen distantly traces her descent. Their founding myth was that they came as immigrants, crossing the sea to Britain back in the mists of time to 'win themselves kingdom'. They rose to be kings of all England and laid the foundations of an English state which still endures. Their remarkable transition from rulers of a small kingdom in the ninth century to emperors of Britain was made in only four generations. Their achievement, in one sense, was a family triumph: from Aethelwulf's day, possibly, but certainly from his son, Alfred, through *his* son Edward and grandson Athelstan we can see them holding on to a family design. Alfred defeated the Danes, consolidated Wessex, created a network of forts and new towns, altered the nature of the military organization of society, and also laid the foundations for the recovery of learning. Edward's military deeds changed the whole shape of southern Britain, conquering permanently the populations of the Midlands and eastern England, English and Danish.

Athelstan turned the kingdom of England into a fact, the 'first to rule what previously many kings shared between them'. Then with astonishing rapidity came the empire of Britain, with all ten Celtic rulers of the British mainland acknowledging his overlordship. He was the most powerful ruler since the Romans, and to a degree was aware of it: 'the fields of Britannia were consolidated into one,' it was said. They were lords of the *Orbis Britanniae* – the 'world of Britain'. This last idea is of particular interest. In Roman times, a tradition had arisen in the West of a 'tripartite world', *triquadri orbis* – that is, Europe, Africa and Asia. Britain, however, as befitted its geographical placing out 'on the edge', was another world, an *alter orbis*. It was with a conscious sense of history, then that after 928, only fifty years after Alfred was burning cakes in the swamps of Athelney, his heirs now claimed to be rulers of the 'whole of the world of Britain'. When they beat their Celtic foes in 937, the victory was hailed in court as the greatest since their ancestors first came out west to Britain 'over the broad waves to carve themselves a kingdom'. This moment was recognized by Geoffrey of Monmouth in the twelfth century as the key moment for the Celts: a turning-point in the Matter of Britain and the Matter of England.

Clearly something very important had happened, but the sources are so scanty and uneven that it is difficult to see exactly what or how, and this period has always been viewed as one of the shadowiest in our medieval history. I say scanty, but in some senses the documentation is rich: the law codes, for example – records of the king's lawmaking councils – and numerous charters include some magnificent originals written by the king's scribes. In the past few years, closer dating of scribal hands has also made it possible to identify many more books produced in Athelstan's reign. Quite a rich haul it is too, ranging from the Church Fathers to Virgil. But when we get to the king and his motivations, the preoccupations of the modern biographer, the story is almost blank.

This gap in our knowledge was the subject of a brilliant essay by J. Armitage Robinson in 1922, which showed what could be recovered from unconsidered trifles, scraps and fragments not normally considered by historians: book inscriptions, destroyed manuscripts, relic lists, entries in calendars, notes in later catalogues. But the narrative is still lacking, and along with Offa, Athelstan remains one of the two greatest English rulers for whom biography fails. The problem is compounded in part by the sudden failure of the *Anglo-Saxon Chronicle*, whose very rich narrative from the 880s to 920 gives out with no warning. The *Chronicle* is virtually non-existent for the 920s and 930s, except for the later insertion of the famous poem on Athelstan's victory at Brunanburh. It leaves us with nothing with which to make a narrative. At least, that would be so were it not for William of Malmesbury.

William was born in south-west England soon after the Norman Conquest. He says he was of mixed parentage, which presumably means that his mother was English and his father Norman. William was librarian at Malmesbury in Wiltshire, John Betjeman's 'queen of hilltop towns', with its fine setting above a loop of the Avon. Malmesbury was the site of a seventh-century monastery inside Iron Age defences; and Athelstan was buried there. Today the abbey is a magnificent fragment which is now the parish church, where the king's fourteenth-century tomb chest with its recumbent effigy is still pointed out. Athelstan is still something of a hero in the town: there's an Athelstan Bus Company and an Athelstan Garage, and when a skeleton was recently found in a tomb in the abbot's garden there was quite a brouhaha in the *North Wiltshire*

Advertiser and on TV as to whether the king himself had been found (he hadn't).

In the 1120s, William of Malmesbury set out to write a history of England. He saw himself in the line of Bede, and indeed his confidence was not misplaced: he was the best English historian since Bede. With a foot in both camps, his was in a sense an act of restitution: to restore to the English their history after the shattering impact of the Norman Conquest; to show the Norman rulers the rich history of the land they had so violently seized. He had a wide-ranging mind. His, for example, appear to be the first serious remarks in Britain about Islam and its prophet. William was not above editing texts and improving their Latin in the process, but he had a critical sense: 'I'll give you the received opinion, but with reservations' is a typical remark. And it is William who gives us our only detailed narrative on Athelstan two hundred years on. Since his time, its contents have always been accepted as the key source for this crucial period in which a kingdom of England emerges. But unfortunately (how often that word crops up in medieval history!) William found the source for his account in unusual circumstances, and has left us with a problem which has always been knotty and has recently become controversial. For William says he found his account in a hitherto unknown manuscript which only he ever described – and of which no trace has ever been discovered.

Here's William's account of his discovery of the old manuscript. It's a good story worth telling in his words. The reader will note William's typical lofty aspersions on bad style (as a scholar he was something of a snob), but at the same time one may warm to a history buff sharing his enthusiasm:

Concerning this king a firm opinion is still current among the English, that no one more just or learned administered the State. A few days ago I discovered that he was versed in letters, from a certain obviously very old book, in which the author struggled with the difficulty of his matter, unable to express his meaning as he wished. I would have appended his own words here for the sake of completeness, if he did not range beyond belief in praise of the prince, in the style which Cicero, the king of Roman eloquence, in his book on rhetoric, calls bombastic. The custom of that time excuses the diction; the affection for Athelstan, who was then living, lends colour to the excessive praise. I will add therefore, in a familiar style, some few matters which may be seen to augment the record of his greatness.

There follows in the printed edition eight pages of William's summary of the lost work, including, unusually for William, direct quotes by 'this poet' of two chunks totalling sixty-three lines of verse. Enough on the face of it, one would have thought, for the experts to be able to discover exactly what the lost book was. But it is a curiosity that although this has been seen as the key account of the unification of England for several hundred years, its contents and language have never been closely scrutinized. I'm no Latinist myself, but I well remember as a graduate student looking at it and assuming that William had tarted it up in his own style: William's quotes from the lost book simply did not look like a tenth-century text; they weren't like the impenetrable writings of that time by people such as Wulfstan the Cantor. But then didn't William say that he would put it over in a 'familiar style'? One assumed that he had worked over the direct quotes in the Latin of his own day. But no. In 1980, Michael Lapidge showed that William's quotes were composed in the 1120s, and worse, suggested that they were made up, as what was in them was just 'manifest flights of fancy'. Such was Professor Lapidge's (richly deserved) standing, that in no time at all William's 'very old book', the key narrative source for this period, was brusquely excised from the record, and one could read everywhere that Lapidge had 'conclusively disproved that William used an ancient poem'. This was perhaps not exactly what Professor Lapidge had intended, but one only has to turn to any of the scholarly literature on the period written in the past fifteen years to find that William's account of Athelstan is now regarded as 'treacherous', 'dangerous' and even 'worthless as evidence'. William, in short, was a faker and his *Life of Athelstan* was no more.

I wonder, though, whether the case on William's mysterious

'old book' should be reopened. After all, William says unambiguously that everything he gives in this section of his account of Athelstan was from the lost book, which, he says clearly, was a single poem in tenth-century Latin. It was in 'the style of that time', the work of 'this poet from whom we have excerpted all these particulars'. William knew very well what that style was, as he explains elsewhere. William also specifically says that he is not going to give the lost author in his own words but in 'familiar style': that is, in the style of William's own time. So we would expect something which has been modernized, whether in the prose paraphrase or in the verse quotes; and that apparently is what he gives us. So can the modern verdict on William's story be wrong? Did the 'obviously very old book' really exist? And if so, what was it?

Proof of the pudding, as we shall see, is in the content of William's précis; but without going into too many technicalities, we should first say a word about William's Latin. My hunch is that William's text is rather like a palimpsest, a page of vellum whose original text has been rubbed out and written over, but which is still visible underneath. Rather as a modern translator would, William has tried to give an impression of the lost book, and in many places his account shows traces of the older text underneath it. Vocabulary, syntax, favourite words, even line ends and internal rhymes – all show traces of the tricks used by poets of the tenth century. His opening looks as if it is modelled on the sixth-century poet Venantius Fortunatus, who was much in vogue in the tenth century but not in William's day. Similarly, William's big set-piece of Athelstan's coronation is modelled on the banquet scene in Virgil's *Aeneid*, just as is the consecration-scene in a tenth-century poem on Saint Swithun – indeed, the two works show close verbal parallels in several places. These hints are enough for us to wonder whether William has not done exactly what he said he would: given us a shortened version of an ancient book, in 'modern' language, making heavy editorial snips but preserving some of the vocabulary and even the word order. The proof, though, is the content. Is William's account really riddled with 'flights of fancy', or does it come from an early and good source? What follows is

my tentative reconstruction of the 'very old book' last seen in the
Middle Ages: the lost *Life of King Athelstan*.

> A royal son prolonged a noble line
> When a splendid gem lit up our darkness.
> Great Athelstan, glory of the country, way of rectitude
> Noble integrity, unswervable from the truth.

A high-sounding beginning: William gives this in verse in direct
quotes. As was the custom in Viking Age biography, the lost book
evidently began with a eulogy about the king, recalling his ancestry
and punning on his name: *aeþel stan*, 'noble stone', or 'splendid
gem'. Then it took us on through his *pueritia*, his childhood;
adolescentia (aged fourteen to twenty-eight); and on to his maturity
and the kingship. But close to the beginning – significantly – was
a wonderful tale which takes us to the heart of Alfred's court,
perhaps not long before Alfred died, aged fifty, on 26 October 899.
Athelstan was a little boy, five or six years old, with 'graceful
manners and handsome looks'. He was presented to his grandfather,
who 'affectionately embraced him and gave him a Saxon sword, a
jewelled scabbard, belt and cloak'. This tale is often dismissed as an
anachronism, a knighting ceremony from William's own day. But
there are a number of ninth-century Frankish stories of young
princes being invested with arms. Such rites of passage usually took
place during adolescence, at fourteen or fifteen; but such ceremonies
might be carried out as young as four or five, especially if there
was a pressing political need to advertise the succession. The four-
year-old Louis the Pious, for example, was placed on a horse with
a sword and belt in the presence of the armed following of his
father. Nothing told more clearly that the job was first and foremost
to fight and defend the kingdom against its enemies. Not surprisingly, kings could become stressed-out people if they didn't have
strong nerves and hardy constitutions. Look at Alfred, with his
nervous illnesses and hypochondria; his writings full of the cares of
rulership. Many of his line died early: Eadred at thirty-two, in
agony from rotten teeth and mouth abcesses; Edgar at the same

age. It was a tough job with many psychological, physical and intellectual demands. So best let the boy know early about the *via regia*: the royal road of Christian kingship.

The 'knighting' of the little boy, then, is far from being an anachronism. The story of Athelstan's investiture rings true, and in its details – the 'affectionate hug' – it sounds like a witness's reminiscence. One wonders whether the story was perhaps told by the king himself, or by an eyewitness who passed it on to the author of the lost book. Indeed, we can get closer still to that day, for by an astonishing chance – given our shadowy knowledge of this period – the story of the young prince's investiture is confirmed by a poem (entered in a slightly later manuscript) which was written by a foreign poet called John. The poem is addressed to a young prince called Athelstan, and it is an acrostic. In the Latin, the first letter of each line, reading down, spells his name, and again we have the pun on his name, *aepelstan*, 'noble stone'. Though of no literary merit, it is one of the most delightful poems in English history:

> Little prince, you are called by the name 'sovereign stone',
> Look happily on this prophecy for your life.
> You shall be the 'noble rock' of Samuel the seer,
> Standing with mighty strength against the devilish monsters.
> Often an abundant cornfield foretells a fine harvest.
> In times of peace your stoniness will soften, for
> You are more abundantly endowed with the holy eminence
>   of learning.
> I pray that you may seek, and that God may grant, the
>   promise of your noble names.

It's a touching moment. From William's story and the evidence of the manuscript poem we can imagine the scene at the royal court: Alfred the doting grandfather honouring the well-mannered and handsome little boy, presenting him with the cloak, sword and belt; then the hug, and the prayer for the future. Alfred, no doubt, had half an eye on keeping his elder brother's children out of the succession. Alfred was the last of five brothers who became king; they were all dead now, but the king had at least one nephew who was grown up and resentful. So this is a political gesture. Athelstan is his only grandson at this moment, so whether the boy's mother is married or not, he is carrying a lot on his little shoulders.

And for the occasion, one of the king's circle of scholars produces the little poem for the boy: a puzzle which even now needs some headscratching to work out, and no doubt had to be explained in English to the boy. Perhaps the poet John was there in person, and was applauded for his ingenuity. He was probably John the Old Saxon, whom the English called 'John the Wise', one of the king's scholarly helpers. John had written two similar poems, one rather sweetly encouraging Alfred to 'run confidently through the fields of foreign learning'. Young princes were often tutored by learned clerics in the royal circle, and it would be interesting to know whether John was Athelstan's teacher. He, too, was buried at Malmesbury: perhaps a further hint as to their relationship?

The lost *Life* went on to say that at his grandfather's behest, Athelstan was brought up away from his father, fostered in Mercia in the court of his aunt Aethelflaed and her husband Earl Aethelred. This story has also been rejected in the recent condemnation of William's account, but it makes good sense. The Mercians had lost their own kings by now, but they still had their own assembly, and Mercian sensibilities were strong, as kings of Wessex forgot to their cost. Asser says Alfred's wife, Athelstan's grandmother, who died in 902, was Mercian, and he had also met Alfred's Mercian mother-in-law. Again a chance survival helps us throw some light on this, a paraphrase of a lost charter of Athelstan's first year, published in 1939 but strangely ignored since. In this document the thirty-year-old king is surrounded by his Mercian friends as he ratifies his first known act of State. He promises to protect the Church of St Oswald in Gloucester, confirming a promise made long ago, 'a pact of paternal piety' made with his uncle, Aethelred. His uncle died in 911 when Athelstan was about sixteen years old, so the promise must have been made after the saint's relics were moved to Gloucester in

909 and before Aethelred's death two years later. The phrasing of the charter suggests strongly that Aethelred, who had no son of his own, was indeed Athelstan's foster-father as William states. It is interesting too to see that the teenage Athelstan was already devoted to the memory of the English saints, as he would remain so conspicuously all his adult life.

With these hints and fragments, suddenly we seem to break through the barrier of unyielding sources and touch on a real life: the six-year-old with his little sword and cloak; the adolescent's solemn promise to his aunt's sick husband, his foster-father, to protect the saint they loved. The psychologist might be tempted to read more into his filial reverence towards his uncle than the evidence warrants, but the evidence does strongly suggest that William's story about the king's fostering was true. We have hardly got beyond William's first few lines, and yet his text has already turned up trumps with absolutely intimate information. I think we can be sure he had indeed found the lost *Life of King Athelstan*.

Let's push on, browsing through its pages, courtesy of William's précis. We are told that the little prince already loved learning at five or six. So now, says William, he was sent to school to imbibe the honey of learning, and he became fully literate. From this part of the lost book William gives a brief quote in verse:

At his father's command he was given to the learning of the schools
He feared strict masters with their rapping rods
And eagerly imbibing the sweet honey of learning
He did not spend the years of childhood childishly.

According to William's critics, this passage is another of William's 'manifest flights of fancy'; but birching was the rule in Carolingian schools and there is no reason at all to doubt this story. A famous ninth-century dialogue between teacher and pupil spells it out: 'Learn now boys! The age for learning passes swiftly . . . youth flies by so don't squander the time you have . . . and lazy blighters will be given a good thrashing!'

Then, says William, still in verse, the young prince was trained
in arms (reminding us that this is, above all, a tale of war):

> Soon, dressed in the flower of young manhood
> He took up the study of arms, at his father's order.
> Nor did the demands of war find him wanting
> As later his kingship also showed.

Anglo-Saxon nobles were trained to fight from a young age, and
royal and noble wills of the time are full of the warlike trappings
of their class: treasured swords, fine horses, inlaid war-gear,
described with loving attention to detail. Such weaponry had a
talismanic power: the Avar sword from Charlemagne which Offa
owned was carefully whetted and buffed by the royal sword-polisher
two centuries on. Athelstan's sword was shown in the treasury two
centuries after that. So the little prince with the bookish bent
became a warrior. Like all his class, he would have fought in wars
by his late teens, perhaps already beginning to gather the reputation
which later 'struck his enemies with fear . . . by terror of his name
alone'. On these early years there may be more still to come out
of later sources: a twelfth-century notebook, for instance, has an
interesting story that Athelstan in his father's reign was sent on a
diplomatic mission in Danish territory, where he 'adopted some of
their customs'. But on this period of his life William allows us only
a brief glimpse of sore knuckles in the schoolroom and a sore
bottom in the saddle.

Meanwhile, his father, King Edward, who may never have
married Athelstan's mother, had twice married, and both women
were consecrated queen. There were lots more children. Royal
families at that time were at least as complicated as modern ones,
with factions pulling against each other, queen mothers fighting
for their sons, hungry athelings prowling; not to mention Athelstan's
uncles, the sons of Alfred's older brother, who were still also
resentful. Deals no doubt had to be struck which would make the
recent horse-trading in the House of Windsor seem relatively
sedate. So far as we can tell, peering through the shadows of the

early 920s, Edward's designated heir as king of Wessex was not Athelstan, but his younger half-brother Aelfweard. Aelfweard, then in his early twenties, was the eldest son of Edward's first queen, and 'his father loved him above all the rest'. Then in July 924 Edward died, and Aelfweard died suddenly sixteen days later. Foul play? It is always a possibility in medieval royal families. Athelstan was then proclaimed king by his Mercian friends and a long delay followed before he was crowned in Wessex. The problem was no doubt the future succession and Athelstan's birth 'to an inferior consort', according to a version of the story told to a German ambassador not long afterwards. Athelstan may not have been 'born in the purple', but the younger princes who were next in line were not old enough to be king at such a critical moment. Someone was needed who had proved his worth in battle (and was acceptable to the Mercians too). Put like that, there can have been no doubt: 'Athelstan stood out among Edward's sons,' said one later chronicler, recalling Asser on Alfred, 'not only because he was the oldest but because of the vigour of his counsels, the elegance of his manners and his capacity for rulership.'

A deal with Athelstan was brokered. Edward's first queen Aelflaed was dead; her son Eadwine was only in his teens. The princes Edmund and Eadred, sons of the young queen Eadgifu, were for the moment out of the equation: the boys were babes in arms. Athelstan, then, would be a 'caretaker king', as the Germans put it, and William confirms this when he tells us Athelstan agreed not to marry, but to raise the young princes to be the next kings: 'with selfless care . . . bringing them up as if they were his own'.

This reconstruction is to an extent conjecture, but it is what William says, and I believe it is what happened, and was referred to in the lost book. The deal worked too: Athelstan's death saw one of the few uncontested English successions between the ninth and the thirteenth centuries. It worked because he stuck to his side of the bargain.

The old book then moved on to the big set-piece on the coronation, based on the great banquet in Virgil's *Aeneid*: the king is crowned with a diadem, harpists play, dishthegns and butlers scurry, and bishops hover ready to tell him what to do. William gives some of this in verse:

> The royal palace seeths and overflows with kingly splendour
> Wine foams everywhere, the great hall shakes with the loud tumult
> Pages scurry, dishthegns rush about on their tasks,
> Stomachs are filled with delicacies, minds with song;
> One strums a harp, another replies with praises,
> There sounds in unison: 'To you the praise, To you the glory, O
>   Christ!'
> The king accepts this honour with grateful eyes
> Graciously bestowing due affection on all.

With that the tale moves on in prose to tell the story of the king's wars, the making of the kingdom and the empire. It describes him doing all the things Dark Age kings did: driving out pagans, defining frontiers, rewarding his faithful followers. First, the York Vikings are driven out, their fortress destroyed and their treasure divided among Athelstan's armed thegns. So Northumbria comes under southern rule for the first time, and with that, in 927, England emerges as a political unit roughly within its present boundaries. The empire of Britain followed swiftly. As paraphrased by William, the lost book told how the north British kings submitted near Penrith where the customary rituals of submission, and the baptism of the son of the Scottish king, took place at the old monastery of Dacre mentioned by Bede.

This section of the lost book, as William shows, was full of vivid detail. The captured Viking king Guthfrith is feasted for four days 'with extravagant conviviality' – and then let free: 'an inveterate pirate going back into his element like a fish to water'. When the Welsh kings submit at Hereford, they agree to pay a huge levy of gold and silver and cattle, but also promise to give him falcons and fine hunting dogs 'trained to sniff out their prey from every nook and cranny', another surviving hint of the lost poet's phraseology. A contemporary Welsh poem corroborates this story, expressing fury, dismay and disbelief at the size of the tribute. Next the lost author turns to the subjection of the Cornish, who till recently had had their own kings. The Tamar is made the border; and Exeter is restored as a centre of trade, 'rich in merchants who come from everywhere to buy and sell . . .' According to William's source, Athelstan refortified the city with walls and towers, and though this has often been disputed, not all the ashlar in Exeter's walls is Roman, and a new stone-by-stone survey of one stretch has proved that it was refurbished – with crenellations – in the late Old English period. Game, set and match to William of Malmesbury.

So Athelstan is now ruler of Britain, and the lost book went on to give a description of the man himself: both looks and character. In the words transmitted by William, we can still detect echoes of Einhard's Charlemagne, the key text for the early medieval ruler cult. Here is William's paraphrase of the lost book on its hero:

He was easy and charming with the servants of God, affable and courteous to the laymen, serious out of regard for his majesty to the magnates; friendly and down to earth with the lesser folk, out of sympathy for their poverty, putting aside the pride of kingship. He was (as we have learnt) not beyond what is becoming in stature, and slender in body; his hair (as we have ourselves seen from his relics) flaxen, beautifully plaited with braids of gold. He was much beloved by his subjects out of admiration of his courage and humility, but like a thunderbolt to rebels by his invincible steadfastness.

Texts like this have to be taken with a pinch of salt, of course. Like Asser's *Alfred*, it was written for a purpose: the cult of the ruler. This was not necessarily what the king was actually like, but what a clerical author expected a king to be. Indeed the model here may be Asser, who also stressed Alfred's munificence and his affability (*maxima affabilitate et iocunditate*). But there were other influences. The line 'not above what is becoming in stature' (i.e., of medium height), for example, is taken from Einhard on Charlemagne. My translation of the line about the king's hair – 'plaited with golden braids' – reflects the custom of the time among men.

This sounds like a genuine description of Athelstan from the lost book, and the Latin usage in which it is expressed, one might guess, came from the Roman poet Horace who was known at first hand in England only in the mid tenth century.

In the tradition of Carolingian royal biography, the author of the lost book now turned to Athelstan's standing in the eyes of foreign kings, giving us otherwise unknown details on foreign diplomacy and the marriages of royal ladies to overseas potentates. A highlight of this section of the book as William gives it was the description of a Norwegian embassy to York bearing a gift from the redoubtable old King of Norway, Harald 'Fairhair': 'a fine ship with a gilded prow, a purple sail, and inside overlapping rows of gilded shields . . .' But this is capped by what even in William's paraphrase is a wonderful scene, describing the treasures brought by an embassy from Hugh the Great, Duke of the Franks. Laid out before the king are rare perfumes 'never before seen in England', precious jewels, a gold diadem, war horses 'champing on bits of ruddy gold' and a 'vase of onyx carved with such subtle engravers' art that the cornfields seemed really to wave, the vines really to bud, and the forms of men really to move' (clearly a classical heirloom, this). But it was the holy relics over which the poet most drooled: for unwrapped before the king's throne were the sword of Constantine; a nail of the Crucifixion fixed in its pommel; the Lance of Longinus, from the treasury of Charlemagne himself; the standard of St Maurice; a portion of the Crown of Thorns; and this:

A piece of the holy and ever adorable Cross enclosed in crystal, where the eye, looking through the substance of the stone, could make out the colour and shape of the piece of wood . . .

Dazzling images, in a scene repeated by many later writers. It would not be possible today to assemble such a collection from all the surviving pieces from Anglo-Saxon England. In France, the treasures of ninth-century St Denis may still be seen in the Louvre and the Cabinet des Medailles; the Holy Lance and other treasures of the first German Reich survive in the Schatzkammer in Vienna; but frustratingly, virtually nothing like this is left from England, unless it be the Carolingian rock crystal which hangs today in the Early Medieval Room in the British Museum, still on the chain by which it could be hung round the neck, its back grooved to hold a wooden sliver of the True Cross. Athelstan's relic, William tells us, was given to Malmesbury, where a fourteenth-century tradition records that he wore it round his neck in his battles. Unfortunately, my inquiries at the British Museum came up with no record of the provenance of the crystal reliquary before it entered the Franks Collection, from whence it came to the Museum in 1867. (Whether the splinter of wood itself survives is another question, but a relic of the cross which was in the royal chapel in the seventeenth century is still preserved at Downside Abbey near Bath.)

The last part of William's précis describes the great event of the reign: the fateful invasion of 937 and the battle of Brunanburh. William moves back into verse again, no doubt heavily abridged, but clearly a close rendition of a tenth-century text:

> He spent five and three and four years
> Ruling his people by law, subduing tyrants by strength,
> When there returned that hateful plague and ruin of Europe.
> Now barbarian savagery descends on Northumbria
> Now quitting the ocean the pirate Anlaf camps on land
> Mouthing forbidden and savage threats.
> To this Bacchant fury, at the will of the king of the Scots,
> The Northumbrians give willing assent:
> And now puffed up with pride they frighten the air with words;
> The natives submit, the whole province gives in to the proud.

Next comes a remarkable passage, which can only reflect the realities of the mid tenth century. The North has fallen to the invaders; the king is implored to attack, but delays and delays. And now, in a surprising twist, our unknown author says he was criticized for his inaction:

For since our king, who was faithful and energetic in his youth
Thought his service long done and whiled away leisure hours,
They devastated everything with incessant plundering raids
Driving out the peasants and setting fire to their fields:
The ripening crops withered in all the fields:
The ruined cornfield mocked the farmer's prayer.
So many were their footsoldiers, such was the barbarians'
Mounted strength: a numberless host of cavalry.
Eventually the voice of protest roused the king;
Not to let himself be branded thus:
That his people had meekly given in to barbarian arms.

This passage is clearly no flight of fancy. The idea that Athelstan of all people could be criticized for lassitude and complacency is inconceivable as a forgery of the twelfth century, and in Malmesbury of all places. This must be a reflection of the anxieties of the time. Kings were expected to be ever vigilant, 'on a watchtower', armed, always ready to attack the pagans. And Athelstan was not a thirty-year-old any more, basking in glory, but a hardbitten king in his mid forties now with his back to the wall, facing the ultimate test of nerve – and luck (*fortuna*) – that other great quality needed by medieval kings along with constancy, fortitude and greatness of soul. A text like this was obviously produced within living memory of these events, perhaps as an encouragement to less successful or less experienced successors, of which there were several in the half century after Athelstan's death. Behind it perhaps we can glimpse something of the nerve-shattering events which led up to the 'Great Battle'.

The battle itself is truncated to a few lines of verse by William, and with that he ends his paraphrase of 'the poet from whom we have taken all these particulars'. The king died exactly two years after the battle, on Wednesday 27 October 939 in Gloucester, and, as he had instructed in his will, was buried at Malmesbury. His brother Edmund led the cortège. Going off into the realms of speculation, one would expect a tenth-century royal biography to have ended with a description of the king's death, the funeral and a eulogy. As it happens, in a later section of his book William does in fact give us an unattributed description of Athelstan's funeral procession, with very circumstantial details of the holy relics and treasures carried along with the coffin. In another work, William gives the king's 'epitaph' in verse: '[Here lies] the Honour of the world, grieved by his country, the path of rectitude, the thunderbolt of justice, the exemplar of purity.' When the king died, says this text, 'the sun was in the sixth of Scorpio' (the sixth of the kalends of November, i.e., 27 October). Though sometimes dismissed as another of William's concoctions, the Latin of this text has many parallels with tenth-century poetry. Particularly eye-catching is the use of *munditia*: an ancient word meaning 'purity' in the sense of chastity, and a very unusual word to use of a Dark Age king, most of whom were inveterate womanizers. Did the king not only not marry, but remain celibate? We simply do not know, but one might suspect that this 'epitaph' was in fact adapted by William from a eulogy of the king which followed the account of his funeral and burial, and with which the lost book ended.

What we have got here, I think, is the skeleton of a full-scale life of the king. William says his extracts add up to a 'small amount', only a part of the whole. At a guess, what he gives us is the equivalent of at least 300 verses. The whole thing, then, must have been several times longer, comparable perhaps to the 1,500 lines of Frithegode's poem on Wilfrid, or even the 3,000 lines of Wulfstan the Cantor's poem on St Swithun. It may be that more is still to be recovered elsewhere, if only we knew where to look.

So where did William find his old book? At such a distance, this might sound like looking for a needle in a haystack. But if the lost work is attested anywhere in surviving medieval library catalogues in the British Isles, there is only one possibility, and that is in 'the great and famous library of these islands' which we have already entered in the story of John Leland: Glastonbury.

William had close relations with Glastonbury; he wrote about its history and made many visits there. And there, in the library catalogue of 1248, is this intriguing item, apparently one composite manuscript: 'Letters of Alcuin, of Alcuin and Charlemagne and

The Wars of King Athelstan, and a Glossary of diverse grammatical words. Life of St Wilfrid. legible.'

It sounds almost too good to be true, but 'The Wars of King Athelstan' would be a good description of William's lost book. As for the texts apparently bound up with it, this collection of letters of Charlemagne and Alcuin on the 'royal road' of Christian kingship could not be more suitable as the preface to a royal biography. The collection is rare in this period in England. There are only two English manuscripts, one intact in Lambeth, one a fragment in Chicago; both date from Athelstan's reign and perhaps one of them was the item in the catalogue. The whole compilation sounds very much like a classic *speculum regis*, a 'mirror of princes': perhaps written for one of the king's successors: Edgar, Ethelred, even conceivably Ethelred's son Athelstan, who was named after his great-uncle. It was written at a time when the king's memory was enviously regarded, as his old protégé Aethelwold put it, looking back as 'one of those who can remember Edgar's predecessors . . . They were men of mature wisdom, hard to overcome in any strife . . .' There can hardly be any doubt he was thinking of Athelstan. Perhaps, indeed, the lost book came from Aethelwold's circle.

That's enough speculation for one day, but I hope at least that I have shown that the modern verdict on William's mysterious 'old book' deserves appeal. The book was real enough: as real as Asser's *Life of Alfred*. Excerpted and paraphrased by a reliable twelfth-century historian, where Asser was copied and interpolated by an unreliable sixteenth-century bishop and bibliophile. If only we had it today it would be our key source for this fascinating moment in English history. There is, I suppose, even hope that one day a scrap might turn up, like the fragment of a seventh-century copy of Isidore of Seville which turned up recently in the binding of a ledger in Longleat, where odd remnants of the great library of Glastonbury found their way. But that, one has to admit, is a very long shot!

9. The Story of a Book

'A manuscript, naturally'

(Umberto Eco, *The Name of the Rose*)

Medieval palaeography may sound as dull as ditch-water, but in fact the study of old manuscript books is often thrilling detective work. Not for nothing are the monkish hero of *The Name of the Rose* and Brother Cadfael among the most popular creations of modern detective fiction. The palaeographer Bernard Bischoff, who was not a man given to flights of fancy, described that electric moment when the manuscript sleuth strikes gold (in his case, the discovery of the great eighth-century English scholar Alcuin's autograph marginal directions to his copyists):

There is a self-renewing excitement in the experience a palaeographer can create for himself through his work: it feels the same as it did the very first time. Something causes him to linger over a manuscript until the unexpected dawns on him, and then, in the blink of an eye, the barrier of the intervening centuries seems to fall away . . .

One such book is a little psalter in the British Library, which is a wonderful example of what an old book can tell us. Like all handwritten books, it carries its history with it, in layers of time: in its additions, scribbles, marginal notes and annotations it tells us something of its purpose and use, its journeys and owners, even perhaps a hint of what its readers felt. The book was written, so the experts tell us, in the early ninth century in Francia, in or near Liège, at a time when Francia was producing the most beautiful books west of Byzantium and Baghdad. The book is written in

Carolingian minuscule, which some think the most beautiful and practical handwriting ever devised in the West, one of the great scripts of the world. It's a psalter containing the psalms of David: poems which for nearly 1,000 years had been the greatest source of solace to Christians everywhere – and to Jewish people, of course, for a lot longer still. It is tiny: five inches by three and a half, and about two inches thick. In the Dark Ages, such books were carried around as pocket books, used for private reading or prayer. But this is not just a book of psalms. It is crammed with other material, mysterious and fascinating, which tells the story of a strange and remarkable odyssey.

When you open it, the pages are rubbed by use at the edges and stained by damp and age. Fortunately, the beautiful little miniature paintings in it are undamaged, the lapis blue on the opening page still fresh and bright. Books now are accessible to all: millions are printed every year, many of them pulped or remaindered when they fail to sell. But books were a different matter to Dark Age people. No book was made uselessly in the Dark Ages, for creating a book involved big choices: it took up large amounts of time and resources. It was an effort to make one. The calfskin or sheepskin had to be treated, scraped, stretched, cut, folded, pricked, ruled, then inked, painted and gilded. To make one of the great Jarrow Bibles took the skins of 500 sheep and the labour of dozens of brethren. So not surprisingly, the finished article was almost magical to people of the Dark Ages: the most intricate and colourful thing they would ever see.

Books are famous [wrote a tenth-century poet], they enable humankind to fully cogently express their opinions . . . for him that thinks on things they make stronger and confirm the steadfast thought. They uplift the mind of everyone from the enforced necessities of this day-to-day life . . . Victory they send to every steadfast person.

If you think such sentiments overdone, remember that this was a time when learning had been smashed and books destroyed; when hardly anyone could read Latin, and hence the connection with the past had been broken. Nowadays the threat is the same, but at the opposite end of the scale: information overload and the crushing banalization of the Internet. It is hard to put oneself back to a time, and a mental state, when, as one English cleric put it, it was 'by no means certain that the written word will survive'.

Because they were such precious currency, books also travelled. They were begged, borrowed and not infrequently stolen. Books could have great adventures: a volume now in Durham was known as 'The Gospelbook of St Cuthbert that got soaked in the Solway'. A book in Utrecht carries on its cover sword marks said to have been made on the day Boniface the apostle of Germany held it over his head as he was cut down by Frisian pagans. Some travelled much farther afield. A French writer in the twelfth century mentions a volume of Orosius's *History* in the Old English translation of Alfred the Great, which had belonged to the Emperor of Byzantium, Manuel Comnenus. It worked the other way too. A Muslim writer, Abul Hasan Al-Harawi, who died in Aleppo in 1215 and who wrote a guide to the pilgrimage places of Iraq, describes how he gifted a manuscript of his work to the King of England, presumably Richard the Lionheart, who was in Aleppo in 1198. No doubt Richard had translators in his pay, Christian or Jewish, who could read Arabic, but if Al-Harawi left any trace in English literary history, it has yet to be found. Such real-life adventures in books rival the wonderful inventions of Borges.

To return to our book, Cotton manuscript Galba A XVIII. Its pages are still in good condition, for vellum, unlike paper, will last and last, so long as it is looked after. Paper, on the other hand, which only becomes widely used in the West after this time, does not keep well. On my travels I have handled beautiful Korans and Ferdowsis from the seventeenth century – in the crisp air of Kabul, in the desert heat of Mashad, and in the must of Multan – and everywhere their paper is crumbling. Vellum, on the other hand, need never be destroyed, except when it falls to bits from over-use. Some medieval books, when you open them, have still got a creamy-white unused look; the stiff vellum crackles a little when you turn the page. But softened up by constant use, by the natural oils of the hand, well-used books are supple. This one was well used.

The book was in England by the early tenth century. That much is sure from the added scripts, to which we will return. But there are no contemporary clues to its ownership. Not until the sixteenth century, the time when, as we have seen, so many of the ancient libraries were broken up and destroyed. Then the book seems to have come into the hands of a Winchester priest called Thomas Dackomb. Dackomb bought a number of books which had belonged to the Old Minster at Winchester, the burial church of the West Saxon dynasty, where many of its kings' jumbled bones still cram painted boxes along the nave wall.

After he bought it, Dackomb scribbled a note in Latin inside the cover on the first folio, which translates as: 'Psalter of King Athelstan purchased by Thomas rector of Colebrook Winchester, in 1542 price –' (The price was originally on the manuscript but has been erased.)

Dackomb had been rector of the Church of St Peter, Colebrook, and a minor canon of Winchester Cathedral. At the time of the Reformation, when the great monastic libraries were being broken up, he accumulated a small collection of manuscripts, including several purchased from Winchester houses. In many he wrote a similar note about provenance or ownership, without making extravagant claims, so it must be possible that he had reason to connect the book with the king – a tradition handed down, perhaps, or most likely a now lost inscription (Athelstan, as it happens, left book inscriptions on many of his book gifts, several of which have survived).

Of course, it is possible that Dackomb was taken in by a salesman's patter: an unscrupulous bookseller trying to hike up the price of the book. But that chance is slight given Dackomb's position. So was it true? Is it Athelstan's book? The question has intrigued me for many years, ever since I first had the privilege of examining the manuscript when I was a student.

King Athelstan was the founder of the kingdom of England. He was the first English king to be portrayed in a painting. His looks are described by William of Malmesbury: 'his hair yellow, beautifully braided with golden wires'. We cannot get as close to him as we can to Alfred, in his own words, but in other ways we possess some very intimate details. We know something of his interests: like Alfred, he was a religious man, obsessed with the cult of saints and their relics. He was interested in books and gave many as gifts, of which a dozen survive, some bearing inscriptions possibly dictated by the king himself which ask the reader to 'pray for his soul'. In his lawcodes we have a glimpse of revulsion against the cruelty of his time: 'the king sends message that he feels it too cruel to execute twelve-year-olds as he sees everywhere is the case'. He was someone with that characteristic medieval mixture of the warlike and the pious, unpalatable to us today, but still recognizable as a type in, say, Shakespeare's *Henry V*.

Like his grandfather, Athelstan was a patron of foreign scholars. Like him, he may have set up a court school with foreign scholars, and his court was visited by holy men from far afield, like Maelbright McTornan, the Coarb of Armagh. It was small beer compared with the court schools of Charlemagne and his son and grandson, but we now know Athelstan's court included the greatest scholar of the age, Israel of Trier, the man Bernard Bischoff called 'the last of the great European court scholars'. If Dackomb was right, and this was the king's psalter, then what we have is no small national treasure: the most intimate testimony to this shadowy but remarkable man, the king who, it was later said, was 'the most learned and just ever to rule England', the founder of the medieval and modern English state.

So what does the book have to tell us? Nothing directly attests Athelstan's ownership, but in its many additions there are some intriguing clues. The main body of the psalter contains the 150 psalms of David, followed by a dozen pages of canticles and other Latin prayers, including the Gloria, the Creed and the Lord's Prayer. This text was written near Liège in a lovely small Carolingian minuscule with golden initials. Then, sometime around the 830s or 840s, the first additions were made. Some private prayers were inserted in front of the psalms, for the adoration of the Cross; a further group was added after the psalms; and then on a flyleaf obituaries were entered of some high-ranking members of the Carolingian royal family, including Charlemagne himself and some of the Frankish rulers of Italy. The owner of the book, now apparently in Italy, was obviously well connected, someone with reason to commemorate in prayer the family of Charlemagne, and possibly associated with a house of women. So the first clue in the story of the book: an Italian connection.

The next additions are in an entirely different hand: a square minuscule commonly found in Wessex in the first decade or two of the tenth century. The book had now come to England. There, early in the tenth century, a metrical calendar of a kind used by the Irish was written down by an English scribe on eighteen leaves added to the front of the book: it's a small compressed script, half the size normal in manuscripts, done with great care, with red initials and headings. Also painted on the calendar are little pictures of saints, and the signs of the zodiac still fresh in their colours. The dates are counted both Julian style and Roman (with ides and kalends). The calendar has an entry for each day, with a few lines of verse at the beginning and end of each month; it also gives the hours of day and night (November, for example 'has fourteen hours of night and ten of day'). Notes at the end of each month on the sign of the zodiac briefly mention the weather, sometimes with charming little details: the ripening fruits of September, for example, the vine 'giving forth abundance' in October, and festive December. Inside the body of the calendar, the change of seasons is also marked, as on 7 November: 'The start of winter, shivering with frost . . .' One imagines that the owner perused its pictures with some pleasure: it is still a lovely thing to hold.

The main purpose of the calendar is as an almanac of saints' days. Each day has a line of verse (thus, 12 May: 'Saint Pancras by his great merits went to heaven'). The calendar is followed by notes and a diagram to show how to work out the movable feasts, all of which adds to the impression of a book designed for use, a mnemonic, like the religious diaries popular for prayer even now: a Dark Age Thought for the Day.

Two entries in the calendar enable us to home in more precisely on date and place. For also marked into it were two obituaries, of Alfred the Great on 26 October 899: 'King Alfred died on the seventh' [of the kalends of November] 'and is also held in affection' [i.e., even though he was not a saint] and on 5 December 902 his wife Ealhswith, 'the true lady of the English'. This clue narrows things down. It suggests the book might have connections with Winchester Old Minster (where Alfred and his wife were buried) or with the royal family. It also shows that the calendar was written after 902, as indeed the handwriting would suggest. It could be from any time in the next decade or two.

So there is our next clue: the little book was now in the hands of someone who had reason to commemorate Alfred and his wife in prayer, indeed to put their names in a list of saints, in a book designed to be used for daily prayer. Now if we keep in mind Dackomb's claim – that this book belonged to Alfred's grandson – it may be worth remembering that there is a story that just before Alfred died he had prayed for a happy reign for the five- or six-year-old Athelstan, invested him with a cloak and sword, and 'seeing the boy was of handsome face and good manners affectionately hugged him . . .' We might guess from this that the boy held his grandfather in special regard – though so too, no doubt, did Alfred's son Edward, and his other children and grandchildren.

Much more could be said about the calendar and its list of saints for commemoration throughout the year. The saints are mainly Roman – famous saints like Laurence and Maurice – but some are Celtic (Columba, Patrick), some English (Theodore, Augustine, Boniface), and a number are Flemish, like St Bertin, or Breton, such as Samson. But the list is old-fashioned. Interestingly, as befits its date, it doesn't include the two English saints turned into 'national' saints in the early tenth century, Edmund and Cuthbert.

The cult of saints and saints' relics was one of the biggest currents in the intellectual life of the Dark Ages. It generated a vast amount of comment and speculation in the ninth and tenth centuries: saints' *Lives*, martyrologies, relic lists, and gazeteers of saints' resting places, not to mention sermons and poems like the *Menologium* which mentions the festivals observed 'at the behest of the English king throughout the kingdom of Britain': this was all part of the way the divine order was believed to interlock with the earthly. Saints' shrines were focuses of royal power, and their patronage was one way of increasing a sense of unity in the State. Alfred's son Edward the Elder, a shadowy figure, who was perhaps not literate, certainly followed the cult of saints, corresponding with foreign churches. Edward's son Athelstan, though, is the most famous patron of the cult of saints in English history.

The next additions to the book are four miniature paintings of unique importance in the history of English art. We cannot tell whether they were done at precisely the same time as the calendar (i.e., roughly 902–20) or a little later. They are: a Christ in Majesty, with rows of saints, nuns, martyrs and confessors; another Christ in Majesty with the relics of the Crucifixion; and an Ascension with the Virgin Mary. A Nativity was cut out long ago, but miraculously survives in the Bodleian Library in Oxford. Paint rubbing on a later folio shows there was a fifth painting, probably a Crucifixion, of which a later copy exists. It is possible that there was a sixth too, a Trinity.

The story of this picture cycle is fascinating, for its sources lie deep in Mediterranean Christian art. Indeed, they take us back to some of the very earliest illustrations of the Bible text. The closest parallel to the Ascension, for example, is a scene in the Byzantine Rabbula Gospels painted in AD 586 at Zagba in Mesopotamia. Some of the clues lie in the detail. By the Virgin are long spindly plants. Very similar plants appear on miniatures in some of the oldest codices: in the Barberini Gospels, in a sixth-century Byzantine Genesis now in Vienna, and in the seventh-century Ashburnham Pentateuch in Paris. The later copy of the lost Crucifixion has also got these strange spindly plants. Another feature which links all these pictures with very early painting is their use of name tags and inscriptions across the picture. These labels are found in two early and important books: the Ashburnham Pentateuch and, most interestingly, the late-sixth-century Gospels of Augustine in Cambridge, a Late-Roman book from Italy which, tradition says, was brought by St Augustine on the mission of 597. There can be hardly any doubt that our artist was copying similar pictures.

So, consciously or not – and why not consciously? – the artists of our pictures were going back to early Christian origins, to ancient painted books held in England, most likely in Canterbury, the home of Augustine and of Theodore of Tarsus, the Greek scholar who became Archbishop at Canterbury in 661. Theodore was educated at Antioch and Edessa and would have been the most likely source of rare Mesopotamian or Syrian art.

The purpose of such paintings was for prayer: these images of Christ, and Mary, the ranks of saints, confessors and virgins, were a focus for prayer, and in this light a detail in one of the paintings may be another clue to their patron and his taste and interests. When you open the book, the first image you see on the inside of the second folio is of Christ, seated in majesty with the instruments of the Passion: spear, sponge and cross, holding out his hand to show the mark of the nail. The colours are still vivid, with the bright blue of ground-up lapis lazuli. There is a famous story of King Athelstan receiving the relics of the Passion from Hugh the Great, Duke of the Franks in 926; among them the spear, a nail, and parts of the Cross and the Crown of Thorns. We know that the king was deeply attached to the relic cult: could this picture have been added because of his own interest? This attractive idea depends on the date the paintings were added to the book: if they were done at the same time as the calendar, then we must probably abandon this link.

The story is still not over. For now we reach what are in some ways the most interesting of all the additions to the book. At some point in the 930s, to judge by the scribe's handwriting, three or four quires were added at the end of the book, of which twenty pages still survive (the book as we have it is defective at the end – a page or possibly more has been lost). These were by a new scribe, in the good, regular hand of a royal clerk, although the initials are fairly brusquely blocked in oranges and blues. On these new quires were written 150 short prayers, each one forming a short meditation inspired by the psalm text. These were composed in Rome in the fifth century A D, and by Athelstan's day the use of these collects, as they were called, had fallen out of fashion. But they are very beautiful prayers, which surprisingly to this day remain for the most part untranslated into English – though there was a version done in Elizabethan times:

Make us O Lord like a most fruitful tree, planted in Thy sight, that we, being watered by the showers of Thy grace, may bring forth to Thee plenteousness in due Season . . .

The psalms were very popular in the early Middle Ages; especially for kings, who liked to see themselves represented as David, the warrior and the psalmist, praised for his warlike abilities and his learning. So the psalter was a prime book of instruction for Dark Age princes, a handbook of solace, consolation and guidance in time of trouble. In it the key lessons could be learned. David's dire situation facing his foreign enemies, for example, spoke volumes to kings beset by the Vikings. Likewise his injunctions to embrace learning and place one's trust in God.

So the addition of the collects makes sense, though one would dearly like to know whether personal choice played its part in putting this ancient series of prayers together with the psalms. Who did it, and whose idea was it?

The most remarkable additions are saved for the very end. On the last page (folio 200) is a Greek litany – a prayer for the saints – in accurate Greek, transliterated into Latin letters. It begins with a list of saints' names for use in chanting in prayer, and is followed by the Lord's Prayer. Turning over the page, there is the Creed and then the Sanctus prayer. At the bottom of the page this breaks off incomplete; but it is clearly the prayer from the main Greek liturgy of the holy oblation which follows the Creed and which is still used today by the Greek Orthodox church:

Holy Holy Holy, Lord of hosts; heaven and earth are full of your glory. Hosanna in the highest. Blessed is he who comes in the name of the Lord. Hosanna in the highest.

So what are Greek texts doing here in an Anglo-Saxon manuscript of the 930s in an accurate transliteration? There was quite a vogue for Greek in the Dark Ages – though few could actually read it – but why would a tenth-century English owner have wanted these particular texts put in his psalter? The answer lies in the content of the Greek texts.

This particular litany came to England in the second half of the seventh century: a Latin translation made in the eighth century survives with a much fuller list of sixty-two names, which has been abbreviated here. As Edmund Bishop noticed long ago, the litany in fact goes back to the time of Archbishop Theodore of Canterbury, a Greek from Tarsus who came to England in AD 667 and who transformed learning in England. Its closest analogues come from Late-Roman Syria, and its combination of Greek, Eastern and Roman saints, some from Antioch (in whose archdiocese Tarsus lies) rather suggests that it was composed by Theodore himself. Most likely, Theodore brought it to England. Like the paintings, the litany (and presumably the other Greek texts) go back to the defining moment of English Christian history.

It is clear that someone in the 930s assembled these Greek texts for our unknown patron, who appears more discerning the more we find out about his tastes. Who was he? Interestingly enough, the same cluster of Greek prayers is found in three other manuscripts, now in the Vatican, in Leningrad, and in London. Though the collection clearly originates in St Augustine's Abbey in Canterbury, it is found in these manuscripts in a dossier of the last of the great court scholars of the Carolingian age, Israel of Trier. Israel was almost certainly Irish in origin, and his extraordinary life seems to have taken him on extensive travels, to Auxerre, Rome, Canterbury, and later Trier, Verdun and Aix, before he returned to Trier where he died in the late 960s. His interests were wide: he was the author of a commentary on the neo-Platonic text of Porphyry of Tyre; he wrote a revision of the standard teaching commentary on Latin grammar, and may also have compiled an anthology of saints' lives which included the famous eighth-century *Voyage of St Brendan*. Israel appears to have been a major figure on the

European scene; indeed a tenth-century Frankish writer says he 'made Britannia famous through the whole world of the liberal arts'. For a period, Israel was one of the scholars attached to the court of King Athelstan. As the Canterbury Greek texts found their way both into his dossier and into the Galba psalter, then we might guess that Israel himself was instrumental in assembling the texts for his patron. Our search has led us back to the person named in Thomas Dackomb's note: King Athelstan.

It is time to pull the story together. We have elucidated something of the inner tale of the book, a biography as rich as any person's life. But what can we deduce from that about its outer journeys? Some of the leaps must be guesswork, but the basic story is clear. Written in France in the early ninth century, the book first went from Francia to Italy. The Frankish royal obituaries show it was in a North Italian house in the 840s or 850s, and perhaps one connected with women. Then it came from Italy to England at some point between 850 and 900, in the lifetime of Alfred the Great. If we ask how the book might have passed from a North Italian church to the English royal family, there is one obvious link. The pilgrim trail from England over the Alps to Italy was well trodden throughout the Viking age. When he was king, Alfred sent many embassies to Rome with alms, especially in the 880s; but as it happens, Alfred himself went as a little boy in the summer of 855–6. So did the book return with him?

In the papal archives there is a description of the 'knighting' ceremony of the seven-year-old Alfred by Pope Leo IV, in a letter to the boy's father, King Aethelwulf of Wessex:

We have now graciously received your son Alfred, whom you were anxious to send at this time to the threshold of the Holy Apostles, and we have decorated him as a spiritual son, with the dignity of the belt and the vestments of the consulate, as is Roman consular custom, because he placed himself in our hands.

The papal account mentions that a 'multitude of people' had come with Alfred on what was a dangerous journey, struggling through the Alpine passes, frozen by snow, risking attack by Saracen pirates. Once they got to North Italy, though, they found hospitality in towns like Lucca and Pavia, which were well known as stopping points for the English. The laws of Pavia especially provided for English merchants, and the towns were furnished not only with hostels, but even, in the case of Lucca, brothels staffed by English women. Pavia was so frequented by pilgrims from these islands that there was a hostel there, known as 'St Mary of the British'. The numbers who took the road to Rome at this time were huge, and though coming from a relatively poor and underdeveloped country, the British were generous in the gifts they brought with them, as a hoard of English coins dug up on the Forum and dating from around 940 shows. In this way the English reestablished their links with Rome after being cut off from their spiritual heartland by the Viking invasions.

Pavia, on the main route to Rome, had a special English connection. Alfred's kinswoman Aethelswith was buried there, and Pavia and its sister churches received special gifts at this time from the Wessex royal family. In this light it is interesting to look at the English names which were entered for prayer in the *Liber Vitae* at nearby Brescia. The church of S. Salvatore (today S. Giulia) at Brescia was a royal nunnery with a very high profile with the Carolingian royal family in the ninth century. It also had a dependent church at Pavia. In its book of commemoration from the 850s are the names of Alfred, his father Aethelwulf, and other members of the West Saxon and Mercian royal families. These entries show intimate contacts with Alfred's family and point us to exactly the kind of exchange which might lead to English royalty possessing a psalter from a North Italian house for women.

There perhaps is the connection. The journey that the book made is sure, even if the precise date and route are uncertain. Indeed, the Alfred connection invites another speculation. Alfred's biographer Asser talks of Alfred's 'little book', which he constantly carried on his person, in which were the daytime offices of the Church and some psalms and 'certain prayers which he had learned in his youth'. This, Asser says, he expanded with 'flowers of wisdom' collected from different masters, all of which were assembled in the little book which 'eventually grew to be nearly the size of a psalter . . . and which he called his enchiridion, his handbook, as he kept it to hand day and night'. Alfred's little book and our royal psalter are clearly not the same. But our tiny pocket psalter looks very much like a companion piece to Alfred's handbook. Asser speaks of Alfred's love of the psalter, and Alfred's translation of the first fifty psalms into Old English has survived. So though our psalter is not Alfred's 'handbook', he had just such a psalter for his personal use. We may ask ourselves whether it was the inspiration of Alfred's handbook which led to the psalter being expanded with other prayers and texts for his grandson.

That is perhaps to let our imagination run away with us. Of course we cannot prove who owned the book prior to the 930s. What is clear though – or as near as could be after a thousand years – is that the book did indeed pass down to Alfred's grandson, just as Thomas Dackomb claimed in 1542. The calendar was added when Athelstan was a boy, including the obituaries of his grandfather and grandmother. The metrical calendar of saints perhaps reflects a key interest of the king, who when he was fifteen had already promised his uncle to protect their favourite saint Oswald. Athelstan later revitalized the whole cult of saints in England, so there was 'scarcely a shrine he did not enrich'. The cycle of pictures showing saints, martyrs and confessors, and the instruments of the Passion, added around this time, reflect that interest. Presumably the king carried the book with him and used it in daily prayer and reflection, 'reading from it every day to acquire wisdom'.

Then, around 930, Israel came into Athelstan's service. While in England, Israel assembled his dossier of Greek prayers from the papers of Theodore which he found in St Augustine's Canterbury. This was seminal stuff and the king himself, no doubt, would have been interested: perhaps indeed the material was assembled at the king's request. It does no harm to imagine the king staying at Canterbury on his itineraries – we know he was there in 929 when he met a German embassy seeking a marriage alliance. So let's imagine one night in the royal hall in Canterbury Theodore comes up in conversation, and subsequently the king is shown items from the Theodore archive which are explained to him by one of his court scholars who knows Greek – perhaps Israel himself. The king's imagination is fired by the antiquity, authority and authenticity of the texts. He has a royal scribe enter a selection of the Greek material into the back of his psalter, transliterated so the texts could be read out. The significance of the prayers for a Christian king is obvious; they represented the current of pure eastern Christianity – from the horse's mouth, as it were. Such texts had a holy aura to them. The king would naturally have known the Latin text off by heart. Now transliterated into Latin letters, the king could speak the Greek text in his prayers too.

So with the Greek additions at the back, the book reached more or less its final form. The king was now in his mid forties, probably worn out by the exertions of his job. He died in October 939 in Gloucester and was buried not in Winchester but at Malmesbury. The news could have got up to Northumbria within three days, and there the clouds of war were soon gathering, his old enemies scenting blood. The great king who had 'struck his enemies with terror' was gone, to be replaced by an inexperienced eighteen-year-old. Down south, fears were expressed soon enough of a new Age of Iron: of the 'many perils to shake the empire'. The new king Edmund moved in his own associates, men of his own genera-tion like Dunstan, to be his intellectual bodyguard. Israel perhaps found himself out of a job. He wrote an elaborate and clever poem to Archbishop Robert of Trier (an old associate) asking for employment. Soon he would be back on the Continent starting a new phase of his astonishing career.

The new king was crowned only a month later. The dead king's royal treasury, the contents of his private chapel, his personal books and the relics which he carried around with him, found their way back to Winchester, where much later they are mentioned with the things 'kept with the king's halidom, the king's gems' in a shrine at the Old Minster at Winchester. The little psalter, the king's own treasured volume, was perhaps among them. At any rate, then or later it came to the Old Minster, the founding house of Wessex, where its connection with Athelstan was remembered and perhaps commemorated by an inscription noting Athelstan's ownership. This, I assume, would be the now lost inscription on which Thomas Dackomb based his assertion in 1542 that this was the king's book.

As for its later history, we know the book was in Winchester in the eleventh century, when a now-lost inscription was entered on a blank page recording the gift of a gold cross to the Old Minster by Bishop Stigand: the same Stigand who later became Archbishop of Canterbury and crowned Harold Godwinson on the fateful Epiphany of 1066. The book presumably stayed in Winchester through the Middle Ages until the cathedral library was broken up in the 1540s, and it is at this point in the story of the book that Thomas Dackomb makes his entrance. A minor canon at the Cathedral, he was a bibliophile. He may well have known the book; perhaps he wanted to make sure it was saved; but he bought it from the king's agents who were selling off books by the cartload. It was Dackomb who saved this precious relic of English (and British) history for later generations, which might otherwise have ended up in a furnace, dismembered for the binding of a ledger, or even, as John Aubrey records, torn up for toilet paper.

The book subsequently belonged to the bibliophile Lord Lumley in the early seventeenth century, then by 1612 had passed on to the great collector Sir Robert Cotton, who signed the book on the same page as Dackomb. In the early hours of Saturday 23 October 1731, fire raged through Cotton's library at Ashburnham House in Little Dean's Yard, Westminster, destroying many priceless books, some of which we have met in these stories: the fifth-century Greek Genesis, with its 250 illustrations; the earliest text of Gildas; the unique manuscript of Asser's Alfred. Thankfully, our psalter was hardly touched in the fire, though manuscripts close by on the same shelf were ruined, and some of the blackening around the edges of the early folios may be due to the effects of smoke and 'engine-water' that night. Today it is still virtually intact, with all its additions; a book whose various contents reach back to the very beginning of Christianity in England, and indeed to its roots in the

Near East; a text whose travels speak of the intimate connections which bound England to the Continent and Rome in the ninth and tenth centuries; a book whose tale evokes the hardships of the pilgrimages across the Alps by which those links with Rome were tenaciously maintained during the Viking Age; a manuscript which perhaps even has something to tell us of the personal tribulations of our rulers in the Dark Ages, of the simple piety and faith of men and women in dark times. Out of such roots our culture emerged. And on such thin threads our real heritage has hung.

PART THREE

Landscapes and People

'We plough the fields and scatter': a sower at work, from the Luttrell Psalter of *c.* 1340, which perhaps depicts scenes from the village of Irnham in Lincolnshire.

10. The Last Bowl-Turner of England

'I go in search of England . . . I leave the place where London ends
and meet a bowl turner . . .'

H. V. Morton, *In Search of England*, 1927

It is out of print now, and you can pick it up for a pound or two
at many a second-hand bookstall, but *In Search of England* was one
of the most successful books ever written about England. It sold in
hundreds of thousands, running through a dozen printings in its
first two years. It came at a signal moment after the First World
War, as Morton said looking back in 1961, just as cars began to be
present in the landscape. The countryside was still largely hand
tended; the tremendous mechanization of farming during the
Second World War had not yet taken place, 'the plough team
jingling home was still a characteristic sound in many villages,' he
wrote. That was a touch artful, of course – Morton was a Beaver-
brook journalist and he knew very well how to balance the mystical
with the down-to-earth, or with irony. But it was in truth a time
of tremendous social change and a time when people were starting
to question the future of England. The debate was encapsulated in
scores of books and magazines, in county guidebooks, and for the
first time captured in photography for the masses.

Morton's journey, as he said thirty years later:

was written in a light-hearted mood within ten years of the end of the
First World War, when I had found my feet in civilian life and was able
to travel about in a small car of a kind which was then becoming popular.
I knew little of England, and set off at random, finding my way from
place to place with no plan except to enjoy myself.

'I believed that I was dying in Palestine.' The epic beginning gives the book its power. The inspiration for the journey lay back in the traumas of the Great War, after which Morton, like many, feared that Britain and England would never be the same. He looks back to his days in the Near East and remembers, with an echo of Henry IV, that he vowed that if he survived he would make a journey, a kind of pilgrimage, to get to know his own country. That is the aim of his journey.

So one spring day in 1927 he sets off, driving out of London in a little blue Austin to see what lies off the beaten track, going 'as the mood takes me'. His first day's drive took him out on the old A4 past Datchet, Eton and Windsor and into the countryside beyond. There an incident takes place which sets the tone of the whole journey. From Windsor he crosses into Berkshire (those boundaries still mattered then), and then in the late afternoon, after a gusting shower, he sees a little lane which he follows, apparently at random. It leads him to Bucklebury Common, 'aflame with gorse . . . trees . . . rain . . .'. There, out of the blue, he meets a man in the lane; the man was carrying a wooden bowl, a beautiful elm bowl.

'That,' he said, 'is the work of the last bowl-turner in England. He lives over the hill at Bucklebury. You ought to see his workshop, for you will never see another one like it!'

The 'chance' meeting, as we shall see, was not in fact uncontrived. Morton was a crack journalist, and he had not come by chance to Bucklebury. He goes on up through the wooded wastes of Bucklebury Common to find the bowl-turner. Eventually he comes to a tumbledown hut on a green knoll with elm logs piled up outside. A scene from a fairy tale. There he meets the bowl-turner. His name is William Lailey: 'a shy middle-aged faun. His cheeks were red, and his healthy country face shaded by a floppy green hat.'

Lailey, we learn, just loves turning bowls. He never felt happier than when holding a good bit of elm to the lathe. His was a family business, says Morton. His father taught him how to make *treen* – as the wooden trenchers, drinking cups and bowls were called in the local dialect. His grandfather, too, had been a woodturner. Now he was the last 'treen man'. They go into the workshop, and Morton sees Lailey's machinery with amazement: a primitive pole lathe, a Heath Robinson contraption fitted up with all manner of pulleys and strings. 'The floor was deep in soft elm shavings, and across the hut was bent a young alder sapling connected to a primitive lathe by a leather thong.' On it Lailey turned elm bowls by hand . . . bowls with a 'marvellous grain, a fine smooth finish, and two neat lines round the outer rim'. Such wooden bowls had been in general use from prehistory to early modern times, until they started using pewter in Elizabethan times; then wood was only used by the poorer people. Then in the eighteenth century came china and glass. No one wanted wood anymore, except the poor, who still used wooden bowls. And in Bucklebury forest, the art of making 'treen' had never quite died out.

(The word Lailey used for his wooden trenchers, drinking cups and bowls, by the way, is interesting in itself. *Treen* is a dialect word from the Anglo-Saxon *treowen*, from Old English *treow*, meaning 'tree' or 'wood'. It means 'made of wood'. It is picked up by dictionaries in the seventeenth century, but was clearly a rural word going back to very ancient times. Such stuff still provided Lailey with a living in the 1920s in a rural backwater of Berkshire, making bowls as they must have been made in the days of Alfred the Great.)

Meanwhile, Morton engages Lailey in conversation. Then comes the key exchange, the inciting incident of Morton's whole search for England:

The bowl was roughly finished.

'It wants titivating up of course,' he explained, 'and the inside will make another smaller bowl.'

The alder sapling sprang back vibrating: a clumsy primitive marvellously efficient invention, and in it – and many more now lost to us – the secret of those beautiful handicrafts of antiquity which remain to astonish us and to confound our modern machinists.

'Boys won't learn work like this now,' he said. 'It's not as easy as it looks, and unless you learn when you're a lad you can never catch the knack of it.'

He uncovered a pile of beautifully turned bowls of all sizes in a corner of the hut. I saw what the man in the lane was so proud of – each bowl had the individuality which only a man's hands can give to an object. 'You could make a lot of money if you wanted to,' I told him.

'Money?' he said with a slow faun-like smile. 'Money's only stirring up trouble, I think. I like making bowls better than I like making money.'

'Will you say that again?'

He leaned against the door of the hut, his homely brown face shaded by his green floppy hat, and said it again, slightly puzzled, and feeling, I think, that I was in some way 'getting at him'. But you will have guessed that I wished to hear for the second time the voice of the craftsman, the lover of his job, the proud creator of beautiful, common things; a voice that is now smothered by the scream of machines.

I went on down the green hill feeling that my search for England had started well.

The authorial voice could be William Cobbett's there. Part of the line of English radical writing on the rural tradition which comes down through Cobbett, Hudson and Massingham to moderns like Richard Mabey or the Common Ground group. You can see Morton's agenda in the exchange with Lailey, which gives us the key to the whole journey: a chance meeting on the first night out from the great wen with a remarkable man: a traditional Englishman who could speak for England before the age of the motor car; a man whose fathers would have said the same to Cobbett or Defoe. Yet this was not a chance meeting. A number of scholars of rural life had already noted the extraordinary survival on Bucklebury Common: the Victoria County History, for example, wrote about it in 1880. A book on rural industries published in 1921 described Lailey standing at his lathe in a kind of pit (in the accompanying photograph, the back of the hut appears to be sunk well below ground level, a fact curiously not described by Morton). There's no doubt that Morton had read one of these accounts and had gone to find Lailey. Looking at the old Ordnance Survey maps from the 1920s, long before the days of the M4, it is clear that if you were driving on the A4 from Reading and turned off at Midgham station, you would never have found your way to Bucklebury Common by chance. But Morton's job was to tell the story as well as possible, and like the good journalist he was, his instinct was spot on. In fact, as the extraordinary tailpiece to the tale shows, Lailey's story was even more remarkable than Morton could have ever guessed.

William Lailey died in 1958, aged ninety. He was unmarried and had no direct heirs: he had stopped using his lathe some years before. Within a year of his death, the land was sold and the workshop was demolished. But the gear in it was so unusual that it attracted the interest of the new Museum of English Rural Life at the University of Reading, and one of the lathes was saved (it can still be seen at the museum). Before its destruction, the hut itself was recorded and photographed (the photos can be examined in the museum). It was a very interesting construction. It had an inner and an outer chamber; the whole thing was about 20 × 13 feet, the roof supported by eight posts of rough-hewn oak. The big central posts had a tie-beam morticed to take the heads of vertical studs for a central partition; an inner door led through the partition down into the workshop. But the sketches and plans show that the inner workshop had one very strange feature: it was *sunk three feet beneath ground level*, its sides lined with elm boards nailed to staves. The pit was so filled up with wood shavings and debris that the Reading researchers didn't see the significance of this pit at the time.

The Reading researchers, though, were able to establish something of the workshop's history from documents and photographs. Documents of the 1820s mentioned a Lailey making a hut on the Common and it is possible that this was a rebuilding. Until the 1860s, the hut had been thatched. From then until 1912 the roof and walls were covered with corrugated-iron sheets. Then in 1912 the roof was rebuilt and tiled, and this was still its state when William Lailey showed it to Morton in 1927. In 1938, the walls were replanked with deal weatherboards. In the late 1940s the now-rotten tie-beam was removed, along with the partition, which was not replaced. By then Lailey had pretty much given up work. His workshop stayed that way till it was demolished in 1959, the eight oak posts still just as they had been when built (or restored) in the early nineteenth century.

The two pole lathes used for turning the bowls had been placed in the sunken section of the hut, lit by two shuttered windows. Lailey's lathes were newly built in 1880, though one was altered in Edwardian times to enable wooden ladles with handles to be turned – to help meet an order for wooden gunpowder ladles in government munitions factories in the First World War (a revealing insight into the way such small-scale cottage industries were harnessed for the war effort). This is the lathe you can now see in the Reading Museum of Rural Life: it is essentially no different from those used in the Iron Age.

The northern half of the hut, the part which was not in the pit, was used for sawing elm logs and for trimming. All that planing, chipping and turning produced vast quantities of wood waste, shavings and sawdust, which accumulated on the sunken floor around the lathes, especially heaped up against the foot of the walls. The whole room became so filled with shavings that neither Morton nor the Reading researchers recognized how deep the floor was. But the shavings were essential for making work possible in the hut in cold weather. The hut had no form of heating, except that produced by the slow decomposition over the years of the compacted mass of wood shavings. Heaped up by the walls, they covered the chinks in the lower cladding on the walls and kept the interior of the sunken hut remarkably warm and dry: a primitive form of insulation and underfloor heating. Outside there were no gutters, but the rainwater which fell off the thatched overhang would have been absorbed by a mound of earth and wood debris surrounding the hut.

Though the significance of the sunken room was missed by the Reading researchers, strangely enough Morton hints at it when he writes of the moment when Lailey opened the door and he peered inside: 'To say that 800 years seemed to have stopped at the

door conveys nothing. The room was an Anglo-Saxon workshop!'
Astonishingly, as it turns out, he was absolutely right.

The 1959 records and photographs of the hut in Reading, and
some photographs taken in the 1930s when Lailey was still working,
reveal a hut that conformed in every respect of construction and
layout to a type only known to Dark Age archaeologists. These
so-called *Grubenhäuser* – sunken huts – are found in fifth-century
Anglo-Saxon England; they were built by Anglo-Saxon migrants
who came into Britain at the time of the fall of the Roman Empire.
In fact, Lailey's hut solved many problems of design and function
which archaeologists had been unable to resolve from the excavated
remains of the huts – namely from their post holes and the shadow
left in the soil by their rotted timbers. In excavation reports (and
popular books) you often see reconstructions of these sunken huts,
with their roofs sloping from the ridge pole almost down to ground
level on both sides. You can see this, for example, in the Saxon-
village reconstruction which is a tourist attraction at Stow in Norfolk. But clearly if such huts were not houses but workshops, they
had to have good headroom. Fixed equipment like lathes or looms
needs space, height and light, like any industrial or craft process.
So the excavated weaving huts at West Stow were probably at least
five or six feet high above the ground to admit looms and give
light. Lailey's hut, in fact, was ten feet high to the eaves in the
sunken section; each lathe lit by a window. The archaeologists at
West Stow found no trace in the excavated huts of gullies for
rainwater, but the huts were probably surrounded, like Lailey's, by
a berm of earth protected by vegetation. Lailey's hut also solved
the archaeologists' problem of the entrance: none of the thirty-four
sunken huts excavated at West Stow seemed to have a door. Lailey's
hut showed that you stepped down from the outer room into a
chamber lined with horizontally planked walls, probably with a
wooden threshold.

So what the Reading researchers had seen on Bucklebury
Common in 1959 was precisely the kind of hut found on the
primitive industrial estates which clustered round the halls where
Dark Age aristocrats lived. Kings in the Heroic Age of Sutton Hoo

and *Beowulf* were great consumers. As they moved from estate to estate, they got through vast quantities of food, and each estate would have needed a huge number of plates and utensils, not to mention tables, benches and tools. In the tenth century, gatherings on the big festival days ran into hundreds and sometimes thousands of people, all descending for a few days on to a small royal estate for a particular saint's day, or for a lawmaking jamboree, or to witness the hegemonic rituals by which kings kept their thumbs on recalcitrant vassals. So semi-permanent service industries grew up around Dark Age courts, with workshops making textiles, and wooden cups and plates. And these workshops were built in the same way as the houses used by poor Anglo-Saxon immigrants back in the fifth and sixth centuries: a mark of the Third World immigrants who came into the British Isles at the end of the Roman Empire.

This poor, indigenous building custom survived unbroken till modern times. It is possible that sunken huts had always been on the common, and it is even conceivable that Lailey's hut itself began life in Old English times, though every bit would have been renewed over time. At the very least, we can say that Lailey's eighteenth- or early-nineteenth-century ancestors had built a hut in the same way as their Anglo-Saxon forebears, and that it stayed in use until the mid twentieth century.

How had that happened? It is partly explained by the isolated situation of Bucklebury itself. The village is now prosaically placed between the M4 and the railway from Paddington to Bath. It lay, as the Old English would have said, between the Kennet and the Thames, between Ashdown and the forested hills along the Hampshire border which stretch from Inkpen Beacon to Windsor. In Morton's day, the village was still an isolated place, as one can see on the 1920s Ordnance Survey map that Morton took with him. 'The extreme isolation of Bucklebury before the coming of the motor car,' said Johnny Myres, the great expert in the Anglo-Saxon migrations, 'is difficult to convey to those who have not known such areas before 1914 or even 1930.' There was a stage-coach route along the Bath road three miles to the south, and the GWR main line, whose nearest station was Thatcham. But

Bucklebury, Myres said, 'was not on the road to anywhere'. The tangle of lanes and tracks among the woodlands north of Thatcham made it extremely hard to find the bowl-turner's hut. Morton says he all but gave up his search.

The history of the place also casts light on Lailey's story. Formerly held by the Mercian kings, Berkshire was taken by West Saxons in the ninth century. Bucklebury itself was the centre of a hundred, the ancient unit of administration finally swept away in the nineteenth century but of Dark Age or even earlier origin. In 1086, in Domesday, the name is garbled by the Norman assessors as *Borgedeberie*; the form in the thirteenth-century Hundred Rolls – *Burghildeby* – shows the place was called 'Burghild's burh'. '*Burh*' can mean 'fort', but in the earlier Old English period usually means a defended farm – probably its meaning here, as there's no Iron Age fort on the spot. Burghild was very likely the daughter of King Kenwulf of Mercia (796–819). In Domesday Book the place is a royal estate, and doubtless it was earlier too, belonging to the Mercian royal family, then to the West Saxons: an important and lucrative holding in the fine forests of Berkshire, finally coming down to William the Conqueror.

The landscape here was always heavily wooded. Even in the late 1990s there is still a belt of woods from the Kennet across to the M4, the remains of the medieval forest which once covered the whole area between Newbury and Reading. Some of today's names of the separate woods and copses are very ancient: Carbin's Wood is recorded in the 1330s, and Hawkridge Wood in the north of the parish is mentioned in a land lease of the mid tenth century. So woodworkers were probably always important in the local economy. The earliest surviving indication of this is a grant in 956 made by King Eadwig, 'ruler of Albion', to the monks of Abingdon to provide timber 'for the building of the church of St Mary at Abingdon . . . a wood called Hawkridge with its fields, constituting a little more than 60 jugera' 'an old Roman land-survey measurement'. As was customary in such land grants, the text includes a description of the boundary features of the estate, which was clearly defined in part by a boundary hedge or fence. These bounds have never been worked out, but the area is clearly the northern part of Bucklebury Parish, bounded by the River Pang, and it contains the common where the Laileys later lived:

These are the bounds of Hawkridge Wood. First on the River Pang. Then to the ditch. Then up the ditch to the boundary enclosure [a hedge or fence]. Then to the wooden cross then along the boundary hedge to the thorny clearing. Then on to the bridge ford. Then by the hedge to the stone way. Then from the stone way along the *wyrtwala* [edge of the wood or foot of the hill] to the flax acres then still along the *wyrtwala* to tit-mouse pond, and from the pond to Cuthwulf's cottage sites; from the cottage sites to the River Pang. Then up midstream back to the ditch.

Armed with a large-scale map and hiking boots, it is relatively easy to find the trail of the surveyors of 1,000 years ago. The bounds begin north of Bucklebury, and go clockwise up the river, perhaps on the western side of the river, which they cross at a bridge or ford. The boundary then turns east, perhaps near today's Hawkridge House, then along the north side of Hawkridge Wood, past an ancient pond near Cook's Copse east of Magpie Farm. Then going down east and south of today's Hawkridge Wood it meets the Pang again about a thousand yards east of Bucklebury. As one would expect in an area of dense forest, the landmarks named in the charter are few and far between. It mentions a 'stone way' (perhaps an old Roman road) and a ford, then 'tit-mouse pond', which may still survive – there are several ponds in the woods here – but it is difficult to say for sure which it might be. Next the bounds mention 'the thorny clearing', perhaps a woodcutter's landmark in a dense forest; they also mention a point where the wood touches open country at 'flax acres' (we know flax was cultivated in the Pang valley in Marlston, the next parish, in the Middle Ages, and there is still a Flex Field in Marlston). The bounds pass a *cristen maelbeam* – a tree or post with a crucifix: the kind of wooden cross you might see in rural areas where there was no church nearby. Nearer the Pang, the charter mentions 'Cuthwulf's cottage sites': evidently a cluster of huts in the forest where the woodsmen or labourers worked and lived. Cuthwulf was perhaps a woodcutter, and, for all we know, used a pole lathe in a little sunken 'woodhouse' just as the Laileys did.

Scanty as its information is, then, the charter gives us a glimpse, however brief, of the life of the woodsmen and their families over a thousand years ago in Bucklebury Parish: the ancestors of the Laileys. Later accounts mention dozens of big trees being felled to furnish the monastic buildings in the tenth century. This eventually led to the clearance of the forest round Bucklebury itself, though it is still there in a great arc between the Pang and Kennet.

So it is safe to say that Bucklebury was an old community by the time it was recorded by the Conqueror's surveyors in 1086. And woodworking was its life. The Norman surveyors described the place in four separate entries. First, there was still a small royal holding, assessed at 2 hides. Then the main manor with a population of 18 villagers and 16 smallholders: these were just heads of families – we should think of about 150 people in total, with 20 ploughteams; there was 1 slave; a church; 11 acres of meadow and enough beech wood to graze 100 pigs. Then there was land of the Norman Count of Evreux also in Bucklebury; land formerly held by the Saxon lord Leofwin – with 3 villagers, 4 smallholders with 2 ploughs, 8 slaves, and a mill on the River Pang. Finally, a tiny holding of 1 hide lay 'inside the forest' and never paid tax: a lady called Aelfhild held it in 1066. Among these villagers, no doubt, were the ancestors of the medieval woodworkers of Bucklebury.

As one might expect with a dense, large forest, the woods were carefully managed, and Bucklebury stayed important as a centre for woodworking. In 1466, for example, John Goddard of Bucklebury contracted to make thirty-seven desks and benches for the Divinity School in Oxford. A big business contract, this one; John was evidently a good woodworker, but he is described in the contract (which survives) simply as a husbandman, i.e., of the same kind of status as the Laileys. These glimpses – the Anglo-Saxon woodsman Cuthwulf, John Goddard in the fifteenth century – are surely glimpses of Lailey's background too.

The Lailey family is known in the villages around Bucklebury over several centuries. Parish registers, wills and other documents from the sixteenth to the nineteenth century describe them mainly as agricultural labourers, though William's father is listed in censuses and registers as a 'bowl-turner'. Talking to Morton, William spoke of several generations in the trade. We know from parish records that his grandfather – also William – was a bowl-turner. He lived from 1782 to 1871 – they were evidently a robust family. William probably learned his trade from his father James, who died in 1834 aged 88. Another Lailey, Richard, who was member of a jury in 1738 and constable in 1750, may have been James's father. Local court documents show that the Laileys had a 'woodhouse' on the waste in 1820, when they were fined by the court baron. In 1826 this is described as a workshop; it was still there in 1834, and James's widow Elizabeth still held it in 1862. In 1927, William was making bowls in his father's and grandfather's shed, in the kind of workshop used by his medieval forebears.

The bowls and trenchers they made, it should be remembered, were the normal tableware for the majority of people until at least the eighteenth century. At Abingdon's Guildhall there survives a great cache of fifteen dozen beautifully made square wooden trenchers discovered earlier this century. With them were treen bowls and a large treen dish, a score of round trenchers and a mass of pewter plates: the old table-settings for the town's civic feasts. The poor would have used similar settings until very recently, as Oliver Baker remembered as late as the 1930s, in a wonderfully tactile evocation of a forgotten way of doing things:

I have heard old people say that when the newfangled crockery ware began to supersede the plates of wood and pewter, many people extremely disliked them because the noise of the earthenware plates, and the scratch-ing of the knife on the flinty surface of the glazed tableware, was so painful after the noiselessness of the trenchers and the silken softness of the pewter, and set their teeth on edge.

So the roots of the Laileys and their trade making 'treen' go back well into medieval times, providing small-scale domestic stuff for their locality, bowls and trenchers, where craftsmen like the God-dards handled bigger orders for the nearby towns. We can't prove they were always there, but most likely they were, as far back as the Anglo-Saxon community on the royal estate of the eighth century. At that date, sunken huts would have been constructed and used as workshops supplying the needs of the royal estate for tools and implements, and possibly larger commissions. Perhaps, just as in 1914–18 and at other times of need in our history when weapons have had to be manufactured, the cottage industries of the common woods were required to manufacture spear staves for the Viking wars, or pikestaffs for the Armada Home Guard. Against such a traditional background, it is not surprising that woodworking and bowl-turning should have carried on by pole lathe until the late 1940s in what was to all intents and purposes an Anglo-Saxon sunken hut.

This remarkable way of life survived into the twentieth century and died out in the course of it, in a century when the pace of change accelerated dramatically and uniformity of culture was imposed from the Second World War onwards. When Morton looked back on his memorable journey thirty years on, in 1959, he said this:

Reading it again I am surprised to discover how little it has dated. In spite of the social revolution the English background remains much the same, neither has the English character altered. Anyone making this journey today will meet much the same kind of people and hear the same stories.

Now, seventy years on from the first publication of his book, we could never say that. Morton's memory of his journey included images almost inconceivable to us today:

a generation of old people who were to be seen at cottage doors and on market days . . . their humour expressed in a strong regional dialect . . . who were a link with the nineteenth century, and they had certain solid virtues and values which were rooted in an older England . . .

People like the Laileys. Of course, Morton's lament for an older England sounds plainly nostalgic, coming as it did on the eve of the age of the Beatles. But it contains a real truth, in terms of the transmission of our traditions. All history is change, of course, and nothing can ever be as it was. It is the pace of change which marks our century out. This, and the modernism of the late twentieth century, with its mass media and common culture, has hastened the end of this continuity of lifestyle, of the givenness which has come down from the past. A past represented in microcosm in the sunken hut on Bucklebury Common, and in the craft of William Lailey, whose family still worked in same way as their Anglo-Saxon ancestors.

11. Tinsley Wood

'Last night I killed a man in Brunanburh'

Jorges Luis Borges

When I first saw the wood it was already in the last years of its long life. I was a teenager at school in Manchester, on one of my frequent bus journeys into Yorkshire, a county much more blessed with history and antiquities than my own. And the search which had led me to Tinsley Wood was one of the most famous unsolved mysteries of British history.

The story takes us back to the Viking Age. After Alfred the Great's desperate struggle for survival against the Vikings in the 870s, his successors were able to create for the first time a kingdom of all England. Then in the 920s, Alfred's grandson Athelstan gained the submission of all the Celtic kings in mainland Britain, becoming the most powerful ruler in these islands since the Romans. But he was surrounded by enemies. In Scotland, Strathclyde, Wales and in Viking Northumbria, many feared the rising power of the southern English. (History, of course, would prove them right.) In 934, presumably to forestall them, Athelstan invaded Scotland as far as the fortress of Dunnottar in Kincairdineshire, and his fleet struck as far north as Caithness. The crunch came three years later in 937. That autumn a coalition of Athelstan's enemies, drawn from all over Britain and Ireland, invaded England. The air was full of threats drawing on the most ancient racial antagonisms between the Celts and the Saxon newcomers, 'the palefaces' as they were called by the Welsh. 'Now we will pay them back for the 404 years,' wrote a Welsh poet. 'We will drive them out at Aber Santwic' (Sandwich, where tradition said the Anglo-Saxons had first landed in the fifth century). At the same time, in a Celtic school exercise from the south-west, a schoolboy smacked his lips at the prospect of the forthcoming 'gigantic battle' in which the English king would be humiliated for his overweening arrogance. For a moment it must have seemed touch and go as to whether England would survive at all.

Finally, late in the year, leading an army drawn from Wessex and Mercia, Athelstan attacked the invaders and in a huge and savage struggle won a decisive victory. The site of the climactic battle, according to the *Anglo-Saxon Chronicle*, was a place called Brunanburh. It was the most famous event of the era. According to a member of the royal family writing fifty years on, the man in the street still called it 'The Great War'. It was recorded in Irish, Welsh and Pictish annals, and may be noted on the Continent at Trier. The greatest of all Welsh prophetic poems, the *Armes Prydein*, the 'Great Prophecy of Britain' in the Book of Taliesin, tells of the build-up to the invasion, and gives vent in impassioned language to the Welsh hopes of victory. Contemporary poems about the battle include the famous vernacular panegyric in the *Anglo-Saxon Chronicle*, which was translated by, among others, Tennyson and Auden. A Latin poem mentioning the victory survives in a beautiful Frankish Gospel book given by Athelstan to Canterbury, and now preserved in the British Library. After the Norman Conquest, the battle became the stuff of legend and was widely circulated in songs, legends and folk tales, such as the twelfth-century story of the Viking leader Olaf Sihtricson disguising himself as a minstrel in an effort to assassinate Athelstan in his tent on the eve of the fateful confrontation. The battle forms the centre-piece of one of the best of the Norse sagas, *Egil's Saga*, whose hero fights as a mercenary on the English side. In the fourteenth century, the age of *Sir Gawain and the Green Knight*, vestiges of the tale could still be found in the romances of *Athelston* and *Guy of Warwick*; in the latter, Athelstan's hero fights the Danish champion Colbrand the Giant 'for to make England free'. The memory of Athelstan's victory and the glamour of his court were slow to fade; he bestrode the Elizabethan stage in Thomas Dekker's *Old Fortunatus*; in the eighteenth century,

David Garrick played the victorious king in a hit show on Drury Lane, with a prologue spoken by the 'Genius of England'; in 1841, *Ethelstan, or the Battle of Brunanburh* played in the London theatre. Even in the twentieth century, Brunanburh has inspired poets as diverse as David Jones (in his First World War epic, *In Parenthesis*) and the Argentinian Nobel Laureate Jorges Luis Borges, who wrote a laconic 'Brunanburh AD 937' in his *Gold of the Tigers*. Such was the strange afterlife of the story.

But where was Brunanburh? No ancient source tells us. For the last three hundred years antiquarians and historians have puzzled, but to no avail. Over forty sites have been suggested from Devon to Dumfries, but none has passed rigorous scrutiny. In 1930, J. H. Cockburn proposed a site near his home town in the Don valley in South Yorkshire. There, by the ancient southern frontier of the Northumbrians, near the site of a Roman fort known as Templeborough, was a village called Brinsworth – Brynesford in Domesday Book in 1086. The name had already attracted attention. In 1913, A. C. Goodall had written a study of the place names of South Yorkshire which included an interesting note suggesting the name might be relevant to the Brunanburh question: no doubt this was Cockburn's lead. The name, it has to be said at the outset, is not strictly analogous to the name of the battle site. Brunanburh means 'Bruna's fort' (or 'the fort by the Bruna'), and another tenth-century writer calls it Brunandun, 'Bruna's hill'. Brynesford, on the other hand, appears to represent 'Bryni's ford' (though this is not quite certain: Norman scribes were notoriously variable on Old English names). Cockburn's book was a tissue of implausibles, false etymologies and wrong-headed history, stitched together with all the zeal of a local enthusiast (by training he was actually a lawyer working in the coal industry). He had the battle raging over a thirty-mile front across the South Yorkshire coalfield, and identified almost every Viking Age place name with the events of the war. But Brynesford has always seemed to me to be in exactly the right place. The area had been the main war zone in the struggles between the North and South English in the seventh century, and again in the Viking Age, precisely in that critical time between the 920s and the 950s. A twelfth-century chronicler, John of Worcester, gives some support to this idea when he says the invaders landed in the Humber. In any case, the site of the battle can hardly have been much further south, for otherwise, why did no southern chronicler have any idea where it was? When I was fifteen I first went to have a look.

I went by bus from Manchester to Sheffield. I took with me tracings of the relevant parts of the 1855 Ordnance Survey maps (this was before the era of photocopying!). Drawn at six inches to the mile, these are beautiful and informative maps. On them it was possible to read some of the history of this landscape even before setting eyes on it. Here was the ancient landscape with its field patterns and demesne farms – settlements which went back to Domesday Book, and maybe far beyond. But here too was a landscape already, by 1855, irreparably changed by the impact of industrialization. In fact, it was one of the most devastated tracts of land in industrial Britain: here was the Midland Railway, the Sheffield and Lincolnshire Railway, the Sheffield canal, Tinsley iron foundry and the Catcliffe glass works. Everywhere on the map one could see the pock marks of old open-cast coal pits, and the spoil tips of the new deep collieries which were being dug throughout South Yorkshire in the 1850s, bringing a great influx of migrant labour from Wales and Scotland. And yet still there in the middle of the map, west of Brinsworth village, was the distinctive butterfly shape of Tinsley Wood, a shape which could be traced back through earlier maps of the area as far as the early seventeenth century. It was over a mile long, just as it was described in Domesday Book in 1086:

In Tinsley in 1066 Ulchel, Agemund and Archil had five carucates [units] of land for tax, where four ploughs can be. Now Roger [de Busli – the new Norman lord] has one villein [semi-freemen] and three sokemen [freemen] there with one plough, and the share of one mill, and ten acres of meadow. Pasturable woodland one league in length and eight furlongs wide. In the time of King Edward it was worth four pounds, now twenty shillings.

In Sheffield Public Library I transcribed the account of Tinsley and Brinsworth written by the great Yorkshire antiquarian Joseph Hunter in his *South Yorkshire*, published in 1831 and still the best work written on the region. As far back as Domesday, Tinsley had been the more important settlement, and the medieval church was here. In Hunter's day Tinsley was still an agricultural place, a pretty village with its 'antient chapel', though it had been tied to the industrial economy of Sheffield since the building of the Don navigation in the eighteenth century. Then Tinsley Wharf (which opened in 1751) had become one of the main outlets for Sheffield manufacture, and for the products of the hundreds of rural metal-workers living in the villages roundabout. But even as late as 1831, Tinsley village still felt like countryside. Hunter was especially taken with Tinsley Wood, which he thought was 'probably a remnant of the antient forest verdure of Brigantia', and where, as he noted in passing, Walter Scott had set *Ivanhoe*:

The paths through the wood to the neighbouring villages have the air of native tracks. There are points in them at which we have vistas of forest scenery of great beauty; and there are recesses in these woods where the depth and grandeur of solitude may be felt. Had the author of *Ivanhoe* been as well acquainted with the scenery in this neighbourhood as he is with his own forests and fells, he might have given more of individuality to the site and environs of Rotherwood. As it is, the mind is left in some doubt where upon the map Rotherwood is to be placed; but it could not have been far distant from Tinsley and Brinsworth.

More to the point, Hunter saw that the wood corresponded to that recorded in 1086 in the Domesday Survey. A mile and a half long by a mile wide, its northern part had begun to be felled to open up new agricultural land during the population boom of the thirteenth century. Medieval rentals preserved among the Wentworth family muniments in Sheffield library mention fourteenth-century tenants like Robert Heryng 'of Chapelwood' clearing away woodland for arable. By the sixteenth century, the original wood had been greatly diminished in the north, where the land was now

part of the common fields. But in 1831, when Hunter described
it, the southern part of the wood was still a mile across, and there
was no record of this part ever having been cut down or replanted.
It was safe to assume that Tinsley Wood represented the partial
survival of an Anglo-Saxon forest.

By the time I got to see the forest, though, on a blustery day
in 1963, it had virtually gone. You could still see where it had
been. It was marked by a long line of trees between a farm field
and a golf-course which had been laid out on reclaimed colliery
ground. The wood was now little more than a pleasant walking spot for local people. It had probably been destroyed over the
last hundred years by industry, surface smelting and open-cast
mining. On closer inspection, though, to my considerable surprise,
the medieval forest ditch was still visible, running for some 400
yards along what had been the eastern edge of the wood. The
Ordnance map marked this line as the parish and county boundary,
so one could be fairly certain that it preserved the medieval – and
presumably the Domesday – lie of the land. So at least part of the
Anglo-Saxon landscape was recoverable. It was an encouraging
start.

From this last vestige of the forest, I walked across the field to
the highest point of the landscape, on the fringe of a modern
housing estate. Here had stood the medieval (and Domesday) manor
farm of Brinsworth until its demolition in the 1950s. At this point,
a couple of miles south of the Don, the land rises to a prominent
hill, White Hill, with fine views northwards where the valleys of
the Don and the Rother open out in all directions. Here the gap
between the forest and the Rother is more than a mile wide; to
the south, though, below White Hill, the forest and the river come
much closer together – about 800 yards apart. Now, curiously
enough, this is exactly how the battlefield is described in the
thirteenth-century Icelandic tale *Egil's Saga*, though such works
are generally held by scholars to be so unreliable in matters of
historical fact that it was difficult to know what to make of what
was on the face of it a remarkable coincidence. Suppressing my
excitement, I walked down from Brinsworth to Tinsley.

The birthplace of Christianity in England? Many of Glastonbury's mysteries remain
be solved.

18. George Lailey, bowl-turner of Bucklebury, in the sunken hut with his pole lathe: an Iron Age tool still in use after the First World War.

19. Hawkridge Wood north-west of Bucklebury 1977. An Anglo-Saxon document shows that the forest was used by wood-workers in the mid-tenth century

. Lailey, *c.* 1930, around the time he met H.V. Morton.

21. Bury Barton in north Devon. The classic isolated Devon farm with its courtyards and animal sheds. The triple ditches of the Roman fort are clearly visible, hinting at a history going back long before the Conquest.

22. The thatched chapel at Bury, now a cart shed, was consecrated in 1434.

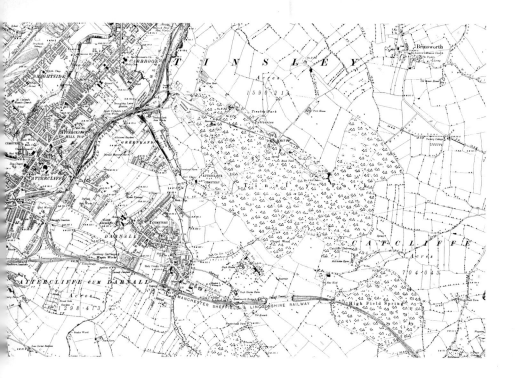

. Tinsley Park on the six-inch Ordnance Survey map of 1889. The wood is mentioned in
omesday Book in 1086 – its distinctive butterfly shape, shown on Elizabethan maps, is
w gone.

. The Church of St Lawrence, Tinsley, c. 1900: the Victorian rebuilding has left no clues to
(Anglo-Saxon?) origins.

25. All that remains of Tinsley Wood is the tiny strip shown to the left of the photograph, by the bypass into Sheffield. Was this the site of the Viking Age 'Great War'?

26. Bede's church at Jarrow on the Tyne, founded in 683; in the foreground is the River Don. Here Bede wrote his *History of the English Church and People*.

& **28.** Two landscapes. Unchanging upland Britain (top): typical Devon hill–farming
ʌntry looking towards Iddesleigh and Dartmoor – an archaic world which has survived to
end of the twentieth century. The industrial landscape of the north at Monkwearmouth
ottom): the site of Jarrow's sister monastery, founded in 672. Since this picture was taken in
3, shipbuilding on the Wear has gone, and so has the colliery, first recorded in the
ȷlfth century.

29. The 'community of the realm' in 1911: the opening of the village hall in Peatling Magna, Leicestershire.

30. Group photograph from 1975 of the Leicester Barbudans in front of Codrington Park, a house paid for by the labour of their ancestors from the mid seventeenth century onwards. On the far right is Sir Simon Codrington.

Tinsley itself in 1963 was just an extension of the industrial sprawl of Sheffield, already far from Hunter's pretty agricultural village. There seemed little prospect of learning anything from its present-day condition, but I headed for the chapel. It was set back from the main road in a small, square churchyard at the end of a little lane. Still out in the fields in Hunter's day, in the Middle Ages it must have been a small rural chapel within the forest itself. It was dedicated to St Laurence. First recorded in the early thirteenth century, its fabric was dated by Joseph Hunter to 'hardly later than the first century after the [Norman] Conquest'. This raised the exciting possibility of a Late-Anglo-Saxon structure. But to my great disappointment, nothing was left of what Hunter saw. As so often, in their zeal to build anew, the Victorians had destroyed the ancient chapel of Tinsley in 1877. Nothing was left of the original church. They did not even appear to have reused any of the architectural fragments in the rebuilding. Luckily, an old engraving in the vestry gave an idea of what the building had been like – clearly Late Saxon or Early Norman, to judge by the windows: Hunter had been right. I asked around for more details, to no avail, though a neighbour mentioned a local tradition that there had been a church here before the Norman Conquest – made of wood, so it was said. There is, however, no church recorded for Tinsley in Domesday Book, and though this is not as conclusive as it sounds – there are many cases of pre-Conquest churches being omitted by King William's compilers – with no documentary support, such a flimsy local tradition could hardly carry any weight.

But could the chapel still have been Anglo-Saxon? The dedication to St Laurence was very popular in Anglo-Saxon England, especially in the north. Only sixty years or so after St Augustine's mission, King Oswy of the Northumbrians received precious relics from the pope, including some of St Laurence, and this has been connected with some early dedications in Durham and Northumberland, and a cluster on the southern border of Northumbria in South Yorkshire. Writing in 1899, Frances Arnold-Forster concluded that many of the English dedications to St Laurence are:

of such an early origin that it is impossible to trace them back to the period when they were first bestowed . . . In cases too numerous to be recorded the architecture of the church proclaims it to have been built at least in Norman times; but even here the probability is that in many instances the dedication-name goes back far behind the existing structure.

Tinsley would fit nicely into that pattern. But there was no proof which would take us back any further than the old engraving in the nave. Or was there?

There was clearly something out of the ordinary about its origins. It had not begun as a minster or a parish church, but seems always to have been described simply as a chapel. It had therefore probably been set up for a particular purpose by a wealthy patron. Joseph Hunter thought the origin of the chapel was perhaps as the domestic chapel of the local lord (in Domesday Book, the Norman Roger of Bully). After the Conquest, it was one of dozens of manors dependent on Roger's castle ten miles to the east at Tickhill in Derbyshire, and had a strange condition attached to its tenure: every year at Michaelmas its owner had to take a pair of white gloves to the lord of Tickhill, and receive a hawk to keep over winter. (This was possibly a hangover from Anglo-Saxon days, as similar arrangements can be found in the pages of Domesday Book.) Later in the Middle Ages we find the chapel attached, as it still is, to the grand collegiate church of All Saints at Rotherham (an undoubted Anglo-Saxon foundation, by the way, whose mother church was the important Dark Age royal centre of Conisbrough: 'the king's fortress').

In addition, though, Joseph Hunter noticed something extremely interesting about Tinsley chapel: it had a royal connection. In the Middle Ages, the chapel had received a royal stipend for the performance of a special chantry service – a service for the dead. At the time of the Reformation, this service was recorded by King Henry VIII's commissioners, with a cantarist (probably the vicar himself), and a small annual value arising from land and tithe. It was put down by royal act in the first year of Edward VI's reign. However, the chapel was not then converted to secular use, but carried on as an outlier of Rotherham parish church, performing the care of souls and, as was said in 1546:

to mynistre to the seke people, as when the waters of the Rothere and Downe [i.e., the Don] are so urgent that the curate of Rotherham cannot to theym repayre, nor the inhabitantes unto hym nether on horseback or bote . . .

Surprisingly, though, the service for the dead continued to be performed. Most remarkable of all, payment of the royal stipend seems to have resumed, and continued to be made long after the Reformation. As late as the seventeenth century, as a letter of 18 October 1660 showed, the king paid to the minister at Tinsley 'a stipende heretofore and alwayes allowed to the said chappell'. This subsequently lapsed and was renewed in 1710, in 1718, and again in 1818. The payment only seems to have stopped finally with the abolition of what were known as church 'peculiars' in 1847.

Of course, England is full of similar extraordinary survivals of ancient custom. But what was the origin of this royal connection? Why had this tiny and utterly insignificant place received such a royal gift for so long? And why did it need a cantarist? Tinsley was not a royal manor, and as we have seen, the main text of Domesday Book has no mention of any royal holding there. But curiously enough, when we turn to the 'recapitulation' at the end of the Yorkshire folios, there *is* just such a note, to the effect that the king held seven bovates of land attached to the manor at Tinsley. This small parcel (or parcels) of land can hardly have added up to more than a hundred acres, but on the six-inch maps from 1855, with their minute delineation of local boundaries, three detached portions of Tinsley parish are recorded which might match this. They lie on White Hill within Brinsworth parish; two of them are tiny, each the size of a small field, but the third comprises about eighty acres around White Hill farm, close to the old manor house of Brynesford. Sometimes such pieces of land can be relics of very ancient tenurial arrangements. Were these parcels the king's land mentioned in the Domesday appendix of 1086? If so, what was the origin of this little

royal holding? And why did the Crown carry on paying an allowance
to this obscure chapel in South Yorkshire right into the nineteenth
century? Had the church perhaps started as a royal chapel, or
chantry, where masses and prayers are said in remembrance of dead
souls? At the time I couldn't answer that.

There was no question though, that this was a fascinating historical
landscape. Even a schoolboy could see that. On the high ground
north of the Don was a big Iron Age camp, Wincobank, and an
ancient dyke system which ran east–west along the Don: probably
in origin the frontier works of the Brigantes, which were later used
as the fortified border of the Northumbrians in the seventh century.
In the 1950s, excavations had shown, too, that the main Roman
road north from Derby to Castleford and York, Riknild Street,
went right over the White Hill at Brinsworth, crossing the Don at
an ancient ford by the Roman fort of Templeborough. So the hill
straddled the main military route out of southern England just south
of the Northumbrian frontier dykes. This seemed to me – and still
seems to me – a crucial factor in the story. The excavator of the
road (and also of a hitherto unknown Roman settlement on the
hill) was Dorothy Greene. A stalwart of the local history society,
she had retired now. I went to see her out on the Whiston Road
in a little Victorian terrace whose front wall shone with cardinal-red
brick polish. Donkey-stoned steps led to a stained-glass door with
leaded windows. Behind lace curtains, we drank tea and ate parkin
off bone china. Dorothy was a kindly, grey-haired lady, not the
sort you'd associate with dirt archaeology; but her digging experience went back to the excavation of the Roman fort at Templeborough during the First World War, and no one knew the area better.
After tea I pulled out a green cloth-backed school exercise book
and my old maroon fountain pen, and I listened to her story.

'Cockburn's book is not really scholarly,' she said in a soft
Yorkshire accent, 'especially all his stuff about place names. But
you can still find some useful ideas in it. He may even have been
right that Brunanburh was somewhere near Brinsworth. There
was a local tradition that there was a battle fought on the White
Hill, you know, between Nursery Farm and Catcliffe – that's

by the Rother opposite Tinsley Forest, on the southern slope of White Hill, at the narrowest point between the wood and the river.'

'Where does the tradition come from?'

'Oh, I heard it years ago, before the Great War, from one of the farmers. All the children heard it at school. It's just one of those traditions. No evidence, mind. Perhaps it was based on finds made long ago. I don't know.'

'A battle when?'

'Oh, none can say. Some say Romans and Britons. There's lots of Roman traditions around here: the Roman Rig, the Roman Fort, you know.' She paused. 'But this might interest you. There was a Roman temple on White Hill.' This came as a surprise – she hadn't mentioned it in her published dig report in the *Yorkshire Archaeological Journal.*

'Now you know I expect that there was another name for the site of the battle of Brunanburh – this appears in the chronicle of Simeon of Durham, who is a very reliable twelfth-century writer with northern interest and knowledge. He calls it Weondun, which very likely means the hill where there had been a pagan Roman sanctuary or temple. The great Anglo-Saxon scholar Sir Frank Stenton thinks this is reliable evidence which might help locate the site, because such place names are quite rare – and they only crop up south of the Humber.'

'But you don't mention it in your report.'

'The trouble was, it was a rescue operation before the new estate was built at Brinsworth. We started digging up a bit of road and ended up finding a small town which we never even guessed was there. The whole dig was never published. There wasn't the time, and it would have been far too expensive. But we found the platform of a temple. I'm absolutely sure of it. It was at Canklow on the northern side of White Hill. It's a perfect spot for a Roman temple, by the main road north, on a hill by the border with the Brigantes. Now look at the name of the Roman fort down by the Don. Templeborough. It's always been assumed that this is just an antiquarian name. It can't be traced back earlier than the sixteenth century. But sometimes these local traditions go back a very long time: I wonder if it could be a memory of the temple on the hill? And the "borough" part of the place name might have been in colloquial use for centuries – the meadow by the fort site has always been called "Burgh field" by Rotherham folk: that could well come from an Old English word *burh*, meaning a "fortified place". We don't know anything about Templeborough in the later Saxon period – the only known find is a Middle Saxon brooch, but we know that the Roman fort at Doncaster was a Saxon settlement in Athelstan's day. So maybe Brunanburh, the fort in the *Anglo-Saxon Chronicle*, was actually the Roman fort itself. Have you considered that?'

I had a last look over the Rother valley before heading for home. The sun was already setting over Sheffield. In the days before the trans-Pennine motorway, it was a long bus journey back to Manchester that night. It had been an exciting day, and my mind was racing. There was no firm proof, but the facts all fitted: the landscape, the Roman road, the temple, the fort, the frontier dyke – and, for what it was worth, the local tradition which Dorothy had mentioned. The events of autumn 937 had started to take on a life of their own. By the time the bus reached Belle Vue on the outskirts of Manchester, I had imagined the whole thing. The invaders' devastation of northern Mercia after harvest time. The southern English advance out of Mercia around the time of the festival of All Saints. The Celts and Vikings taking a defensive position on the hill between the forest and the river. In my mind's eye I could see old Constantine, king of the Scots, 'the hoary-headed traitor' as the English called him, parading the crozier of Columcille before his chiefs as the chill autumn dawn came up. There, too, was the English king himself: a piece of the True Cross in a crystal reliquary hung around his neck, and in his hand the famous sword which was still preserved as a relic in the royal treasury over two centuries later. He was only forty-two, but a hardbitten and successful king now facing the supreme test of his nerve and luck. Then the grim struggle – 'immense, lamentable and horrible' as an Irish annalist said – and the terrible slaughter in the river valleys.

And then the immense booty left behind by the defeated armies, described in poems of the time in Homeric terms:

wide corslets decked in red gold . . . beautiful ornaments, shields and broad swords, helmets and hip swords, war trappings of heroes inlaid with gold, treasures more splendid than any among the sages can tell.

That surely was how it had been? And perhaps it was. But without proof, this was all just imagination. And reluctant as I was to see it at the time, there simply was no proof.

Ten years passed before I saw Tinsley Wood and White Hill again. After postgraduate research into the later Anglo-Saxon period, I got my first job as a journalist in South Yorkshire, covering another part of the rich history of the area: coal strikes and industrial history. For someone straight out of the ivory tower of Oxford, it was a gritty baptism into the world of real history. South Yorkshire had become the focus of the miners' momentous (and fateful) struggle with Edward Heath's government. That time I frequently made the journey down to the coalfield, to get the latest opinions from the pit leaders at Sharlston, Elsecar, Wath: Old English names all. In the interim, the landscape at Tinsley had gone through truly dramatic changes. In the mid sixties the main London to Yorkshire motorway, the M1, had been driven right across the hill in a great sweep from the east, over the Rother and then curving northwards over Tinsley village, overshadowing the little chapel on a huge viaduct which took it across the Don valley. An immense coking works had been built over the site of Tinsley Wood, with a vast marshalling yard cut into the hill below Brinsworth. Only a strip of Tinsley Wood still remained. The hill had been devastated. Tinsley itself was now one of the most blighted places in the British Isles. Down by the Don the Templeborough steel works belched black smoke; the Don itself flowing sluggishly through a scum of oily debris and white detergent to the roar of steam hammers and blast furnaces. But the chapel was still there, and the chapel, I felt, was somehow the key to the mystery – if indeed there was still a key left at all.

I was still curious about the Norman or Saxon origins of Tinsley chapel and the strange story of its royal connection, which had been maintained for so many centuries. Medieval kings, we know, were prone to commemorate anniversaries – especially for the souls of the dead. William the Conqueror's foundation at Battle and Henry IV's chapel at Battlefield near Shrewsbury are the best known, but there are others further back in time. After his victory at Assandun (Ashingdon in Essex?) in 1016, in which the 'flower of England' fell, Canute built a church to have perpetual masses said for those who had died. Indeed, not so far from Tinsley, near Cuckney in Nottinghamshire, a chapel at Edwinstowe may mark the spot where the Northumbrian king Edwin – St Edwin – was killed by the pagan Penda in 633. As late as the thirteenth century we find King John providing a stipend for a hermit to live and pray there. With a battle as famous and momentous as Brunanburh, in which members of the West Saxon royal family had died, it seemed inconceivable to me that Athelstan, of all people, with his well-attested obsession with the cult of saints, would not have left some remembrance. It was just a hunch, I admit based on what I thought I knew of the king's personality and the custom of the time. But it rang true. Could there, then, be any significance in the saint or saints commemorated in Tinsley church?

As I have said, St Laurence was a very popular Old English saint. He appears in many pre-Conquest litanies and prayer books. Laurence's intercession was especially invoked in war. He was a martial saint. And with their calendrical view of the world, early medieval rulers took this kind of thing very seriously. Athelstan's contemporary, Otto the Great of Germany, for example, elected to fight his crucial battle against the Hungarians on St Laurence's day, 10 August 955, and founded a church in the saint's name as thanksgiving for the victory. Athelstan, so I thought, would have done the same. Perhaps he might even have dedicated a memorial chapel to St Laurence. Laurence's date, however, was no help for Brunanburh, which was certainly fought later in the year, perhaps in late October, most likely in November. But there was a calendrical commemoration at Tinsley which was more suggestive. For in the record of King Henry VIII's commissioners, the service for the dead maintained in the chapel at Tinsley was stated to be in a chantry of St Leonard. Was this just a slip for St Laurence? Perhaps, but St Leonard's day is 6 November – just when we might guess the battle to have been fought. It was a hunch worth following up.

The purpose of these perpetual chantries was the commemoration of anniversaries, usually through the saying of prayers for the dead, on the day of their death, to lessen the time souls spent in purgatory. Chantries became very popular in England from the twelfth century onwards; but the custom of founding such chapels was already widespread in the ninth century in Francia, and there are many examples of the institution of perpetual prayers on death annivers-aries from the early tenth century in England – especially, as it happens, in the reign of King Athelstan. Several times in the land grants of the 930s Athelstan attaches the condition on the mortgagee of praying for his soul. Some of these services were long-lasting: at Penkridge in Staffordshire, there was still a king's chantry in the fourteenth century to celebrate mass for the souls of the tenth-century kings who were thought to be the founders of the church; at Durham, Athelstan himself still received prayers on the day of his death until the Reformation. So what, if anything, was the significance of St Leonard's chantry at Tinsley? And when was it established?

St Leonard seems to have been a Frankish hermit who lived in the sixth century; he was very popular from the twelfth century, especially among prisoners of war. Unfortunately, his cult appears to be a Norman import into England. His only appearances in Anglo-Saxon litanies are post-Conquest insertions into two Old English manuscripts. Most of the twenty or so surviving Anglo-Saxon calendars which have been printed are blank on his day; some give the obscure Breton saint Winnoc; none names Leonard save as a Norman addition. Where Athelstan, for example, possessed relics of Winnoc, Leonard does not appear in any early relic list. So, on the face of it, it is extremely unlikely that this dedication to St Leonard could be pre-Conquest. Indeed, to underline this point, the famous medieval hospital of St Leonard in York, which was allegedly founded by Athelstan, was only dedicated to the saint by King Stephen in the twelfth century. Even in the case of churches with certain pre-Conquest fabric, such as Stanley St Leonard in Gloucestershire, the dedication itself is not certainly pre-Norman. Of course, it is still not quite impossible that the chantry itself could have been Anglo-Saxon and rededicated in the twelfth century. But no sensible researcher would depend on it. The saints of Tinsley had led to a dead end.

I returned to Tinsley for the third time on a squally spring day in 1981. I was still convinced that Brunanburh should be sought somewhere in this border region between the Mercians and the Northumbrians (indeed, I had just published an article arguing as much). At Doncaster museum, I had a chat with Malcom Dolby about his new excavations which had uncovered massive ditches outside the Roman defences there: the town had been an Anglo-Saxon *burh*, and place-name evidence had now identified a line of Viking Age forts along the Don valley, most prominent of which was Conisbrough, 'the King's *burh*', where the great Norman castle stands today. This gave an even better context for the lost fort of Brunanburh. But although I had gone into print with my theory, I had to admit the clinching evidence was still missing. Meanwhile, at Tinsley, the hill and the forest had gone through still more changes since the mid seventies. A new bypass, the A57, had been built from the motorway leading straight into Sheffield. It cut through the southern end of what remained of Tinsley Wood. Part of the medieval ditch still survived, and behind it a straggling line of ash, elm, an old oak or two – the last few trees left of the mile-wide forest recorded in Domesday and described in 1831 by Joseph Hunter. The story of the wood was almost over.

My last visit to Tinsley was in the summer of 1999, well over thirty years after the first. Further dramatic changes had once again transformed the whole area of the Don valley. The steelworks had closed after centuries of metalworking in the region, part of the massive contraction of British heavy industry during the early years of the Thatcher government. The huge works at Tinsley had been shut down and dismantled after only twenty years of life. The collieries had all gone too, in the aftermath of the great miners' strike of 1984, when the depot at Orgreave, south of White Hill, had been the scene of one of the worst confrontations in the longest strike in British labour history. The Conservatives' pit-closure plan of the early 1990s had been the last straw. The river road past Templeborough was silent now. At Tinsley, the vicar Colin Gibson showed me the surviving pieces from the old church, fragments of Tinsley's history: the seventeenth-century parish chest, communion table, coffin stands, and plate. In the vestry was still the old engraving showing the Norman door seen by Joseph Hunter.

'There's a local story – I heard it from my predecessor – that there was a fire in the old church a couple of centuries ago. Destroyed the best part of the Norman building. So what you see in this engraving is largely an eighteenth-century reconstruction of the medieval church, using some of the original bits. When the Victorians rebuilt it they did away with the lot: built a nice new serviceable church for the growing industrial population of Tinsley. Really there's nothing left of the old church. Nothing at all. Architecturally speaking, it's a ghost.'

'What do you know about the story of the Saxon church?'

'Only that there's supposed to have been a wooden church here in Saxon times. That's the tradition. That's all I know. I'm not local, of course. My predecessor was working on a history of the church before he retired. Unfortunately, no one knows what he did with the manuscript.'

He pottered about in the vestry, putting old flowers in the dustbin, wiping a film of oily dust from the window ledge. From outside came the constant roar of heavy lorries over the Tinsley viaduct. At the end of the church path, in the shadow of the viaduct, the streets were windswept and desolate. All these steel and mining communities had been devastated in the last fifteen years. And so history moves on, from the Vikings to the miners. Landscapes are shaped and reshaped, devastated and restored. Forests grow and are cut down. Battles are fought, and forgotten. Pits sunk, mined and closed. Cycles of destruction and rebirth. Wounds left that heal in time.

Going back to the mystery of Brunanburh, I have to say that I no longer think the site can be located with any certainty. Of course, I don't deny that something might turn up which changes that gloomy conclusion. Things still do: for example, a lost Old English charter copied into a Tudor antiquarian's notebook; or a medieval rentbook with the key place name noted in an estate survey; there is even the chance of a stray archaeological find, a spear head, perhaps, or a sword pommel dredged out of a river bed. But those are all long shots. I am still sure that the general area is right – it can hardly have been much further south, otherwise how would southern and Midlands annalists have failed to record where it was? But, for the moment at least, I've come round to agreeing with what Alistair Campbell wrote in 1938, that by now 'all hope of localising Brunanburh is lost'.

The schoolboy history enthusiast in me still clings to a different conclusion. He cannot quite let go of the conviction that White Hill at Brinsworth was indeed the site of the battle of Brunanburh. He believes that Athelstan did not omit to commemorate his dead kinsmen and friends, and that St Laurence's church at Tinsley is the memorial chapel he established with a small gift of land and a stipend which continued into modern times. But regretfully, the historian in me has to tell the schoolboy that this story is pure imagination, and not history.

You may think, then, that the search has been fruitless. Just a series of unsubstantiated leaps of the imagination. But to me, it sums up the joy of historical research. I can't pretend that my long trawl through the documents and landscape history of these two South Yorkshire parishes has brought me much closer to understanding the dramatic events of the tenth century. But what it did do was illuminate a corner of the English landscape. What I carry with me from my search is a sense of the layers of our history – symbolized in concrete by the Roman road, the canal, the Victorian railways, and the motorway (itself destined to be ancient one day). And there are the layers of history in terms of people's lives, too: Arnkel, the Saxon farmer of Tinsley; the medieval colonists, like the Heryng family, grubbing the forest; the metalworkers, canal engineers and railway navvies; the miners' families 'scratting' for surface coal in Tinsley Wood in the strikes of 1893 and 1984; the newcomers on the post-war housing estate at Brinsworth; Reverend Gibson and his dwindling flock at Tinsley today. But on this particular journey through time, two things especially stick in my memory: the ancient chapel of Tinsley with its mysterious predecessors, whose Victorian ghost still stands under the viaduct; and above all, Tinsley Wood itself – the magnificent forest of Domesday Book, whose origins must lie even before the Bronze Age, in the wild wood which covered Britain after the last Ice Age. The forest still seen by Joseph Hunter in the 1820s, with its glades and walks, 'where the grandeur of solitude may be felt'; now just a straggle of trees along a municipal golf-course, in earshot of the unceasing noise of the motorway.

In summer 1999, over thirty years since I had first stood there, I met an old man in Tinsley Wood. He was a former miner from Orgreave out walking his dog, an old grizzled terrier with rheumy eyes. They were alongside the fairway in the last of the trees by the roundabout on the A57. It's a high, exposed spot now, and there was quite a breeze. 'Aye,' he said, 'my grandad told me it were a great forest here once: they used to play here all day long when they were kids. A grand place.' His grandson will only read about it in books.

12. A Devon House: to Domesday and Beyond

One spring day nearly twenty years ago, I was on my way from Exeter to the north coast of Devon, heading across the heart of the county to the ancient church of Stoke St Nectan at Hartland. From Exeter, the Barnstaple road leaves the black mass of Dartmoor on the horizon to the left, the names on the signposts speaking of bleak Devon winters: Coldridge, Cold Cottages; the trees bent by the wind that 'tyrannizes . . . rowling upon the high hills and moors in furious gusts,' as a Tudor writer put it. An isolated world, this, till the turnpikes came in the early nineteenth century. It is no coincidence Conan Doyle set *The Hound of the Baskervilles* out here. Such stories found uncanny echoes in real life in these parts. There was the weird tale of the North Devon Savages, for example, whose 'dreadful superstitions' and pagan marriages, 'defying goodness and decency', caused a scandal a century or so ago. These were people who, 'had they lived in Patagonia, would have received the attention of missionaries', but instead drew a reporter from the *Daily Telegraph* in 1871 to file reports which sent shivers down the spines of metropolitan Victorians at their breakfast tables. There were, of course, rational explanations for such strange occurrences, as there still are today, but even at the end of the 1970s such parts of rural England still felt as if they were an enclosed world which belonged to an earlier age, places where one might encounter survivals.

We stopped for petrol at Lapford Cross in the valley of the Yeo. On the steep hill above us, the Ordnance Survey map marked an ancient chapel. While the garage owner filled up the tank, I pulled out my copy of Pevsner, the old Penguin paperback with the famous white cover edged with brown bands. Pevsner had come here in the immediate post-war years in a ramshackle 1933 Wolsley

Hornet to record the buildings of England, in the that far-off time of petrol-ration books, when towns like Exeter were still in ruins from the bombers. His book, another search for England, was a kind of act of restitution: he noted Lapford church and a nearby farm, where, 'according to Mr G. Copeland, a chapel of the manor house is said to survive'. Strangely worded: perhaps Pevsner had not checked his map, since the chapel, in fact, was clearly marked on the 1930s and 1940s Ordnance Surveys after the six-inch Victorian maps. Perhaps he was in a hurry, but Pevsner never went up the hill to check it out.

We were late, but we made the detour. A narrow country lane rose steeply between hedgerows about a hundred feet above the river. On top, we passed a wood full of rooks. In the twilight we could see across to the black mass of Dartmoor. The farm loomed up on the left; it had two courtyards surrounded by a massive perimeter wall of cob, the traditional Devon building material of mud and straw bonded with cowdung. It was a private house, so we just peeped inside the outer courtyard: a great pillared wooden square with a huge thatched inner gate like the cart entrance of a tithe barn. A big mudbrick peasant enclosure, half farm, half fortress; the place reminded me of a small rural chateau in the Midi of France. A little further along the lane, an iron gate led into a yard full of seeders and threshing machines – the place was apparently still a working farm. To the right of the gate was a thatched cart-store, which on closer inspection turned out to be the chapel, with some segments of medieval stone tracery still left in its windows. I pushed open the wooden door and got the fright of my life as a barn owl flapped past my face out of the window and shot off over a mossy pond overhung with trees. The sun had now almost gone, but from the hill there were views in all directions. For a second, time stood still: the place seemed intact, as it might have been about 1820, on the eve of the railways, when upland farming in Devon was still a world of its own, yet to face its modern decline. Soon it was pitch dark and we could barely see a thing: a strange experience for town dwellers as a blanket of darkness settled on the countryside, the only light the distant twinkle of Lapford a mile off.

There was a howling gale by the time we reached Hartland cliffs, the most dramatic part of the north Devon coast. The pinnacles of the old tower of St Nectan's, the tallest in Devon, were lost in cloud, and we took a wrong turning several times in the last mile or two. The hotel near Hartland had a creaking wood-floored bar with a welcome fire and a shelf of books by the window seat. The usual kind of thing for a country inn: old Shell guides; worn-out OS maps; old editions of *Country Life* and *Illustrated London News*; and William Hoskins's *Devon*, the gazeteer for all Devon travellers. After dinner, I settled down in an armchair with the book and looked up the old farm on the hill near Lapford.

Hoskins was the author of one of the most brilliant and influential books ever written about the British past, *The Making of the English Landscape*. He was the recorder and interpreter of a world we have lost; what he called the 'civilization' of rural England, whose origin he saw far back in the Anglo-Saxon period in the Midlands, and even further back in the west and south-west, the highland zone of Britain whose essential character he felt had changed only very slowly over many centuries. Hoskins was a poet of a disappearing world; not of exotic, faraway tribes, but of our own 'peasant civilization', as he liked to call it. With his books and his wonderful TV series, *One Man's Landscape*, he taught a generation a new way of seeing, like a conjuror revealing amazing discoveries right under our noses. Driven by an intense sense of locality, he showed us the hidden patterns below the surface of the English landscape, whether in the rural West Country or a Victorian industrial estate on Teesside. Topography, to him, was the key to seeing what made us who we are. His aim was to recapture the lives lived by the people who had shaped our landscape over millennia.

In a sense, I suppose one could say his work was nostalgic: part of the growing movement between and after the wars to record a past – physical, mental – fast disappearing under the impact of modernity. Arthur Mee, the Shell County books, Pevsner: they were all part of it. But where Pevsner kept a tight rein on himself and delivered the dry facts (for which his arch-critic John Betjeman always lampooned him), Hoskins was unashamedly emotional.

Anchored firmly in the records of the daily lives of ordinary people, his was, none the less, a visionary idea of England.

Hoskins himself was a Devon man, a native of the lovely medieval and Tudor city of Exeter, which was bombed by the Germans and then wrecked by developers, a devastation which he found somehow less forgivable. The history of the Devon landscape was always close to his heart. It was one of Hoskins's great insights that the pre-Domesday landscape of Devon was still recoverable in the late twentieth century. Armed with Ordnance Survey maps, he delved in buzzard-haunted crofts, peered down 'almost impossible lanes', scrambled in the roofs of ancient houses, and dated hedgerows which appeared in documents of 1,300 years ago. Descended from Devon and Dorset yeomen himself, he was (so it seemed) driven by an almost genetic direction finder: it was as if he wore a pair of magical spectacles which enabled him to see through the present, and envision past lives. At a time when the physical past was being destroyed everywhere, and the very idea of continuity was no longer taken seriously, he was demonstrating deep and still tactile continuities. And among his many discoveries was the old house, or *barton*, as they are called in Devon, at Bury near Lapford. This is what he wrote in 1952:

Five miles to the south-east of Rashleigh, on a steep hill above the valley of the Yeo, stands Bury Barton, with a detached chapel by the roadside now used as an implement shed. The farmstead is a good example of a large barton arranged round a courtyard . . . The barton itself is partly of early-sixteenth-century date and partly of a hundred years later . . . Bury takes its name from some earthwork (*burh*) which must formerly have occupied the summit of the ridge on which the farmstead now stands, commanding the two valleys of the Yeo and the Dalch and a wide stretch of country to the east. No trace remains of this earthwork today. It was presumably a small hilltop camp of the type usually found in the late Iron Age, immediately preceding the Roman conquest. When the first Saxon settlers reoccupied the site – most probably in the eighth century or possibly the ninth – this earthwork gave its name to the new farm. It is called Beria in Domesday Book and was then a small manor belonging to the bishop of Exeter, having been given to the monastery at Exeter by Athelstan early in the tenth century . . . At some unknown date this small manor was granted by the bishop to the ancestor of the Burys, who subsequently took their name from their estate. No record of the Burys has yet come to light before the early part of the fifteenth century . . . The last of the Burys died here in 1804.

The waves were crashing around Hartland Point and the wind still beating on the hotel windows when I fell asleep. Hoskins's account had shown what exciting possibilities lay in the story of a single house:

Every parish in Devon has at least one such farmhouse, and some have three or four, each with its own peculiar history. A whole book could be written about them. They, and the men and women they nourished, are a most distinctive part of the social history of England.

This was a history of England not viewed from the point of view of kings and queens; nor even from the more fashionable perspective of radicals and revolutionaries. But it was no less interesting or valuable: the history of a gradually developing continuity, of families and labour, of that profound sense of obligation and cooperation between neighbours and parishes out of which all our institutions have grown. Hoskins felt this was the essential ethos of English civilization, and in particular of the yeoman class, out of which Shakespeare, Harvey, Newton and so many others – including Hoskins himself – came.

It would be fifteen years before I saw Bury Barton again. Then one sparkling sunlit December day I had a chance to see the place properly. In the meantime, north Devon had changed: now a land of ubiquitous weekend holiday cottages – almost, in the mid 1990s, a commuter land. The countryside had become prettified and kerbed with an unnecessary clutter of road signs. But still, the Council for the Protection of Rural England had just announced that this was one of only three major 'tranquil zones' left in England, untouched by industry, major roads and 'development' (a word which made Hoskins see red).

At the top of the lane was the chapel, with its brown ironstone walls and wagon roof, a soft sheen of green moss over the thatch (and a barn owl still nesting in the roof – barn owls are very loyal to their houses). The farmhouse itself had been reroofed in Welsh tiles (in ancient times it would have been thatched with reeds). Walking through the yard, I saw the sun gleaming on the white-washed cob walls of the Tudor barn and cider house.

In the kitchen, Mrs Ramsay made tea and sat down at a big square pine table; she was pretty, slim, in jeans and blouse, her hair in a bob. Mr Ramsay was digging in the garden in his wellington boots. He was a surveyor in Exeter. The Ramsays had been there now ten years or so, and their children were nearly grown up. I sat and stared out of the window towards the moor as she told me what she knew of the house.

'It stopped being the farmhouse in 1943: the farmer built a newer house on the hill in the copse. They still farm ... store their machinery in our barn and in the outer yard by the chapel. The people we bought it from, the Pecks, moved in at that time and lived here for forty years.'

She poured the tea.

'The kids have loved growing up here. It's a magical place. It's a funny house, eccentric, really. It's almost as if it is alive. It has never been modernized, so it still carries all the little additions made by the previous generations. The problem is, it needs a lot of love and care, and it's getting a bit down at heel now. Some of the Georgian window-frames – like this one in the kitchen – have to be replaced now, though of course, as the house is listed, they must be done in exactly the same way. It can be a bit of a burden. You can't go away for any length of time. It needs us here. It's a constant job, really.'

Above the fireplace in the sitting-room was an unpainted plaster overmantel with twining vines and mythical figures, a coat of arms, and the date 1614, with the initials J B and M B.

'That's John Bury's marriage to Mary,' Mrs Ramsay explained.

Upstairs was a warren of rooms. Lathe and wattle and straw stuffing came out of the plaster in an empty back storeroom where the ceiling was sagging. In the main bedroom, the upright posts of what I imagined had once been an open hall came through the floor and disappeared into the roof, framing the room. We peeped into the roof space: there was a huge roof tree, and two crucks with massive beams. There were frequent signs of woodworm.

'Now I expect you'll want to know about the archaeological dig?'

It was the first I'd heard of it.

'They had taken some aerial photographs and discovered that the house was inside a Roman fort.'

Mrs Ramsay took me over the road to the site which had been dug by a team from the University of Exeter. It looked north across the Yeo valley to where Lapford spread over its low hill with the big thirteenth-century tower of St Thomas's church.

'We had the excavation team for several summers a few years back. Professor Malcolm Todd was the leader. He really wanted to dig up the courtyard, to find how far back the house went, but we didn't want to go through that much disruption. Great fun and all that, but they'd have had the kitchen floor up in a jiffy if we'd let them! I'm not that interested in history.'

We walked a hundred yards down the lane past the wood, where there was another spring-fed pond. She stopped and pointed into a field. 'There's the ditches of the Roman fort.'

Once I knew what I was looking for, they were really clear. It was surprising that Hoskins missed them, but maybe he never expected them to be so far from the house.

'Professor Todd thinks there were two camps, one inside the other.' We walked back into the courtyard.

'What else did they find?'

She left her boots at the front door. Inside the porch was something wrapped in newspaper.

'Flints like this.'

It was dark blue, almost blackish.

'They came from Beer Head, about thirty miles away on the

coast near Seaton. The mines there are now a tourist museum. You can go down them.'

'Any prehistoric pottery?'

'I don't think so, but remember these were found out on the edge of the site. The main site they think is under the house and courtyard . . . unfortunately.'

She smiled.

I turned the flint over. It was a clearly shaped scraper and it showed that the hill in the area of the farm had been occupied as far back as Neolithic times: 3000 BC!

I phoned Professor Todd as soon as I got back. He had moved from Exeter to Durham now.

'The dig report is still in the bottom of my drawer, I'm afraid. I'm rector of a college here now and you simply get overwhelmed by the admin. and paperwork. But I hope it will see the light of day in the next year or two. You see, the material became much more extensive than we thought it would.'

'What happened with the dig?'

'It got more complicated after 1984. The house is inside two Roman forts. The larger one probably dates from Vespasian's campaign in the AD forties and fifties, when the Romans conquered the south-west. It's big, more than twenty acres. Looks like more than a temporary camp, perhaps big enough to be a campaign base. It was short-lived, though: dug in the late forties or early fifties, and abandoned by the seventies. Then there's the small one: four and a half acres. It's the best-preserved Roman fort in the south-west. That's the one whose ditches you can see by the copse down the lane. You can trace it all round the perimeter except where the house stands. This was the only one we test dug, and then only on the outer perimeter.'

'What did you find?'

'Traces of wooden buildings. Most interesting, we found bits of flanged bowls – black burnished ware: probably second to early third century AD. Good-quality stuff. It suggests the site was reoccupied later, and possibly by people of some status. I wonder whether perhaps the place had some official function, an administrative

centre, maybe. But what it is really all about, only intensive excavation can tell. All the answers lie under the house. We couldn't
dig the house area as the owners weren't keen. But then something
new turned up. We were also field-walking the whole area, mapping
other sites, and just then we located another settlement over the
valley: at a farm called Rudge. Do you know about Devon rounds?'

'Can't say I do.'

'They are earthwork enclosures which are called rounds in Devon
dialect. Anyway, the Rudge round was a small native settlement
of the same period as the Roman fort. We found the same sort of
thing here as we found in the fort at Bury Barton. It was the same
date, clearly a native settlement linked to the Roman site. We
excavated that in detail. But the answers to what you are looking
for lie with Bury Barton. There may be continuity all the way
through – but how to prove it?'

Domesday Book is always a good place to start, because clues
sometimes exist there which can point you to a much earlier history.
In the survey of 1086 is not only a name but a community, a
population, a local economy: a set of relationships, and a structure
of power and ownership which sometimes may be very old indeed.
You can learn a lot from the cryptic notes of the Conqueror's
surveyors. Their survey of England is listed by shire under landowners. In Devon, the king, as always, is first, then the main
religious landowner in the county: the bishop of Exeter. The
bishop's first section lists his houses in Exeter; the second gives the
ancient manor of Crediton and its appendages. Then comes a list
of twenty-two smaller estates. The first one is this:

The same bishop holds Berie. In the time of King Edward [i.e., before
1066] it paid tax for one virgate of land. Land for three ploughs [i.e.,
ploughteams]. There are four villagers and three smallholders who have
two ploughteams. Five acres of meadow. Worth 7s. and 6d.

In Exeter Cathedral library, there survives a preliminary draft for
the survey of the south-west. It has much more detail, in some
places itemizing every sheep and cow. The entry for Beria opens

the folios of this draft. It is disappointingly unrevealing, though there is a minor difference in addition to the spelling of the name: 'The bishop has three villagers who have two ploughs.' Probably there were three dependent semi-free tenants in 1086.

But is Berie certainly Bury? The lack of any definite mention of the place till Tudor times makes this not quite certain. But no other place fits so well, and being in North Tawton hundred it is in the right order in the list. For anything earlier, the landscape detective draws a blank. The Exeter archives have been very unlucky: burned by the Danes in 1003 and bombed by the Nazis in 1942, to name but two disasters. A few Anglo-Saxon charters have survived – these are the land grants which are the first really detailed information about the early English countryside and which Hoskins used so brilliantly in *The Making of the English Landscape*. But, despite the fact that Bury was owned by the bishopric, no charter exists today, and there is no early reference to the place. Exeter had been endowed with twenty-six estates in the tenth century, but by 1050, when the new bishop Leofric came, he says he found all gone except 'one miserable little place': Ide, just outside the city over the Exe. By 1072, he had restored fifteen of the lost estates, but Berie was not among them. Seven of the original twenty-six remain unaccounted for, and their names have not come down to us. If Bury was indeed part of the original endowment, as Hoskins thought, we can't prove it.

My hope of establishing a pre-Conquest history for the house looked like falling at the first. But there was better luck with the fabric of the house. Hoskins had thought it was sixteenth-century Tudor, but since he wrote his book the house had been examined in meticulous detail by Nat Alcock. Alcock is a Professor of Chemistry by day, whose great passion is recording the ancient vernacular building styles of Britain: his drawings and notes are deposited in the Devon Record Office. His report turned out to be more informative than one could ever have hoped: the carpentry of the roof showed it was probably built in the mid fourteenth century, conceivably even before the Black Death. The surviving fabric of the house was well over 600 years old.

Then the aerial photos arrived. The Aerial Archaeology Survey team of Cambridge University had crossed Devon in the dry summers of the mid 1970s. It was they who had first noticed what were clearly two Roman forts at Bury: this was the clue which had led Professor Todd to dig on the hill. The big one was much eroded, and only just visible on the photographs. From the air, though, taken in low sunlight, the smaller one with its triple ditches was very clear, and interestingly enough, the farm lane and field boundaries precisely followed the perimeter of the fort. The Roman period down here is as yet very thinly mapped – beyond Exeter it is almost a blank – so this was an important addition. It also explained the name. As Hoskins had guessed, the Anglo-Saxons must have called it Bury because it was a *burh* – a fort. It also gave the house a prehistory, for the house was built inside what could have been one of the most important Roman stations outside Exeter. A surprising question then presented itself: could the place have been important enough in Roman times to have had a name?

By an amazing chance, given the fragmentary nature of our evidence, a detailed Roman account of the area has come down to us. It is part of the fullest – and most baffling – Roman topographical source for Britain. The text was compiled by a Christian cleric in Ravenna in around A D 700 and hence is known as the Ravenna Cosmography: a rather grand name for what actually reads like a garbled and disordered index to a Roman road atlas.

The text survives in three manuscripts of the thirteenth and fourteenth centuries A D, so it is at several removes from its sources, which must go back to a Roman copy of a Roman itinerary. Compiled originally under Severus in the early third century A D, the Cosmography covered the whole of Western Europe in massive detail, with a long geographical preface which takes us from Ireland to India (including the whereabouts of Paradise!). It gives 300 place names in Roman Britain, and its first section consists of more than twenty place names in the otherwise blank area of Roman Britain west of Exeter, naming rivers, tribes, capital cities, islands and waystations. This section seems to have used a Roman map, but also contains information based on an official document. This is suggested by its use of administrative terms like *statio*, 'station', meaning a customs post on a frontier, but also a police station or centre of control. Many of the names in the Cosmography, it has to be said, are still completely obscure, and the order is often hopelessly jumbled, but here is the very beginning of the British section as reconstructed by modern scholars. It appears to start somewhere in Devon:

Glano
FI Tavo [i.e., River Taw, Devon]
FI Cenio
Nemetotatio [Nemetostatio]
Tamara [i.e., River Tamar]

Further down the list, among those place names which can be identified, we find another *statio* apparently on the River Dart, the Roman site at Sidford in Devon, Land's End, and Exeter itself.

The fourth name in the Ravenna list, *Nemetostatio*, is one of the most fascinating place names in Britain. For *nemeton* is an ancient Celtic word which means 'a sacred wood'. The word is attested across the Celtic world, in ancient Ireland, Gaul and Britanny. In Britain it crops up in four other places, all of them highly significant. The Roman spa at Buxton in Derbyshire was called *Aquae Arnemetiae* ('the waters of the goddess of the sacred grove'); the hill of Willoughby in the Wolds on the Fosse Way in Nottinghamshire was *Vernemetum* ('the great sacred grove'); the Roman shrine within the Iron Age fort at Lydney in Gloucestershire, may have been *Nemetobala* ('the grove on the hill'); and *Medionemetum*, 'the place in the middle of the sacred grove', was very likely the remarkable prehistoric shrine at Larbert in Stirlingshire. Such groves were often associated with sacred pools or sacred springs; an inscription to Nemetona, the goddess of the grove, was found at the hot springs in Bath. *Nemetostatio*, then, was 'the station in the sacred forest'.

Now, around Bury Barton there is a cluster of *nemet* place names which is unparalleled in the rest of Britain. Thirteen Domesday manors bearing the name are recorded in the area around the Taw and the Yeo. Even today, eight village and farm names survive – among them Nymet Rowland, Broad Nymet and Nymet Tracy. A clue to the distribution of these names is offered by an Anglo-Saxon charter for Bury's neighbouring parish of Down St Mary. Dated 974, it survives in an original parchment sheet in the Public Record Office in London. It contains a physical description of the boundaries of an Anglo-Saxon estate which runs up the Yeo to a point only three hundred yards from Bury Barton. In this charter, King Edgar gifts land to his thegn Aelfhere, 'in the place called in common speech by the name *nymed*'. On the back of the parchment, the charter is also endorsed *aet nymed*. So in Edgar's day the whole area around Bury Barton bore that name. The charter bounds mention the highway (the *herpath*, literally the 'army way': the Exeter–Barnstaple road) and then the boundary continues to 'where rush brook flows to the nymed'. Then the survey tells us precisely where we are when it goes on 'east by rush brook to sheep brook [today's Shobrooke] then up sheep brook to Copplestone' (a ten-foot-high Anglo-Saxon granite marker stone which still stands on the side of the A377, and which is still the meeting place of three parishes). So the old name of the River Yeo was also *nymed*. The river must have been named after the forest through which it passed.

So in the Iron Age there was an extensive sacred wood across this part of central Devon; and the Roman site at Bury was inside this sacred wood by the river 'Nemet'. And with that single ancient word, the search for the history of the house moved inexorably back before the Romans, into the time of the ancient Britons.

So where was *Nemetostatio*? On our present knowledge, there are only two Roman settlements where it could be: North Tawton, or Bury itself. One might perhaps plump for North Tawton, for this was the administrative centre of the hundred in Anglo-Saxon times. But North Tawton is on the Taw, not the Yeo (or 'Nemet') where one might expect *Nemetostatio*. And Bury was a big earth-work: twenty acres is a major site, and it occupied an important position, dominating the road from Exeter to the north Devon coast. So could Bury have been the Roman *Nemetostatio*, later known to the first Anglo-Saxon settlers as 'the *burh* by the Nimet'?

Staring at the aerial images of the Roman defences, it was hard to resist putting two and two together. The Roman fort; the Celtic sacred wood; the spring-fed ponds on the hill, still surrounded by a grove of trees. Hints perhaps: a mere hypothesis, but a workable hypothesis. (And how strange that even in the 1870s, only a mile or so away, the newspapers should have reported dark pagan goings-on, a return to ancestral customs within the area of the ancient sacred forest!) Perhaps people had indeed lived on the site since prehistory. Even though much of it was still guesswork, I felt tempted to make a stab at the history of the house.

Settlers came into upland Devon after the last Ice Age. Then Neolithic farmers made their homes on the fringes of Dartmoor, fashioning their tools from flint scrapers. They chose hill sites, leaving the heavily wooded river valleys which exist even today. In the Bronze Age, with better tools, the uplands were cleared. Then, in the Iron Age, Celtic immigrants planted farms in their thousands across the south-west. And so the pattern of habitation was laid out and the land was named. All the river names here are still British: Torridge and Taw, Yeo and Dach. Later, after the Roman conquest, Exeter became a thriving colony of the Roman empire, with sea links with the Mediterranean which were maintained late into the Dark Ages. But outside the city the land was only lightly Romanized. The region was still essentially an Iron Age society and economy, based on small isolated farms, when the Anglo-Saxon migrations brought a new colonial class spreading from the east during the seventh century. Just as with the Romans, this process was piecemeal and was never completed. The Cornish had their own kings till the ninth century, and Celtic speech only died out here in the eighteenth century. The coming of the English was not a mass migration but the work of warrior groups who settled and married locals. By the late seventh century, Devon was ruled by the kings of Wessex, and a monastery was founded in the old Roman *colonia* at Exeter endowed with lands across east Devon. But the diluting of the Celtic element in Devon was a very long process. British speech survived for centuries, and there are still churches in Devon with Celtic dedications; Clannaburgh, very

near Barton, is still St Petroc's, for example. These were ancient
hill sites linked by hidden patterns in a landscape already ancient
in 1086. The site at Bury on its spur over the Yeo was surely part
of that pattern.

The farms which are characteristic of upland Devon mostly lie
on land cultivated long before the arrival of the English. That had
been one of Hoskins's great insights. He found that many, if not
most, of the 9,500 farms in Devon in 1086 were still in existence
today, usually under the Devon name of Barton.

The map of Devon in the eleventh century would have looked very like
the map today, even on the one-inch scale. Practically all the thousands
of farm names printed on the modern map would have been on the
earlier map, could it have been drawn; and nearly all the thousands of
miles of lanes and by-roads would have existed also.

In fact, a good deal of the man-made landscape – settlement
sites, ecclesiastical sites, estates and their boundaries, roads and tracks
– was probably already in place in the Late-Roman period; some
of it goes further back still.

We are never likely to know the names of the British and English
owners of Bury in the Dark Ages: people like the Saxon Aelfhere,
who owned the Nemet estate next door to Bury. But to speculate
– in the tenth century, when the minster at Exeter was refounded,
twenty-six estates were given to the church, a number of them
former Roman sites. Bury was probably among them. The new
tenant of Bury could have still been British, but most likely he was
an Anglo-Saxon thegn who must have lived in an open wooden
hall with cob walls and a cruck roof, nestling in the corner of the
Roman fort where the house is now. British serfs would have
worked his lands, protected by a ditch and palisade around the
perimeter of the *burh*. That would have been the life of the place
in the last century or so before the Normans. The thegn of Bury,
let us imagine, would have been summoned by the beacon fires
from Ide and gone to fight the Vikings with the 'men of Devon'
in 1002; he and his wife and children would have attended the

great festivals at Exeter, when the relics and banners of the saints were paraded through the streets, and the stories of their deeds and martyrdoms recited outside the minster; perhaps they even bought luxury goods – French wine, a length of Byzantine silk – from traders at Topsham quay.

Then, in 1086, Bury hits the light of day again in Domesday Book after what was already a long history. At that time, three villeins (semi-free peasants) lived and farmed on the hill, under the bishop's tenant. Alongside them were three smallholders. Bearing this in mind and looking at the magnificent Ordnance Survey maps at 25 inches to the mile which were produced in the mid nineteenth century, we can reconstruct the manor of Bury in 1086. It lay south of the River Yeo, and with land for three ploughteams had about 250 acres, much as the farm does today. There were five acres of meadow down by the river, along with woodland for timber and grazing swine. The three dependent farms worked by the villeins in 1086 are still there: Kelland, Pennycots and Edgeley. All three of these modern names go back to Old English personal names – Ecgi, Cylla and Pinna – these were presumably the villeins who worked for the tenant of Bury in the eleventh century. The three smallholders probably lived down by the river; as late as the 25-inch map in 1889, Bury and Kelland cottages are marked by the bridge. The cottagers' huts and allotments had stood here for centuries. These cottagers formed the Tudor underclass and are still described as landless labourers in the seventeenth-century surveys.

At some point after the Conquest, the church in Exeter granted Bury to a family who took the name of the place. Perhaps their ancestors were freeholders who had rented the episcopal manor for generations; we don't know. The family name would run through to the nineteenth century. If one generation had no sons then the Bury daughters took the farm, and a condition of marriage was that their husbands took the family name. This custom can be traced in many other places in Devon, where continuity of place was more important than continuity of person. You became a Bury, or a Seccombe, for example, by marrying yourself to the place, by literally husbanding the patrimony; a striking testimony to the idea that a family took their identity from their place, from their native soil.

Unfortunately, when we reach the medieval history of Bury, the trail peters out for a while. The rich store of documents we have for other parts of England is lacking here. The Hundred Rolls, the records of the inquisition of the 1270s which make up a second Domesday, are lacking for Devon. In particular, the Exeter records are gone. What we would really like to have – manorial accounts, extents, wills, post-mortem lists of chattels – are all missing for Bury. In the standard reference work, the English Place Name Society volume on Devon, a post-mortem of 1503 is cited as the first definite mention of the place. But there are many unexamined medieval surveys and tax lists: no less than seventeen taxes were levied between 1290 and 1334 and they are a mine of information for the local historian. Among these, the subsidy of 1332 was published not so long ago. Among the list of taxpaying freeholders in Devon in 1332, there is no Bury named under Lapford, the parish to which the farm belongs today. But in the neighbouring parish of Nymet Roland, among twenty-two freeholders we find these names, most of which can be tied to still-working farms marked on the large-scale Ordnance maps:

> Wiliam de Bukyngton 2s. [This is High Beckington Farm]
> Matthew de Legh 2s. [There are three Leighs today; this is perhaps East Leigh where there is still a medieval house]
> Thomas de Chilverdon 2s. [Chilverton in Coldridge, still a medieval house]
> Robert de Clyfhangre 8d. [Cleavanger, a medieval house]
> John de Clyfhangre 8d.
> John atte Brigge 12d. [Nymet Bridge]

And there among them is:

> John atte Bury 12d.

So John 'atte Bury' was registered among the freeholders of Nymet Rowland. Nymet Rowland was clearly much bigger than the tiny parish it is now. In 1332 it included the Domesday manors of Nimet, Berie and Coldridge; the whole northern part of the hundred which lay in the land enclosed by the rivers Taw and Yeo – the area of the old sacred wood. So Bury was part of Nymet until later joined to Lapford, perhaps in Tudor times.

The thirteenth century had been a boom time: the population soared from two million in 1086 to five or six million in 1300. But a massive collapse followed in the fourteenth century. The Black Death led to depopulation in many parts of Devon: many isolated farms were deserted between the early fourteenth and the late fifteenth century, their ruins still traceable on the fringes of Dartmoor and Exmoor. The Great Famine of 1317–22 precipitated the catastrophe, but the decline had in fact already started in the early fourteenth century in the less fertile hill-slopes of Devon and the moory landscapes of the far west of Cornwall. Rents were falling long before the great plague struck. Diseases prevalent in animals also ravaged the farming community – just as BSE was to hit Devon so hard in the late twentieth century. In a countryside where smallholders predominated, destitution was soon widespread. At Ottery St Mary in 1334, twenty-six tenants abandoned their holdings because they couldn't pay the royal tenth. In neighbouring Somerset on the manor of Shapwick, three poor itinerant women 'of Devonshire' were fined for gleaning – 'but pardoned because dead'.

Looking out over the bleak ridge south towards Kelland, I imagined it must have been especially hard for the tied peasants who lived in the cottages down where the petrol station now stands at Lapford Cross. With their damp living conditions and poor diets, they were the first to suffer. And decline and death (and plague) were well established even before 24 June 1348, when the Black Death came in a ship through the Dorset port of Melcombe Regis. Later outbreaks in the 1360s and 1370s only served to exacerbate the decline which brought the fifteenth-century population of England down to the level of the late eleventh or twelfth century. As late as the 1490s, outsiders and foreign visitors alike found the land very thinly inhabited. These were bad times to be a farmer.

Back in the house, I scrambled up into the roof. In the torchlight I could see the middle truss timber was blackened with smoke from the days in the fourteenth century when the hall was open to the roof, with a hearth in the floor below. What happened at Bury during the Black Death we don't know for sure, lacking the documents. But the family evidently survived; and here the archaeology of the house itself can help us for the first time in the story. If the surviving fabric is anything to go by, the Bury family in the fourteenth century became wealthy and successful. In the period right after the Black Death, the house was rebuilt. It often happens this way – whether in history or today: families go through great trauma, then the next generation makes a fresh start. At any rate, a new house was built on the site, with the big crucks you can still see inside, bracing the roof. The whole building was around a hundred feet long, with service wings at either end containing the kitchens and the living quarters, including the solar – the owner's bedroom in an upper chamber. The centre of the building was a large open hall, forty feet by twenty-two feet, with an open hearth in the middle of the floor under the roof which survives today, thirty feet high at the ridge. This was the centre of domestic life for the next few generations: strewn with rushes, and lit by torches at night, dark and smoky, but throbbing with life at family feasts and festivals, when the long table and benches were laid out and food and cider provided for friends and neighbours. That was the house in the days of Chaucer's Wife of Bath and Langland's Piers Ploughman and his 'fair fields full of folk'.

Not long afterwards, in the reign of Richard II, the family moved up in the world. They bought Colleton Barton a few miles to the north. (This fact we owe to the Devon historian Tristram Risdon, who was writing around 1630.) Colleton is a grander house, with finer decoration, and from then on Bury became a subsidiary dwelling, a farm for the younger son or daughter. This explains its survival: it was never pulled down, but modernized piecemeal, and it stayed a working farmhouse till the middle of the twentieth century. The three smaller farms which existed in 1086 were sold off around this time. The villein families at Kelland and Pennycots in time rose to become yeomen farmers in their own right, again taking the name of their place: the Kellands, in particular, appear in the local records for hundreds of years. Bury, though, was still important enough to the family for them to build a chapel there. Thirty feet long, in Devon brownstone with a typical Devon wagon roof, it was dedicated to St James, and licensed on 6 July 1434, according to the bishop's register. There was quite a vogue for such private chapels among Devon yeomen farmers in the fourteenth to fifteenth century, and several wonderful ones survive. A measure of the prosperity of a family, they speak not only of faith, but of wealth, status, and the growing desire for private space.

Of the Bury family's possessions, no inventory has yet turned up. But the handful of Devon wills from this time give us a good idea of the chattels of farmers like them, and also of their chief preoccupations: their loyalty to the local church, for example, and their friendships with neighbours. In 1416, the year after Agincourt, John Ufflete of Woolfardisworthy East in Devon bequeaths his armour, sword and shield and horse; but to wives of his neighbours he leaves a gilt cup, a maple-wood bowl, a silk girdle and a gold ring. Among his domestic goods were brass pots, saucers and pans, iron cooking pots, two pewter dishes, a cloak, a candlestick, a mattress and bedcovers.

That perhaps gives us an idea of the Burys just before the Wars of the Roses. It is in Henry VII's day that we get our first contemporary reference to the family since 1334: the death of William Bury in 1503. This was on the eve of the recovery of rural England, the time of the Great Rebuilding, as Hoskins called it. People were beginning to thrive again; and in the landowning classes the Tudor century saw a movement towards more middle-class taste and privacy. The story is there in the architecture of Bury Barton. Up till then, the hall had been open to the roof, with an open fire in the floor. Now come the 'middle-class' innovations: bedrooms, fireplaces and windows. The hall is divided, and a floor inserted. In the roof one may see where the carpenters had to cut into the main timbers to insert the bedroom floor. Chimneys were put in, and downstairs a partition. As for possessions, the visitor would have noticed more furniture – chests, cupboards, tables and chairs, with cloth hangings on the walls. In people's wills there was wider circulation of money: William Richards in 1532 gives £6 13s. 4d. to each of his three sons and five daughters, in addition to other sums of money to his own church, and to friends and neighbours. We are moving into a money economy.

The story of the Bury family's economic life is told clearly in their farm buildings. For now the farm becomes a detailed record in itself. In the Tudor period it was greatly expanded, to judge by the surviving structures. In the Middle Ages there had probably been just one big barn. Now the courtyard is built: the north range of buildings early in the sixteenth century, then a new stone barn 75 feet long. A slightly later building on the north side has a stone floor and large windows. This looks domestic rather than for animals or storage, and most likely was accommodation for the farmworkers, some of whom might have been migrants who came in seasonally. As for the character of farming at that time, the courtyard shows the main economy was still agriculture, grain not stock. These were not easy times for farmers: there were many bad harvests, and in the champagne lands of the Midlands, much unrest, especially where the big landowners were enclosing land for sheep. But the old upland farming life of Devon was relatively untouched. The family were still doing well.

From the sixteenth century, a relative flood of material illuminates the house and the life lived in it. The parish registers of Lapford, for example, start in 1557, and for the first time they give us a full picture of the community, in its baptisms, marriages and deaths. Other evidence of people's jobs and status can be gleaned from the various tax returns, subsidy rolls and 'home guard' musters (which name all the 'habell men' within the parish; the sort of people Shakespeare sends up affectionately in Shallow's Gloucester). From these it is possible to draw a picture of the old yeomen families like the Burys and their neighbours and friends, who formed the basis of the squirearchy of Devon for the next 250 years. This is the beginning of what Hoskins called the Golden Age of rural England, which he placed between Elizabeth's day and the accession of

Victoria; a world rooted in continuity of place and descent. But life could still be unpredictable. The freezing winters of Elizabeth's reign must have been terrible for the poor on the fringes of Dartmoor (1601 is still the coldest year on record). In the Great Flood of 20 January 1606, 'a mighty storm and tempest' killed many when the Taw overflowed. Plague, too, was still a killer. In the plague year of 1597, Shakespeare's company were on tour in nearby Barnstaple to avoid the teeming streets of London, but Devon did not escape: that April in Lapford parish there was catastrophe. The Burys' neighbour Matthew Shorpsheire and his wife Joane Allin lost, in quick succession, five of their six children: Roger (eight), Thomas (seven), and Ralph (eleven days) along with their daughters Joane and four-year-old Anne. Matthew himself died in early May.

The head of the Bury family at this time was Humphrey (1584–1631), who lived at Colleton; his son John lived at the farm. In spring 1614 John married, and the day was commemorated in the downstairs living-room in a plaster overmantel with the arms and initials of John Bury and his bride Mary Arscott. The wedding took place on 25 April at Mary's village of Tetcott (two miles away), according to the Tetcott parish register. Again, the archaeology of the house helps us picture the life of the newly-weds. The present kitchen was built at just this time, with all the latest in Jacobean mod. cons. Measuring 17 by 20 feet, with a larder outside, it had a fireplace with a shaped lintel, and windows with glass panes. People of John and Mary's time might now have a wider range of fancy items in their homes. Ann Burrough of Lupitt, for example, mentions expensive items of household furnishing in her will: 'I leave my son the glass in the windows of the house where I dwell and all the sealing [i.e., the wainscotting] in the hall about the walls of the said house.'

The world of interiors was changing. With kitchen windows and fancy fireplaces, one may sense the good farming stock of Devon entering a world of private comfort, with even the possibility of leisure: unheard of till now, save for the rulers. John Bury may still have gone down to the fields with his workers, but as Hoskins said, with a little exaggeration perhaps, 'Instead of a mattock, the

Stuart or Georgian yeoman reached for a book in the evenings.'

John and Mary had children, including a son, Humphrey. In the 1641 Protestation returns, father and son appear together swearing they are good Protestants and will have nothing to do with popery. Humphrey died young, in May 1646, leaving a son, John. A grandparent now, Mary herself was buried on 5 December 1648, probably in her mid fifties. Her husband John long outlived her. According to the Lapford register, he was buried on 18 December 1664, aged above his three score and ten. We can trace their descendents onwards: they never had many children, as befitted gentry. To marry late and have small families was a pattern long established among the English middle classes. There they contrast with their yeomen neighbours, the Kellands, whose children pack the baptismal registers of the sixteenth and seventeenth centuries. The Kellands survive today. The last Bury died in 1804: the family had probably lived in the same house for over 600 years, and who knows, maybe since long before the Conquest.

Delving in the Ramsays' outbuildings, I had almost come up to date. Here were the remains of the last two centuries of farming on the hill: in the cider-making room, for example, with its Victorian apple-crusher and press. (There is still an apple orchard by the side of the house, probably just for domestic supply and to provide drink for thirsty workers at harvest time.) But built into the wall of the barn which contained the press and the cider-barrel store were broken pieces of a massive, circular granite trough from an older, horse-drawn apple crusher: probably from the early eighteenth century.

Around 1800, the outer courtyard was built, the great pillared wooden sheds which the Devonians call linhays. That signalled a major change in the life of the farm: the shift from agriculture to stock breeding, cattle farming. The smaller open farmyard built in the Tudor age for grain storage was also now enclosed for stock. The collection of farm buildings, twenty ancient and a dozen modern, ends up spanning nearly five centuries. Up till the seventeenth century the farm was largely arable; there was an increase in the number of cattle in the eighteenth century, and a very large increase in the nineteenth century with the demand for beef on every British table. The whole tale of the highland zone of south-western Britain is here in this one place.

The rest of the story of the house can be pieced together from parish registers, trade gazeteers, and the local papers. The last Bury, as we saw, died in 1804; his widow left the place to Captain Richard Incledon, who took the name of Bury. But by the late 1830s the Denshams lived at Bury: an old yeoman family of Lapford parish who are there in Tudor musters and tax returns (and are still there today: it was a Densham who published the Lapford Parish Registers for the Devon Record Society in 1954). In the twentieth century the area entered a period of greater change than at any other time in these islands. The cataclysms of the Great War and then the mechanization of farming ended the old way of life for good. The highland zone of the south-west was left behind in the British economy, though it brought the railways to Lapford and electricity and running water to Bury (the medieval well is still there, though, under the stairs, and still has water). The barton ceased to be the farmhouse in 1943, but the farm is still working next door. By the late 1960s, cattle had been completely replaced by sheep: 370 ewes and some arable, 120 acres of barley and 10 acres of root crops on a total of 250 acres – not that different perhaps from the land use in 1086. In the 1980s, though, cattle were back again: a herd of Frisians grazing the big field below the ridge and enduring the shocks of BSE and the red tape of Brussels. Such was farming life in western Britain in the 1990s, its links with the old hill-farming of the past now tenuous – an archaic life, represented by the last of the old generation who live in isolated cob farmsteads in the bleak valleys up towards Exmoor and the wooded valleys of the Taw and the Torridge.

William Hoskins had been right. It would be possible to take any house and write its story, which somehow would also be a history of part of England itself. My brief portrait of this one house out of so many thousands in the south-west could be much improved and expanded – especially in the past four centuries, when records are so plentiful. There is surely more to come, lying unnoticed in

Devon archives; and the fabric of the house doubtless has more secrets to reveal. The tale I have told with conjectures may yet be provable, if the archaeologists ever get their spades into the land around the house and under the kitchen floor . . .

Not long ago, the Ramsays decided to leave Bury. The children had grown up; the house and its yards, rambling and ramshackle, needed more love and care than they could manage. They put the house up for sale, for the kind of money which buys a flat in my part of London. I confess my heart jumped for a moment as the vision crossed my mind of upping roots and moving down to Devon to live with shades of the druidical custodians of the sacred grove, Aelfhere the Saxon, John atte Bury, Mary Arscott with her new kitchen, little Thomas Colyhole and the rest. My family rapidly dissuaded me. The point about history is that it is gone; it is a world we have lost. 'You'll end up like Jean de Florette,' said my wife. But I confess that I still think about it sometimes with a slight pang of regret. What I loved about Bury (like so many Devon houses) is that it's an ordinary yeoman's house: nothing posh, only three rooms downstairs. In the fourteenth century, the owners were small landowners; yeomen in the later Middle Ages; well-to-do gentry in King James's day. But it was never a grand place, which is why it was never demolished, but always updated piecemeal. So something of the life lived in it over so many generations has come down in the successive layers of the fabric, enabling us still to touch it today. In its ordinariness there is perhaps some key to the English story, in the continuity of life lived on that windswept hill dating back to Domesday and possibly long before; before the coming of the English, before the Romans, and maybe even – if the flints from Beer Head mean anything – before the Bronze Age.

13. Peatling Magna: August 1265

I met Michael again years after I left university, when he had retired. He was one of the great medieval scholars of his day, and by a lucky chance for me he had supervised my postgraduate work. We had lunch at another old pupil's house near Bath. I felt bad that I had never submitted my thesis, though I'd written a piece for his retirement volume, about which he had written to me amusingly: 'I took it as an olive branch from a wayward pupil to a deserted supervisor.' After lunch we walked in the garden; he was smoking the remains of a cheroot (a still cloud of smoke had always hung over his chair in his rooms in Merton Street). Curiously enough, his background had not been from the very beginning in the exacting discipline of medieval history, but in imaginative literature, in the Charlemagne Romances, the great cycle of tales which is second only to the Arthurian legend in medieval European literature. During the war, he had worked in Intelligence; afterwards he went on to professorships and wrote famous books on early medieval history. His work was above all about Europe, but when he retired it was to fulfil a long-held ambition to write a commentary on Bede's History. So Bede was on his mind a lot in old age. Few students of medieval history can escape Bede's impact. There have been many great historians, but few permanently changed the writing and the perception of history in their own civilization, as Bede did. We reached the fence in tall damp green grass at the bottom of the garden. Michael was talking about Bede in particular, and medieval people in general:

'Do you think you can ever know them?'

To me it seemed an irretrievable distance. You make a stab out of the fragments which have survived. Occasionally, with people like Alfred, you think you're getting through to their real feelings.

'No, not really,' I said.

But of course the truth was I didn't know them well enough to be able to begin to know them – if that doesn't sound too much of a contradiction. To know how Bede thinks, you have to start by sinking yourself into his beautiful, clear, simple Latin. A task beyond me. And a lifetime's work. That's what it means to be a true scholar.

'Do you?' I asked.

'Oh yes,' he replied. 'I dream of Bede.' He shook his head as if he had taken himself by surprise. 'He speaks to me. I feel as if I know him.'

I, too, was surprised. It was a side of him he'd never let show. But then, as the poet said, old men should be explorers. I should have been alerted by a lecture he once gave about what it was like to be a poor peasant in the Dark Ages, in which he relaxed his terse lapidary style to let us imagine, for a moment, serfs on the edge of the Maconnais (as I think it was), in a place liable to flood, oppressed by the exactions of their landlords, by the poor level of their material culture – bone pins and wooden ploughs – and by their miserable diet, as they worked to feed their betters; harvesting the pale green patches of cress from their lord's moat to get some iron.

'I feel as if I know him,' he said with a twinkle, as if amused by the admission. His predecessor Charles Plummer, the nineteenth-century editor of Bede, had been famously criticized for over-identifying with Bede's charm, his sweetness (*dulce* was a word Bede used a lot), his 'delight' in study, his generosity to others, his humility, and his scholarly toughness. But therein lies the danger for the historian. You have to put yourself into the people of the past to make them come alive, but you must never forget that when you see them live again, it is your blood which makes them do so. Great as he was, Plummer portrayed Bede as a nineteenth-century Christian gentleman, donnish and saintlike. Michael, more than anyone, was aware of the difficulty, this far on in time, of getting anywhere near the objectives of Bede's work, of understanding *his* rules, of being sensitive to his language, to his meanings. It was a lifetime's job, which now he just hoped he would have time to complete, all too well aware of the unavoidable pitfalls of putting our own values on to the past and the people who lived then.

We trudged on round the garden as the autumn light thickened, treading a mat of sodden leaves. Across the valley, the high-speed train wooshed into the tunnel on Brunel's railway heading towards London, as a veil of rain loosed over the hills behind Bredbury Fort. Then he told me a story.

'You know, there's a story from the revolt of Simon de Montfort in the great rebellion of 1265 which has always intrigued me. It's the story of a village in Leicestershire. A place called Peatling Magna. The Revolt was over. Simon de Montfort had been killed at Evesham. The king's men come into the village armed to the teeth. The peasants tell them to get out, because they are against the community of the realm, the *communitas regni*. Think of it. The peasants tell the king's men that they are against the community of the land! Why? How had they grasped that? And where did the idea come from?'

He chewed on his cheroot and stared across the Avon valley as the first rain spattered heavy drops on the leaves in the garden.

'It always bothered me, that story. You know, our sources are from the high-ups: the kings, the clerics, the tax inspectors. We only know the peasants from what the rulers say about them. Archaeologists can show us what's left of their villages; we can describe their poor diets, reconstruct their diseases, imagine their aching bones. But they never *speak*. Now here's the peasants speaking – and they are talking about the *communitas regni*! How did they know they belonged to a national community? How did ordinary peasants get that idea?'

Michael died not long afterwards. When he died, he left his commentary on Bede neatly completed on his desk, with a request for Bede's last prayer to be spoken at his service, the brief beautiful prayer in which Bede gives humble thanks to Jesus for having been granted his lifetime's work, 'joyfully imbibing your knowledge'.

The memorial service was held in Merton Chapel. It was the end of winter, thick snow. I took the train to Oxford and sat freezing in a pew with the great and the good. Afterwards, I walked round Christchurch Meadow, where all the elms had gone since my student days.

I missed the express back to Paddington and took the stopping train through the snowy Oxfordshire countryside, through Goring, Pangbourne and Streatley, past villages whose people had also resisted their lords in the thirteenth century. (In one place, Newington, they raised a collection of 4d. a head to fight the case in court: perhaps the first-recorded strike fund in British labour history.) On the left, just before the Thames, we passed Ethelred's church at Cholsey, site of a gigantic tithe barn where the peasants had laboured to amass their lord's grain. Here, by the thirteenth century, even the unfree peasants were resisting the demand to give service, pushing in the lawcourts to commute for money, to move from status to contract. Even before the Barons' Revolt, the ordinary peasants of England were involving themselves in politics. As we trundled over the bridge at Streatley, it set me thinking again of the story Michael had told. What exactly had happened in Peatling Magna in August 1265?

The story is told by Maurice Powicke in his great book, *King Henry III and the Lord Edward*. The jury case was printed in 1941 in the dauntingly titled *Select Cases of Procedure without Writ under Henry III*, one of the series of medieval English legal texts published by the Selden Society, an unrivalled treasure trove of social history. The original document is kept today in the Public Record Office at Kew; it was written by a royal scribe of the time in a great parchment roll, Curia Regis Roll number 175, membrane 29. It is one of thousands which survive, testimony to the obsessive accounting, judging and recording of a government for whom written law was a central feature of rule, and was understood as such by high and low. At the centre of the tale is the precise interpretation of a single phrase: the *communitas regni*, or *communitas Angliae – le Commun de Engleterre* as it was expressed by the French-speaking nobility. Writing in the immediate aftermath of Hitler's war, Powicke's understanding of it was almost mystical; for him it was an early conception of the community of England. But let that be for now. Suffice it to say that this August day in 1265 stands precisely midway between our own time and the traditional date of the coming of Cerdic. For us at the end of the twentieth century, it comes at the mid point of English history.

The Barons' Revolt of Simon de Montfort came half a century after the Magna Carta. Then King John had acceded to the barons' demands. Immediately after his death it was reissued in the name of his successor. There are several versions up to 1225, and since then it has come to be regarded by English people, and by all who have adopted English law, as the chief constitutional defence against arbitrary or unjust rule. Its most famous clauses express some of the English people's most deeply held political beliefs. Take these:

39. No free man shall be seized or imprisoned, or stripped of his rights or possessions, or outlawed or exiled, or deprived of his standing in any other way, nor will we proceed with force against him, or send others to do so, except by the lawful judgement of his equals, or by the law of the land.
40. To no one will we sell, to no one deny or delay right or justice.

Later, lawyers found here the basis for some fundamental rights: equality before the law, freedom from arbitrary arrest (a characteristic English conception: freedom *from*, as against freedom *to*). To the king, of course, 1215 was a treaty of peace forced on him under duress by barons who had rebelled against the royal authority. The story reached its climax in the Barons' Revolt of 1264–5, under its leader Simon de Montfort. Simon became a heroic figure, around whom popular tales, songs and even miracle stories gathered: the priceless flower, *la fleur de pris*, 'who died unflinchingly [*sauntz feyntise*] like Thomas the martyr of Canterbury', and who, like him, had no truck with royal power. Simon and the barons were determined to maintain the limitations on royal power granted by the Magna Carta and to force the king to rule within a framework of custom and Common Law. Their movement was particularly attentive to the opinions of the shire, the fundamental unit of local rule. In 1258, in the Provisions of Oxford, the barons attempted to reduce Henry III to the status of a constitutional monarch –

it has been said that 'no other kingdom in Europe had gone so far towards a republican Constitution'. The name of the movement is most revealing: the Barons (who were French-speaking) called themselves the 'community of the realm' (*le Commun de Engleterre*), for they claimed to represent the interests of the country as a whole. They demanded that elected councillors should hold a parliament three times a year, 'to review the state of the realm and to deal with the common business of the realm and of the king together'. It was bound to end in war.

In the beginning, the king was defeated at Lewes and taken prisoner, but then the barons fell out. Opposition to them grew, focused round the young and capable Prince Edward, the future Edward Longshanks (the gloomy autocrat of the film *Braveheart*). Inevitably, the revolt failed. The final dreadful denouement took place at Evesham on the morning of Tuesday 4 August 1265. Simon was trapped by superior forces in a loop of the Avon and stood at bay on the high ground north of the abbey, where today a scramble in the bushes will reveal a decayed monument. It was a slaughter rather than a battle. Montfort was killed, mutilated and dismembered. As they said in a popular song of the time, it was 'the murder of Evesham, for *bataile non it was*'.

After all the turmoil and passion of social revolution, the barons' party was broken and the running of the country was disrupted. The victors rampaged through the lands of Simon's supporters, out for spoil and vengeance, despite their declaration of a state of peace. Old King Henry had been rescued wounded from the battlefield, but was still confused and disoriented. Power was in the hands of Prince Edward. Among the king's men in those first few days there was widespread talk of vengeance.

On Friday 7 August, three days after the battle, the news had already reached Montfort's heartland, Leicestershire. Royalists rapidly appeared in the shire with armed forces. The king's marshal, Peter de Nevill, and the standard bearer, Eudo de la Zouche, moved to take control of the villages of south Leicestershire between Lutterworth and Leicester, an area largely sympathetic to Earl Simon. One of them was Peatling Magna. The village was a small place: we can imagine a dried-mud street in August, lined with timber-framed houses thatched in reed, a more substantial manor house behind massive earthworks, and a stone church with a fine chancel and a typical Leicestershire stone tower which is still there today. The whole place stood in the middle of three great open fields divided into strips, which the peasants farmed cooperatively. In 1265, the population was probably about twenty-five, mainly male freeholders and their spouses and families, with a small handful of dependent peasants, perhaps a hundred adults altogether. It was a close-knit society of self-sufficient peasants, the majority of whom were free men and women – a key factor in the story.

Next day, Saturday 8 August, one of Nevill's grooms tried to go through the village with a cart of supplies. The villagers had strong feelings about this and protested. At this point the groom was confronted by 'some foolish men of the village' (one shouldn't, I know, but it is hard not to recall the language of Mrs Thatcher in the 1984 miners' strike!). The villagers then sought to arrest him with his cart and horses and in the scuffle the groom was wounded 'in the arm above his hand'. On Wednesday 12th, a large company of Peter's men were brought in to take revenge for the incident, and Peter himself now arrived on the scene. It is probably on this day that the key confrontation took place. The villagers confronted the king's marshal. They didn't want him there and told him so. According to Peter, they now accused him and his men of sedition and 'other heinous offences'. It was at this point that they told Nevill that he was 'going against the welfare of the community of the realm, and against the barons'.

It's an extraordinary scene. Remember that the Barons' Revolt has already been crushed and the peasants of the village must have known it by the Friday morning. But the king's marshal is guilty of sedition! More than that: he's against the welfare of the community of the realm (*utilitas communitatis regni*). Not surprisingly, the scene now turned nasty. Peter de Nevill threatened to burn the village down unless he got redress. The men took to the church for refuge. Now the women of the village took the lead, led by the wife of one of the peasants, Robert of Pillerton. Worried that their houses would be burned, they tried to negotiate a compromise, and, according to Nevill, promised that a sum of twenty marks should be paid to him as a fine on the following Sunday, 16 August (a mark was 6s. 8d. – so twenty was a large sum for a small village).

According to the villagers, though, Nevill had demanded sureties, and when the women explained that their men were in the church for sanctuary, Nevill's men had muscled in, roughed them up and dragged them out. The women again tried to take the heat out of the situation, with the help of the local reeve, Thomas, who had some authority. (Thomas was the village representative elected by the villagers to defend their rights in the manor court: these were communities bound by common oath who took responsibility for their fellow members, an ancient principle of English law.) At the women's prompting – but here the two sides would later strongly disagree over the course of events – five freemen agreed to stand as hostages for the payment of the fine, or perhaps were physically coerced by Nevill into doing so. They were poor men, and the rest of the community now clubbed together to provide the hostages with expenses and sent them twenty-seven pennies (a penny from each of their neighbours?). With that, Nevill took the hostages away to prison and waited for the village to toe the line.

But that wasn't the end of the story. The villagers couldn't – or wouldn't – pay the fine, and the unfortunate hostages languished in prison until the the following January, five months later. They had missed the harvest on their own land, which their wives or children would have had to gather with their neighbours' help. The village feast in November had passed them by too, and Christmas, a big time in the medieval countryside, when holidays were almost as long as those we get now. In the meantime, the community of the village had taken their complaint about Nevill's high-handed actions to the king's justices of the peace. The upshot was that the peasants took the king's marshal to court.

The case was not heard until 14 January 1266. Our surviving manuscript account is the record of this hearing. The case had been brought against Nevill by the reeve and six others 'on behalf of the community of the village', claiming that he had used violence against them and that the five hostages had been taken illegally. Nevill was ordered to appear in court in Leicester with the hostages on 14 January 1266, 'to receive and do what is right in the aforesaid matters'. Nevill arrived in a bullish mood, as the clerk noted: 'he declares that he is willing to stand trial if anyone wishes to speak against him'. Nevill denied force and wrongdoing. He had suffered trespass and violence at the hands of the 'foolish' villagers, who had accused him of heinous crimes 'and beat and wounded and maltreated his men'. Speaking on behalf of the village community, Thomas the reeve and the local priest, who were alleged to have agreed the fine with Peter de Nevill, wouldn't let it rest. They strongly denied that there had ever been any consent:

On the contrary Peter by the agency of his men had dragged the hostages out of the church by force and against their will and assent, and led them away and kept them in prison until now, when they have been released by the king. And thereby they say they have been wronged and have suffered loss to the value of forty pounds.

As far as the spokesmen of the villagers were concerned, the whole fracas had been caused by the threat to burn their village down. They and the other villagers had done no wrong, and all the trouble had come from Peter de Nevill and his men, who should never have come into the village in the first place. (One recalls the famous verdict at Featherstone on the fatal shooting in the miners' lockout of 1893. Then a jury of local people baulked at convicting the government of unlawful killing, but wouldn't be browbeaten by the coroner into agreeing it was justifiable homicide: they would only say that the dead had been killed by Her Majesty's Army, adding the rider that they 'very much regretted that the South Staffs Regiment had ever come into Featherstone'.)

However, at this moment it would appear that the villagers could not put up a united front. The five hostages had felt badly let down by their neighbours' failure to pay up and get them released, and they now alleged they had been given up against their will by their neighbours, and had 'lain in prison in wretchedness . . . wherefore they say that as they are free men and of free status they have been wronged, and have suffered loss to the value of a hundred marks'. Thomas the reeve and the villagers denied this, insisting that Peter had 'dragged them by force and unwillingly out of the church and the churchyard . . . and that neither Thomas, nor the others, nor the community of the village in any way meddled in the matter.'

It was now a case of the word of the king's 'beloved' Nevill against the 'foolish' villagers, who were compromised by the attitude of hostages (had they perhaps been threatened or nobbled in prison, one wonders?). At any rate, the case was heard 'before the king', that is, before judges and jury, on 3 November 1266 – not in Leicester but in Warwick. The jury concluded that Nevill had indeed used force, but that he had a fair complaint against them. The women had indeed organized the peace deal 'for fear that the village might be set on fire', but nevertheless the hostages had gone 'at the women's request and with the authority of Thomas the reeve'. Subsequently, when 'the whole village of Peatling' had sent expenses for the hostages, 'they had signified their assent that they should be hostages for money'. In short, the jury chose to believe Nevill's version of the tale.

It was true, the jury said, that all the men of the village had not been present when the hostages were given, but 'they had given sufficient consent afterwards'. The villagers had thus aquiesced in the fine, and they should pay it. Moreover, they had done wrong to the five men given as hostages in letting them lie for so long in prison. They must therefore not only pay Nevill the fine of twenty marks, but also pay one mark to each of the hostages in compensation for lost earnings and time spent in jail. As for Nevill's men, who had forcibly entered the church and used violence against the villagers, they should be arrested. The Peatling Five were then released, and no doubt went home grumbling at the court's award of only a twentieth of what they had claimed. There the story ends. Case dismissed.

Of course, the story begs more questions than it answers. However much we might think the verdict unfair to the villagers, one has to say it is a remarkable testimony to the administration of

English justice at the time that the partisans of the defeated in a civil war should have access to the king's court. The judgment also affirmed that Nevill's men were unjustified in using force, even though it enforced the arbitrary fine imposed on the village under threat of setting fire to the place. The jury's concern for the welfare of the hostages and the unfairness they had suffered is also notable. King Henry's judges deserve some respect: they were in a very volatile political climate, and clearly tried to find some kind of an equitable solution even though they wanted to get Nevill off the hook. Compared, perhaps, with any other legal system of the time, it was a model of equitable judgment: Thomas the Reeve would surely have met a terrible fate in Yuan China – or even Mao's China, come to think of it. Here recourse to the law is understood by the villagers as well as accepted by the king's bully boys. So too the use of writing, negotiation, acceptance of the authority of the state and its instruments. This had been the achievement of the Old English state and the first two centuries of the Anglo-Norman state.

But what are we to make of the peasants' statement that the king's men were against the welfare of the community of the realm? Of course, loyalty to the 'community of the realm' may mean no more than support for the barons even after their defeat. Peatling had been a village of Simon, after all. To some modern scholars, the sense of a community of England so early is an anachronism:

There was little kinship of thought between the aristocracy and their social inferiors, that struggling mass of all sorts and conditions of men who were possessed at best of only the most rudimentary political conceptions.

But the Peatling peasants in court do not quite sound like that. They clearly distinguished the barons from the community of the realm, just as they had distinguished the king's men from it. To accuse the king's men of sedition suggests that they had what we would call a 'political' point of view. And after all, they lived in a 'community of the village', which had a legal existence; they were used to the idea of the 'community of the shire', through which

their own local representatives could have their say. Their use here
of the concept of the community of the realm strongly suggests
that they thought there was a national community to which they
felt they owed allegiance and in which they had rights – and
that this community in some sense stood above the agents of the
government of the time. How had they got that idea?

It may seem a hopeless task to try to illuminate a few words
spoken in haste, passion and danger over 700 years ago, and words
translated into another language for that matter. We are never likely
to know for sure what was in the minds of the people who spoke
them, but it is worth a little detour to make the attempt. Who
were they, the peasants of Peatling Magna that day in 1265, the
rich and poor freeholders; Thomas the reeve; and the women,
some of whom were independent farmers themselves? What did
they think about the great national events which briefly threatened
to engulf them? And what sort of place did they come from?

'Oh, you'll not find much has changed at Peatling Magna,' said the
man at the taxi rank outside Leicester station. He was right. The
village lies eight miles south of Leicester, a booming city today
with a large and vibrant Asian population. Once a Roman provincial
capital and an early Anglo-Saxon bishopric, at the beginning of the
last century Leicester was still only a small town, with a population
of fifteen thousand; a market for the surrounding countryside which
then still came right up to its walls. Since then it has been transformed
beyond recognition, and many of the medieval villages on the south
side of Leicester have been swallowed up by new housing estates.
Peatling Magna, though, is sufficiently far out to have escaped, and
once you have crossed the River Soar the last four miles of the
journey beyond Wigston are through delightful rolling countryside,
in whose woods and meadows one can still see 'the rich and pleasant
prospect' of which Susanna Watts wrote in 1804 in her *Walk through
Leicester.*

The village lies at the foot of the ridge of high ground which
crosses England diagonally from the Cotswolds through Northamptonshire to where the East Leicester uplands give way to the flat

lands of Lincolnshire. In the Middle Ages, this was the very heart of open-field England, which extended from the coast of Durham down to Dorset, and from the Welsh Borders to the edge of the Fens: 'Champaine ground', as John Leland described it, where the wheat-and-bean system of farming has been practised for centuries, if the wills of Tudor farmers are anything to go by. Good heavy soil, giving the 'best corn in Europe' in the south of the shire according to Gabriel Plattes in the 1630s. Good old farming country since the time of the Romans, a land 'whose great manufacture was tillage'.

You come in along a tree-lined country road, once the old medieval cart track which led south from Leicester through Coun-testhorpe, with the Peatling stream over to the left where the mills stood. The village is a small square of lanes with not many more houses than it had in the 1840s. There's been little new building: just a small bungalow here and there tucked discreetly behind hedges, and a modern brick detached house with a conservatory and a well-kept lawn. The Cock Inn is still there, mentioned from the seventeenth century onwards, offering wayside accommoda-tion, though small: two guest beds and stabling for ten horses. Off the main road, Peatling was never an important place.

The houses in the village are mainly eighteenth century, though under the brick skins of some may be the frames of medieval houses. They were built facing on to the lanes, each with a garden, an orchard and a croft. The village has been roughly this size since the late fourteenth century, when there were 150 people over the age of fifteen living here. It had 22 households in 1564 and exactly the same number in the 1801 census, when 170 people lived in the place: 84 males and 86 females (8 per house: much more than today when so many live on their own). It rose to the peak population in its history in the 1840s – nearly 50 houses and 308 people; it sank to 134 people, the lowest since the Black Death, in the 1961 census. On today's electoral roll there are 151 adults. That gives us a measure of the place: a stable community never big enough to have its own market; till recently a self-contained sort of place with its inn, a smithy, a wheelwright and a tailor. Something of that feel still survives, though it is home now to people who work in business in Leicester, and even one or two who commute to London.

The village church of All Saints, scene of the events of August 1265, is still there. It is one of the loveliest in Leicestershire, in a delightful setting on the edge of the village, looking out southwards across a field whose humped mounds mark the moated site of the medieval manor house. You approach it down a narrow green footpath shaded on both sides by hedgerows of hawthorn, chestnut saplings, walnut, an elder or two; the grass under your feet sprinkled with daisies and buttercups. The church was rebuilt in the boom time of the early thirteenth century: this was where the village men took refuge from Nevill's troops. In the churchyard the old tombstones have not been cleared away, and walking through the long grass you see the names of many of the old village families.

Benjamin Smith, for example, came from a long line of black-smiths in the village; though, of course, his is a common name, there have been Smiths here since the Middle Ages. William Pollard, the village wheelwright in the 1840s gazeteers, was probably descended from one of the twelve children of Thomas Pollard, vicar in the 1580s.

The man clearing the grass came over.

'The Pollards died out here only fifteen years ago. Pollard's shop was next to the pub. They were the wheelwrights. Dick Pollard took to drink. His father were the parson. There were some as didn't take kindly to that.'

'What about the Burdetts?' I asked, looking at a headstone from the 1890s. (The Burdetts are in the parish registers from the 1560s, in the fourteenth-century subsidies, and a Peter Burdet and Elena his wife are named in a court case there in 1318, just about within living memory of the Barons' Revolt.)

'Gone now. Now Mrs Cooper at Dunton Basset: she's a Burdett. The Mawbys, they're still here. Dick, Syd and Jack were brothers: they were the bellringers and the gravediggers.'

On the south side of the church, in deep grass, we came to a cluster of large grey headstones, among them: 'Rebecca Flude, widow of Thomas of this parish, died 13 December 1878 aged 83.'

Rebecca is listed in the trades gazeteers from the 1840s as a farmer and grazier. The Fludes are in the parish registers all the way through from the start: 'Ann Floude daughter of William Floude baptized 15 March 1568.'

'Ah,' said the man, 'I didn't know the Fludes. But there's a house on the Willoughby Road they used to call Flude Farm.'

'You know a lot.'

'Only what I know.'

Populations in villages are always shifting. Names change early on, people come and go, move to nearby villages, families die out. In some areas, such as the isolated Devon hill farms, families show unbelievable tenacity and continuity on their native soil, whereas in some villages of the south and east it is unusual in the Middle Ages to find 10 per cent of the same family names a century later. But in the East Midlands and Lincolnshire, the old Danelaw, things are different. Perhaps it is to do with the form of tenure: for these were free peasants, they had a patrimony to hand on. Even in the twelfth century, in documents recording land sales, you sense a pride in ancestry: peasants, however humble, name their parents, grandparents and even great-grandparents. And they stayed put here more than in other parts of England. Some of the families buried in the churchyard had seen much of the story of rural England enacted here: the transition between the eleventh and the seventeenth centuries from a self-sufficient peasantry to a diversified, regionally orientated society of commercial farmers, artisans and landless labourers; the decline of the old way of life in modern times with the migration to the cities. Peatling Magna was still a rural place in 1801, but nearly half its people were now employed in trade or manufacture. A sign of the times, though it was only in the later nineteenth century that the old pattern was finally broken.

'Several old families moved out at that time,' a lady in the lane told me. 'My husband's family came into the village about a hundred years ago. And now, along with the Spokes, we're probably among the oldest here. Most people today are newcomers.'

That represented a major change in the old pattern of village

life. From the evidence of Peatling churchyard, this had been a
very long-lasting and stable community. That impression stood up
to more detailed questioning. Back in the County Record Office
in Wigston, I transcribed the first forty years of the parish registers
from Peatling Magna, which start in 1565, made a selective search in
later volumes, and then cross-checked these with various sources
going back to the fourteenth-century subsidies and on to nineteenth-
century trades gazeteers and poll books. An imprecise science, of
course, and I don't pretend it gives more than an impression. But
even on this limited search, the impression I think is a fair one: at
least nine families seemed to be there from the fourteenth to the
seventeenth century (some, like the Bayles, had risen to the status
of knights and squires by Charles I's day). At least six more families
were certainly there through the sixteenth century to the end of
the nineteenth century, when some of the old families left. Curiously
enough, another half a dozen names on today's electoral roll are
the same as those of people here in Tudor times, though whether
they have lived here continuously I cannot say. Suffice it to say
that for a thousand years, Peatling Magna has been a stable and
rooted farming community with long continuities in its population.
Does that give us a clue about the peasants in 1265?

The tradition of the people was also freedom of tenure, as the
hostages so strongly emphasized to the jury in the court case of
1265. And that pedigree went much further back in time. Freemen
– *liberi homines* – were a characteristic feature of society in these East
Midlands shires before the Norman Conquest. In 1086, Domesday
Book records about 15 per cent of England's population as free,
and these people are heavily concentrated in the old Danelaw, east
and north of Watling Street, in East Anglia, and in Leicestershire
and its neighbouring shires. For them, freedom of tenure meant
that they could buy and sell their land, witnessed under their own
seal; and they owed the feudal lord of the manor no services on his
land. That made them as free as a peasant could be in the feudal
world. In Leicester, the local juries in 1086 recorded a substantial
portion of *liberi homines*: as many as 50 per cent of the population
in the huge soke of Melton Mowbray. In some individual villages

the entire population is free. The Domesday entries for Peatling Magna give the same picture. In 1086 the village had 7 taxable freemen, 1 villager, and 2 smallholders: perhaps 40 or 50 people altogether allowing for their families. The village priest, called Godwin, also had a smallholding. Together with the lord's demesne they farmed 12 carucates of land: about 1,500 acres, with another 25 or 30 of meadow; figures close to the acreage in the Victorian gazeteers.

The reason for this preponderance of freemen and women in the East Midlands has long been debated. But it seems most likely that they were descended from members of the Viking armies who settled here, dividing the land out to farm in the late ninth century. These settlers seem to have initiated more egalitarian forms of lordship and land tenure, and they left a long mark. Even today, many old Leicester names are Viking in origin: Pauley, Tookey, Astill, Herrick, Chettle. In Peatling, some of the fourteenth-century families were clearly descended from Scandinavinan settlers: the Thurkells, for example, had a Viking name; the Gamel family too – they appear as six separate households in the tax rolls of 1377, which rather suggests an old family who had divided and subdivided their holding over several generations.

These freemen and sokemen of Domesday Book, then, were the ancestors of the the freeholders of the later medieval charters and surveys. Indeed, the pedigrees of many well-known Leicestershire gentry families in Elizabethan times can be traced back to this class at Domesday. As a class, they maintained their traditions and rights tenaciously through the Middle Ages, and in parts of the Danelaw even today, in the Lincolnshire Wolds, for example, Scandinavian dialect words are still plentiful in the farming speech, just as up in Yorkshire the shepherds of Hunderthwaite still count in Danish. The fabric of their civilization, as that historian of Leicestershire William Hoskins liked to put it, was the village and the common fields; its social backbone was the free peasantry and the later yeomen descended from them; its central quality the deep rootedness of the families, and a kind of peasant democracy at township level; its ethos thrift, careful husbandry and canny exploitation of local resources. That perhaps gives an idea of the patrimony of the 'foolish peasants' of 1265.

So who were they? What were their names? The thirteenth century is the time when patronymics start to turn into fixed surnames. We can't be sure that Robert son of Eyrick (another Scandinavian name), who lived at Peatling in 1247, was an ancestor of the Tudor Herricks in the village, though it is likely enough. But by the time we get to Peter Burdet and his wife Elena in 1318, it seems pretty certain we have the ancestor of the Burdett family who lived in the village until the turn of the twentieth century. As for the people of 1265, we have only the statement of the roll in the Public Record Office. Representing the community of the village were:

> Robert of Pillerton
> Hugh (his brother)
> Roger Musket
> Thomas Musket
> Thomas the Reeve
> Philip le Clerk (i.e., the village scribe or accountant)

The hostages, all poor freemen of Peatling Magna, were:

> Geoffrey Bertram (their spokesman)
> Simon de Aune
> William Barun
> William, son of Martin of Weston
> Roger of Thorp

So the court case gives us eleven villagers, perhaps between a third and a half of the village's heads of families. Among these names, the Muskets and the de Aunes are well documented throughout the thirteenth and fourteenth centuries; the Thorps for much longer. The hundred rolls of the 1270s with their incredible wealth of detail might have given us the whole picture, but none survives for Leicestershire. For a fuller, though possibly not complete, account of the village, we have to wait till the 1327 subsidy which names twenty-six taxpayers. Among them are names well known in the village in later times: Reyner, Sewale, Gamyl, Pope:

Roger le Conestere	Thomas Poleys
Agnes Boley	Henry Reyner
Thomas Hogeman	Walter Pope
Adam Wymarkes	William Gamyl
John Fraunceys	Thomas le Negle
Adam le Negle	Robert de Thorp
John Sewale	Peter Boley
Henry de Thorp	William de Rowell
John Julion	John Gamyl
Peter Gamyl	John le Lone
William Hubert	Agnes Fouke
William de Oune	John Stotes
Walter de Redesdale	William de Whylughby

So the 'foolish men of the village' in 1265 were in reality people of some standing and experience. They lived in a largely free village, and their customs and traditions had been handed down over many generations. Working in an open-field community, they were used to dealing cooperatively. They clearly also were people used to dealing through the legal institutions of village, hundred and shire, and specifically to using the law and written records. In particular, the smooth running of the open-field strips required regular meetings of the manor court, and the ability to resolve disputes with one's neighbours peacefully. One of the group in 1265 is named as Philip le Clerk, and he was perhaps the village scribe and accountant. But other villagers may also have been literate. Till recently this idea would have been thought highly unlikely. But one of the surprising finds of recent scholarship is the degree to which by this time literacy had become part of a peasant's life. Between the eleventh and late thirteenth century, it is now clear, a revolution swept England; an irreversible shift in modes of communication, as important as that now taking place from print to computers. This shift was from memory to written record. In part, this came about as a consequence of the Conquest, and the need of foreign rulers to record things which had previously been transmitted orally as part of customary law. The change was dramatic, and in historical terms very swift. In 1066, possession of a personal seal (entitling a person to sign his name) was confined to the king. By the later thirteenth century, the time of the incident at Peatling Magna, even serfs might have been required to have them. And as might be expected, literacy was especially useful to the free peasantry of eastern England. Its most obvious practical application, for example, was in the thriving twelfth- and thirteenth-century land market. In the ecclesiastical archives of Lincoln and other places there are literally thousands of documents recording such transactions, witnessed and sealed by peasants. These are often minute deals – an acre here, an acre there – with sub-clauses which would do credit to the most nit-picking property lawyer today, such as the lease which allowed the lessor *inter alia* to 'keep a mastiff chained by day, loose by night'. One Lincolnshire indenture from the 1220s, an agreement between a lord and a group of villagers, bears the individual wax seals of no less than fifty villagers. This growing use of writing for ordinary business shows the development of a literate mentality, which the people of Peatling Magna may well have shared.

Literacy was thus part of the lives of the peasants of 1265, and it had a 'political' application. By then, even manorial villeins, semi-free peasants, were proving able to organize collectively and use the law to fight uncustomary or excessive impositions. Only a few years later, in 1276, at Stoughton in Leicestershire, six miles from Peatling, the tenants took their landlord to court after refusing to do services. This perhaps helps illuminate the tactics of the people of Peatling: their immediate recourse to law, their raising of funds and persever-ance over the months of the case. If feudal society burdened its members with an oppressive and mind-numbing range of customary duties, the same legalism of necessity made them aware of their rights as free people.

The reform movement of 1258–65 was distinguished from all

similar movements in the past by the attentiveness of its leaders to the local opinion of the shires. It was a movement for reform of central government, but also of local government by the king's officials and magnates. The Old English system of shires, hundreds and village courts had long enabled local opinion to have a voice and had endowed the community's leaders with a political consciousness which grew from common responsibilities. (And at root, of course, village societies like Peatling with their communally farmed fields were cooperative by their very nature.) Out of this sensibility grew political aspirations which underlay the assertiveness of the local community at the time of the Barons' Revolt. The community of the village had long had its links to the community of the shire, and as the revolt had shown, the community of the shire now wanted its say in the 'community of the realm'.

So we can make a tentative answer to the question we asked at the start of this chapter. The peasants were surely speaking up for the welfare of the national community, and they did so out of an awareness of such things. No doubt they would have aligned themselves with the anti-government rhetoric of popular songs of the day. Henry had departed from 'good old law'; they saw Simon as the hero in the struggle against not so much this king as his advisers, grasping and overmighty, whose influence was felt as a foreign threat to English liberty and dignity. So they believed Simon's revolt was 'to grant good laws and the old charter too, that so often was granted before, and so often undone'. They believed that England was an old nation whose rulers had brought in too many foreigners who had grown fat on the nation's wealth. Foreigners were riding on the backs of the native English, even though they could not read or write English. After the Barons' Revolt, again and again English writers speak of 'community', of which they claim insistently they are a part: 'our land . . . our people . . . our nation . . .' speaking not for a local regional community but for 'this land'.

In the next decades they and their children and grandchildren would see English re-emerge as the national language, the popular songs and poems of the day replete with sentiments of English nationalism. By the 1340s, the concept of England as a nation was to the fore once more, an association between nation, territory, people and language. The national identity was expressed in various ways: a territory, a history, a set of cultural traditions, a body of legal practices expressed in the Common Law, a single economy with a common coinage and taxation, and also, as we have seen at Peatling, some concept of shared rights. In the thirteenth century, then, a construction of national identity was going on – or more likely, a reconstruction.

Though we cannot prove it, it is not impossible that the peasants of Peatling Magna in 1265 shared these ideas about the nation, or indeed felt they owed their allegiance to the 'community' of the English state: an idea whose roots lay back in the Old English period. This idea of community involves the idea of consent: acknowledgement that the state is the authority, and that it can be separated from its rulers. That, surely, is what the people of Peatling Magna were saying that August day in 1265.

People are the same the world over, of course, but history has shaped them in different ways. What strikes me after years of travelling in other cultures is the combination in English society of respect for individual freedom and respect for the law: freedom *from* allows freedom *to*: the basis of an ordered society. This was a very great achievement whose foundations were laid by Old English law. Of course, the English are deeply suspicious of Utopias, indeed of abstract thinking at all. They have tended to shun any system of thought which claims to have all the answers, whether a religion or a theory of politics, and rightly, of course. The history of the twentieth century, more than any other, shows us that Utopias are to be shunned. The English system with its very idiosyncratic arrangements was worked out over a long time, and largely without outside interference. This was the English people's greatest stroke of luck: to develop their ideas and structures of governance without the constant threat of upheaval. This is not to say that change is not needed now, to overhaul both central and local democracy, to get rid of the unelected second chamber, to redress the failure of civic virtue; but the English achievement was a notable one in history, as can be seen in the many attempts to emulate it. One of the great problems in history is squaring individual and collective rights. This is what makes England one of the most successful attempts in history to form a state where men and women may live in peace, marry, have children, and enjoy the fruits of their labours.

Before I left Peatling Magna, I went back down the lane to the church and had a last look inside: the furniture, the medieval font, part of a medieval screen, the seventeenth-century altar and some lovely early pews, including a group at the back which date back to before the Reformation. On the wall, another more recent list of men of the village:

> To the Glory of God and in Loving Memory of
> White Chesterton
> Henry Cook
> Allan Marshall
> Edward Tilley
> William Tilley
> Who fell in the Great War 1914–18
> Their Name Liveth for Evermore

'That's my father's brother there.' The man with the scythe was packing up.

'He died at Ypres? A lot of men from a small village, isn't it?'

'It is.'

'Do you know, it's said to be the oldest village in Leicestershire. So they say. There were Romans and Bronze Age people here before. It is said the old track where they took the Irish gold came through here from Robin-a-Tiptoe Hill.'

'Really?'

'Peatling's an Anglo-Saxon name, you know. It comes from the person who founded the village here after the Romans. Long ago they found a grave and urns in West Field. Perhaps it was his. Peotla was his name . . .'

He chuckled. 'I suppose that makes us still Peotla's people!'

14. Jarrow and English History

Coming up on the train from King's Cross to Newcastle I treated myself to a pile of dailies and weeklies. The lead news story in the *Northern Echo* took my eye: 'Triumphant return of the Elgin Marbles to the North . . . The Lindisfarne Gospels are coming back to Northumbria.'

Perhaps the greatest of all illuminated manuscripts, the Lindisfarne Gospels had been removed from Durham by Henry VIII's agents in 1537, before eventually finding a home in a glass case in the British Library. In 1998, an alliance of MPs and church leaders from north-eastern England began the final push to get the book back, under the aegis of the Assembly of the North, one of the cluster of medieval-sounding 'parliaments' set up by the New Labour Government in the English regions in the late 1990s.

The Gospels were written in the north-east in the seventh century, and experienced many adventures before finding a safe home in Bloomsbury. After the sack of Lindisfarne during the Viking Age, they had followed St Cuthbert's body in its wanderings across the north, to Crayke, Norham on Tweed, Chester le Street. In the late tenth century they found their way to Durham, where they remained till the Dissolution of the Monasteries, when they were confiscated by Henry VIII's commissioners. In modern times, they have rested in the British Library, but the manuscript was taken up north again, by train, in 1987 and laid open on Cuthbert's tomb in Durham Cathedral on the 1,300th anniversary of his death on 20 March 687. Few who saw its open pages gleaming in the candle light, their swirling geometric patterns glittering with gold and lapis lazuli, cannot have experienced a tingle down the spine.

For some, even in our secular times, this is not just a manuscript whose mysteries are for scholars to dissect, but a holy book, a symbol of divine mysteries. Also, and especially to northerners, the book is still connected with a 'Northumbrian identity', a symbol of one of the greatest periods in English history, the late seventh and eighth centuries. This was the time when the former barbarians of Northumbria created a powerhouse of European civilization. Assimilating elements of Irish civilization, making links with Scots and Picts and contacts with Europe and Rome, they also helped to lay the foundations for the continental *renovatio* under Charlemagne, which marks the true beginning of modern Europe. There were many key figures – abbesses and abbots, patrons, scholars and monks – but the greatest of them all was Bede, the first historian of the English, the man who in a sense defined what England would – or could – be. And Bede spent his life here on the Northumbrian coast, at Jarrow.

Bede's monastery lay just down the Tyne from Newcastle and Wallsend, the last fort on Hadrian's Wall. From Newcastle city centre you cross the river to Gateshead in County Durham, where a towering rust-red sculpture, the 'Angel of the North', attempts to speak the old language of spirits which animated Bede's universe. Follow the signs to the new Bede's World Heritage Centre at Jarrow: through an industrial estate, take the A185 to South Shields, and soon on the left you will see the old back-to-back houses of Jarrow. A former ship-building and colliery town, Jarrow is inextricably connected with two great symbolic moments in English history: the writing of Bede's *History*, and the Jarrow Crusade of 1929.

The remains of Bede's church lie crammed between a Nissan works and a housing estate, in the shadow of a huge oil depot. To imagine the lie of the land then needs a leap of the imagination which Nicholas Pevsner, for one, felt unable to make when he came here to write about Jarrow for the *Buildings of England* series. For Pevsner, the aura of the place was irretrievably gone. But Jarrow can deceive the eye. As a historical landscape it takes some beating. To say the least, it holds a very special place in the English story.

The monastery lay in a crook of the River Don, which enters the Tyne at Jarrow. The Don is now a tiny river, flowing over black mud littered with the debris of pipes, tyres and electricity cables. It is a small miracle that it makes it this far through the industrial wasteland south of the Tyne, through Hedworth, Primrose and the landscaped remains of Boldon Colliery. At the Don mouth, where a Viking fleet was wrecked in a providential storm in 794, rotting wooden piles stick out of banks covered with pink and yellow sedge flowers. An old stone causeway leads from a timber yard across a bridge festooned with barbed wire, seabirds on the fence poles. Below the church the land falls away steeply; here the monks had their garden, workshops and glass foundry. Now the horizon is filled by a slag tip, oil tanks, the cranes along the Tyne, and power lines which pass within a hundred yards of the church.

Jarrow was the ancient territory of a tribe known as Gyrwas, 'the dwellers on the marsh'. That's how the place got its name. Up to the eighteenth century, the church stood on the very edge of the marsh and the great tidal pool of Jarrow Slake (a word which comes from the Old English *slacian*, 'to fill with water', as in modern English, to 'slake' thirst). Engravings of the 1720s show open marsh and water as far as South Shields. Even as recently as twenty years ago, the marsh was still the haunt of flocks of seabirds, until the Slake was used as a landfill for the Newcastle Metro, and the Nissan car works was built on top. Nissan has been a great boon to a once depressed area, no question. But it is incredible none the less that one of most resonant landscapes in the British Isles should have met its final ruin only in the era of Mrs Thatcher, whose strident citation of the lessons of English history was matched only by her obliviousness to what had actually gone into its making.

The industrial transformation of Jarrow, of course, goes much further back in time. In the mid nineteenth century the marshes had already partly been filled in, with the construction of the Tyne Dock. Charles Plummer describes the view from the church in the 1890s: 'the reaches of the lower Tyne resound with the din of shipbuilding, and the roar of factories; and her own wooded banks are bare and black with the smoke of colliery and furnace', a description entirely confirmed by apocalyptic photographs of warships emerging from the Jarrow yards through a fog of tug smoke.

Many of the battleships of Britain and Japan came out of these yards, a connection which left a handful of Japanese Geordies in these parts – but that's another story.

In the early nineteenth century, cramped rows of back-to-back houses had been built right up to the churchyard wall; generations of shipworkers and miners lived and died here. They have all gone now – all that is left is the line of the streets and back entries, hummocks under the grass and weeds. But because of that, today's traveller searching for Bede's England discovers with some surprise (or is it a hallucination?) that though the physical topography known to the Jarrow marchers in the 1920s has been almost obliterated, that of the seventh century has, strangely, begun in places to reappear.

To imagine that landscape you have to stand on the highest point of the Jarrow peninsula, where the Bede World village and Saxon farm is today. Think away the oil refineries, shipyards, cranes and car works, and picture a wide-open landscape with views across the Tyne valley and down towards the sea. It was a typical northern monastic site, like Hartlepool, Coldingham or Whitby; protected by nature, between the marshes and the rivers on a windswept promontory from whose northern edge one could just make out a blue strip of sea at Tynemouth. It was once a wonderful spot, a little gem in a perfect setting: the only hint of modernity then would have been the newly built Christian churches.

It is an exposed site, and in the Middle Ages Jarrow was often attacked. Vikings, Normans and Scots all plundered the place. But the essential structures of Bede's church survived till 1782, when they were demolished thoughtlessly with no record taken: another of the casual losses to Dark Age history which have happened so often, and so late in the day. Finally, in 1965, the archaeologists got their hands on the site, and they have been able to give us a detailed picture of the church founded at Jarrow by a wealthy patron, Benedict Biscop, in 682. Over eleven seasons they uncovered more than could ever have been hoped for, given the modern devastation of the area. There were hints of some kind of Roman predecessor: reused stones, bricks and roof tiles. Pagan burials, too, with grave goods: an eye bead in black glass with red, white and black insets; a large bead in opaque yellow glass from the Iron Age; early Saxon beads. Clearly there had been settlers on the promontory long before the conversion of the Northumbrians in the seventh century. The monastic church was founded in a place where people had lived and died for centuries.

For one of the spiritual powerhouses of the Dark Age in the Western world, the place was tiny. The main church is nearly 100 feet long; an eastern chapel joined to it adds another 50 feet. So the whole building was only 150 feet long. Close by was the cemetery, a refectory (96 by 26 feet) and the monks' assembly hall (60 by 26 feet). Other buildings which we know existed have not yet been found: the monks' cells, the infirmary (where the plague victims lay dying in Bede's youth), the monastic school, the scriptorium, and all the ancillary buildings (not least the brew-house – the monastic rule made generous provision for beer and wine). On the terraced slope above the Don, there would also have been a garden, always important in a monastery. ('The monastic life of solitude has many rewards,' wrote the Frankish monk Walahfrid Strabo in his delightful book on gardening, 'not least of which is the joy of devoting yourself to a garden.')

The finds are displayed in the fascinating little museum in Jarrow Hall, a small eighteenth-century mansion built by Simon Temple. Born to a Westoe shipping family, Temple was one of the pioneers of the industrial transformation of Jarrow: he built a dry dock in Jarrow Slake in 1798; he sank the Alfred pit in Jarrow in 1803 and built the White Cottages as miners' homes abutting the graveyard. In Jarrow Hall are displayed the excavation's finds: fragments of medieval life such as a bronze key, an antler hammer, chisels, buttons, a thimble, buckles, needles, a rubbed coin of Edward the Confessor.

As I stared at the case, a man engaged me in conversation. Young and well dressed, he worked for a multinational dealing in food franchises.

'You see, 370,000 people come through here off the ferries from Scandinavia. They land in the Tyne and then we lose them.'

'Lose them?'

'They go to Scotland; the Lakes; or into southern England. They spend their money in Edinburgh or Stratford. We want them to stay here, and spend some of their money here. So we're looking at options.'

'So where does the history fit in?'

'Well, Bede's World gives the place a public profile. His is one of the names you connect with Northumbria. Putting it crudely, Bede is a brand name up here.'

I narrowed my eyes at the model in the case, which showed the monastery as it would have been in Bede's day. On the slopes below the church, the archaeologists found workshops where the monks and their craftsmen did the stone-carving, glass-making and metalworking, and the tanning (an unpleasant, smelly job). Moored in the River Don there were fishing boats; along the banks of the Tyne there were, perhaps, also the wooden frames which they call yares up here – supporting nets to catch salmon. It would have been mainly a fish diet for the community in Bede's day which, here and in Wearmouth and their dependencies, numbered an astonishing six hundred brethren and workers.

Outside the window, rain had begun to fall in sheets. I sat by the window, undid my bag and opened my Bede.

'I was born on the lands of this monastery,' Bede says – that is, on land which belonged to the Wearmouth half of the double monastery. He was probably born in 673. Later tradition says his birthplace was close by, at Monkton, where Bede's Well is still pointed out on the Bede Heritage Trail. But the Old English translation of Bede's *History* done by Alfred the Great, two hundred years after Bede's day, says he was born on *sundurlonde thaes ylcan mynstres*. In Old English this means precisely what Bede says in Latin: namely, the territory of the monastery, but as the name still survives close by Wearmouth, in Sunderland (*Sounderland* in 1183), it may suggest that Bede's home was on the north bank of the Wear in a little village exposed to the coastal gales which, as all football fans will remember, used to scour Roker Park on Saturday afternoons in winter, swirling the Roker Roar over the stands and across the serried rows of back-to-backs beyond.

Bede's life was uneventful. The nearest he comes to an auto-biography is rather diffidently tucked away in the last chapter of the *History*. Here, writing 'in my fifty-ninth year', he gives a bibliography of his works (and a truly vast output it is too, in science, grammar, history and biblical commentary). In this he also includes a short summary of the only biographical details he thought worth mentioning. No self-advertisement here: 'At the age of seven I was by the charge (*cura*) of my family (*parentibus*) given to the most reverend abbot Benedict, and afterwards to Ceolfrid, to be educated . . .' Of the words he uses here, *cura* means guardianship, care, rearing, charge, solicitude even; his word for family, *parentibus*, doesn't specifically mean parents, and could refer to the wider family. His parents were dead, perhaps, though it is also possible that they were religious people giving a younger son to the church. At any rate, one guesses they were local landowners of thegnly rank.

'I was made deacon in my nineteenth year,' Bede goes on. Below the canonical age, this, which was usually twenty-five: a mark perhaps of his precocious abilities? 'I was made a priest at thirty'. After that he didn't travel widely, except in his mind. It is hard to prove he went further south than York.

As for the life he lived, the rule at the double monastery of Wearmouth-Jarrow was not strictly the Benedictine version, but one worked out by the first abbot, the former nobleman Benedict Biscop. It was put together from the rules of many early monasteries, and 'not just from my untutored heart', as Benedict assures us: seventeen, in fact, among them a place where he had once stayed off the south coast of France, the delectable island of Lerins, where there is still a Benedictine house today. But life at Jarrow was similar to the austere life of the Benedictine order: matins at 2 a.m., then three basic elements to the day: prayer and singing in common in church (four hours), reading and meditation (four hours) and manual labour (six hours). This was Bede's life from childhood.

From the age of seven I have spent my entire life within that monastery, devoting all my pains to the study of the Scriptures; and amid the observance of monastic discipline and the daily charge of singing in the Church, it has ever been my delight to learn, to teach or to write.

('My delight', *dulce habui*, is a favourite and typical Bede phase. He was a sweet person, so far as we can tell from the witness of pupils and the evidence of his own writings.)

The impetus behind the monastic life was to escape the world; to retire to a primeval landscape, which Jarrow once was. Western monasticism began in Egypt, with the express denial of the material world, the rejection of Late Antique city civilization for the wilds of nature, the deserts of the Red Sea. The early monks were 'heroes of the *paneremos*', the 'deep desert'. The Celtic Church in turn sought out wild spots: Skellig St Michael, Iona, Tintagel. Lonely, beautiful places where communities could be self-sufficient, places to challenge the capacity of the individual human being to transform himself or herself, and of such communities to transform society. And therein lies the key to Bede's *History*.

Outside the window, a cloudburst over Jarrow Hall now had the rain pouring down in torrents. Across the car-park, a knot of schoolchildren fled to their coach from the sodden thatched huts of the Saxon village. I went for lunch in the pleasant café in Jarrow Hall and had a chat with Miriam Harte, Director of the Museum.

'Of course, what we show here is tied to the national curriculum. It's split up into one- or two-hour modules. Here you've got medieval monks and the Saxon farm. In summer, we get two or three schools every day. We are completely booked all summer so we have to turn people away. It's very popular and is highly appreciated. I wouldn't say that people really have much awareness of Bede himself as a historical figure, but the kids love it, especially when they come to the farm. They see hill sheep, geese, and other older breeds of animals – big, fat, hairy pigs, small cattle – and they are encouraged to imagine what it was like to live in the seventh century; for example, to get a sense of what it was like to be a boy in the monastery.'

'What else do you think they get out of it?'

'I think they're also fascinated to see what people could do, and what they could make, without technology. Without all the things we have.'

'And what about Bede's religion?'

'Look, most of the kids that come here have never been inside a church in their lives. They don't know what an altar is.' She saw the disbelief in my face. 'But it's true. It may be surprising to people of our generation.' She laughed. 'Mind you, I was brought up in the Republic of Ireland. I went to a religious school from the age of four. But now we live in a post-industrial secular society. Some history they can no longer relate to.'

She paused and looked into her cup reflectively. 'That's not to say that there isn't real value in it, though. Even if you're a kid standing inside that ancient church, and you know nothing about what went on here, you can take something away with you; some kind of aura, perhaps.

'The thing is, too: it's an amazing history here, when you think about it. They went through a heyday and decline in ancient times, and then again in the industrial age: shipyards and mining; and now they're gone. But it will emerge again. I think that when I see Nissan exporting cars from here across the world. And there's still some heavy industry along the river.

'It's had many blows, this community. Something like this centre helps develop a sense of worth.'

'So history has a value?'

'Strangely enough, it's just what we were always taught. History helps give meaning to the present. It's the same for individual people as it is for nations, isn't it?'

The rain was turning into sleet when I went down to the church. It was the most authentic part of the late-nineties Bede's World experience so far. A bitter rain lashing in from the North Sea, leaving a rime of icy slush on my coat. In those days, in the shorter daylight hours of wintertime, vespers were probably spoken by four o'clock, and the monks must have appreciated braziers after compline. The weather on the north-east coast can be very harsh in winter, as one of Bede's pupils, Cuthbert, wrote:

The conditions of the past winter oppressed our people's island very horribly with cold and ice and long and widespread storms of wind and rain, so the hand of our scribe was hindered from producing a great number of books.

I put my coat over my head and ran across the churchyard into Bede's church. It was warm inside, the rain still beating on the roof, and I felt glad to shelter there. In the nave there was a gift shop run by local volunteers, selling religious books, cards, posters, mugs and tea-towels. Very little of the actual fabric of Bede's church remains today, just the end of the chancel through a fine Anglo-Saxon arch. There are no ancient furnishings left, save for a medieval wooden double-width chair in old oak with a high back, said to be Bede's. In the south wall, three narrow Anglo-Saxon windows are overpowered by a huge Victorian one (the walls of Bede's church were high, the windows tiny). Along the north wall of the nave was an exhibition of stones from the Anglo-Saxon church which were found during the rebuilding by Gilbert Scott in 1866. These give us a hint of the decoration: one stone has exquisitely carved birds and beasts in a vine scroll; nature nourishing itself on the true vine. There are tiny hints of the splendour of the old church. It was a typical basilica, like Santa Maria Maggiore in Rome: tall, narrow, white-washed and painted; torch-lit and lamp-lit.

You could easily miss the most haunting relic. During the excavations in the 1960s, some tiny pieces of coloured glass from the seventh century were found lying shattered in the debris. At one point in his *Lives of the Abbots of Jarrow*, Bede describes how Benedict Biscop brought Frankish glass-blowers and glaziers to create what to people of that time were beautiful, almost magical, patterns in glass. These tiny remnants were retrieved by the archaeologists from heaps of rubbish, and have been remounted in lead and reset in the small, round Anglo-Saxon window in the nave. So light once more floods through Bede's glass: we may look through it as he did.

And one more telling fragment. On the wall into the chancel is the original dedication stone, or at least two bits of it, which may perhaps be fitted together to read thus:

The dedication of this Church of St Paul ninth of the kalends of May, fifteenth year of King Ecgfrith, [Sunday 23 April 685] the fourth of Ceolfrith abbot also founder under God of the same Church . . .

Bede perhaps saw the ceremony as a twelve-year-old. His boyhood is now re-enacted by school parties. Inside the door there's a row of monks' cowls on a clothes rack, for schoolchildren learning about what it was like to be a monk, a one-hour module in the national core curriculum. There is a story from that time in Bede's life. In 686, when Bede was a novice at Jarrow, aged about fourteen, an outbreak of plague swept both houses. The tale is told by an anonymous member of the community.

At Abbot Ceolfrid's monastery [Jarrow] all who could read, or preach, or recite the antiphons and responses were swept away, except the abbot and one young lad, nourished and taught by him, who is now a priest of the same monastery, and who both by word of mouth and by his writings commends to all who wish to know them, the abbot's worthy deed. And the abbot, despairing because of [the severity of] the plague ordained that, contrary to their former custom, they should at vespers and at matins recite their psalms without antiphons. For a week they did it this way, with many tears and upset on the abbot's part, and then he could bear it no longer, but decreed that the psalms, with their antiphons, should be restored according to the regular order of service. And all assisting with just himself and the aforesaid boy, he carried out with much difficulty what he had decreed, until such time as he was able to train himself, or get from elsewhere, men able to take part in the divine service.

The boy must surely be Bede himself. Other boys survived, no doubt, but Bede was the most gifted, and he was the one later famous for his writings: the description can only be of him. The story is told in the *Anonymous History of the Abbots* of Wearmouth-Jarrow, which Bede uses extensively as a source for his own history of the

Abbots; but characteristically, he omits this incident – presumably out of modesty.

Outside, the rain was still drumming on the roof and streaming down those ancient pieces of coloured glass.

'Can I help you? Have you been here before?'

The soft Geordie accent belonged to a white-haired lady, glasses on a golden chain, wearing a thick cardigan.

'I have,' I said. 'A few times. They've tidied it up since I was last here, though. Didn't these stones used to be on the floor?'

'Yes, they had to mend the organ and they couldn't get at it.'

'Wonderful place, isn't it?'

'Oh, we have to look hard to see it these days. It's all changing so fast we don't recognize it. Time was that you would say you were from Jarrow and people said sorry. They expected you to be wearing clogs. Southerners who come here not knowing about its history are surprised. They learn a thing or two.'

When she said 'southerners', it was as if she was talking about people from another country.

'To southerners, the name of Jarrow only meant the Depression of the thirties and the Jarrow march. The Crusade set off from this church, you know. Come and look at this.' She walked over to a low table of polished wood. 'This table was made by the Jarrow marchers. They gave it to the church. It's got Abbot Ceolfrith's dedication on it.'

A few others had come up by now. Sam Rowan, the husband of one of the women, was one of the leaders of the march. Molly still lives in one of the old back-to-back streets in Jarrow. She knew the story behind the table.

'So the marchers have a sense of the history of Jarrow?' I asked.

'Why, of course! They wanted to speak up for all England.'

Before I left Bede's church, I had a look in the book of prayers. There were entries about recent deaths, of parents, grandparents and even children. A prayer of a child to a lost dad, an attempt to find the language to come to terms with a murder, and one or two prayers like this: 'For enough money for me to keep my dad and my kids.' The life of secular Britain in the 1990s. People still drawn to the battered but numinous aura of the place. School parties still moved to leave prayers about the pollution of the oceans, the destruction of the rainforests, famine in the Sudan. 'Please pray for people with no food in the Third World,' said a nine-year-old.

It's a small world today. We all hear in no time about drought in Africa or floods in Bangladesh. We are all familiar with the struggles of underdeveloped societies to transform themselves through the agency of civilization, in whatever form. Now it is the age of global US culture and the free market. Not so long ago, it was the creed of communism which promised salvation in the poor countries of the world. Back then, it was Christianity. In the seventh and eighth centuries, it was the barbarians of the West who were underdeveloped; trying to transform themselves through the Church. As Pope Gregory the Great said, they were 'people living at the far corner of the world who till now worshipped only sticks and stones' – members of the Third World compared with the powerhouses of civilization: Byzantium, China, India, the Muslim world. And in comparison their numbers were tiny. But they had a vision of history.

Theirs was a time of tremendous change. The Muslim conquest of North Africa and Spain was accomplished in Bede's lifetime. Near the end of his *History*, he writes of the *gravissima Sarracenorum lues*, 'the most grave Arab peril', perhaps speaking of the autumn of 732 and the great Muslim defeat near Tours by Charles Martel (the moment Edward Gibbon memorably saw as sparing us the muezzin calling the faithful from the spires of Oxford!). Whether that is true or not, Bede watched events with a keen eye as far as circumstances allowed (he would, no doubt, have been amazed to know that there would one day be a mosque for Northumbrian Muslims in South Shields, within sight of his church!). Bede knew about the Arab victories in Africa, their attacks on Sicily and the south of France, and the Siege of Constantinople in 716. The Arabs are mentioned frequently in his *Commentaries on Theology*. Their unexpected and rapid rise to world empire posed a profound theological question. Was it the will of God that the followers of the new prophet had gained such success in the world?

What message was to be gathered from these momentous events?

One lesson was grim yet inspiring: the power of history as an idea. The Catholic Church, the last great institution of the Roman Empire, had once embraced the Mediterranean world, where classical people had lived, as Plato had put it, 'like frogs around a frog pond'. Now as the ancient lands of the Mediterranean fell to another power and another faith, the Roman Church had to look north, just as in the twentieth century it would turn to the Third World for mass support and financial aid. And so, in this turning away from the Mediterranean world of Late Antiquity, a northern European civilization was emerging here as surely as an Arabic Muslim civilization of the Near East and the Mediterranean was emerging.

So what took place here – epitomized in the tale told in Bede's *History* – is that the barbarian nations took on board Roman Christianity and Latin culture, and showed how enthusiastically they could follow the Roman lead and be good Europeans, a part of Christian Europe, building a brave new society with all the optimism of immigrants thrown up on strange shores. They would be the heirs of Rome – and they would leave a great legacy, in their inheritance and transformation of Rome, in their idea of nationhood, in the belief that history is purposive. (Bede, indeed, would pioneer the use of the AD dating system.) They – and Bede in particular – changed society's conception of the past and made people see its relevance for the present.

At the very heart of this is a fable told by Bede, almost like a fairy-tale. One day, in an Italian market-place, Pope Gregory the Great saw some young and fair Anglo-Saxon slaves on display for sale. When asked who they were, he was told *Angli* ('English'). He replied, 'That's good: for they have angels' faces, and they will become co-heirs with the angels in heaven.' The story was told and retold. In later years, Gregory was always seen as the real father of the English Church, and his gentle pun about the English stuck: 'they are still inordinately proud about it . . .' said a later writer. The tale offered Bede the metaphor which helped him give a shape to the English past, and a metaphor which proved uniquely valuable to the future. The English were in some sense a chosen race. And

ever after they were *English*: not Saxonish, Jutish, Norman French,
or anything else they might have been. So when the West Saxon
kings of the tenth century set out to make 'England', they did so
with the conscious model of Bede's united *gens Anglorum*, and
within its physical limits. Perhaps they even hoped to re-create
Bede's 'happiest time'; to achieve that visionary quality which Bede
imparts to his vision of Albion as a Promised Land. It was elegant
and clever, but also, one suspects, genuinely felt. So Bede is the
first and greatest historian of the English, the man who at Jarrow
first gave form to the idea of the English nation, and his book
crowned the Augustinian mission – it is the defining history of the
origins of the English nation. England's political creators, in fact,
were not Angles but Saxons. Nevertheless, today we are still English.

So that's why Bede's Jarrow has a special place in the English
story. With its sister house at Wearmouth, Jarrow became one of
the greatest centres of culture in the West. The founder, Benedict
Biscop, and his successor Ceolfrith made many visits to Rome in
search of books to help create an English civilization. Ceolfrith was
able to bring back to England some of the earliest and most influential
Western books, fragments of which are still being discovered.
Monkwearmouth-Jarrow became an international centre, small
scale but of incalculable influence. Confident in the promise of the
Christian message, wealth was ploughed in by willing royal families
and by an aristocracy who revelled in the links with Europe and
Rome, in the beautiful productions of its scriptorium, in its music,
painting and words; also in the transforming power of Christian
civilization which in violent times enabled Germanic kingship to
reinvent itself, and to remake society.

All these creative strands combined to make a golden age.
Missionaries like Boniface and Willibrord went to Germany;
scholars like Alcuin were at the forefront of the Carolingian Renaissance. Of this time, only fragments survive now. All we can do is
sift the wreckage. But though manuscripts are a great deal more
fragile than stones, some have survived in much better condition
than Bede's church. As modern knowledge of the scribes of Jarrow
has grown, scholars have identified their hands in other books of

the seventh and eighth centuries: in the wonderful Stonyhurst Gospels, which were buried with St Cuthbert's coffin in 1104; in the beautiful Durham Gospels; and in the two key early copies of Bede's *History*, now in St Petersburg and Cambridge – the latter begun in his own lifetime at Jarrow and probably copied from his autograph text. In fact, of all the surviving manuscripts written in eighth-century Northumbria, by far the largest number (over forty) come from the Continent, especially from Germany, which was Christianized by Anglo-Saxon missionaries in the generation after Bede. These may seem small numbers, but that is the measure of the eighth-century Renaissance.

Of the most famous Jarrow creations, we have recently received fresh illumination. Abbot Ceolfrith commissioned three huge bibles – one for St Peter's, Jarrow; one for St Paul's, Monkwearmouth; one a gift to Rome. These must have been among the most beautiful books ever made; each one weighed 75 pounds and it took the skin of 500 sheep to provide the vellum pages for each. Only in 1886 was it discovered that the Codex Amiatinus, one of the greatest treasures of the Laurentian Library in Florence, was in fact Ceolfrith's gift to the Pope in 716. The oldest complete Latin Bible in existence, it was so brilliantly done that it had not been recognized as the work of an English artist.

Amiatinus was thought to be the only one of the three great books of which any trace survived. Then, out of the blue in 1889, in a Newcastle antiquarian bookshop, a leaf turned up which had been used as the wrapper for a book of accounts: a fragment of another of the great Bibles. Ten more leaves and a fragment of an eleventh were found in 1911 at Wollaton Hall in Nottinghamshire. Then, only recently, the parchment wrapper of a small volume of ancient deeds was discovered in a country house in Dorset. Cut from an ancient Bible, it turned out to be another fragment of the same book. Perhaps more pieces remain to be found. Meanwhile, in Florence, the survivor of the three great Bibles, the Codex Amiatinus, which Ceolfrith sent to Italy as a gift of thanks, stands as a symbol of the age in which the likes of Theodore, Ceolfrith and Bede created the foundations of English culture – and the idea of England.

This is defined in Bede's *History*. Translated into Old English by Alfred the Great, studied in the tenth century by empire builders as a founding text, more than 150 manuscripts survive even now, proof of Bede's popularity in Western Europe. It was translated again at the point of the great divide, the Reformation, by Thomas Stapelton, who recommended it to Queen Elizabeth as a testimony to 'the true Catholic faith of Englishmen'. Bede's greatest work, according to one tradition, was begun in 725. It was finished in the late summer or autumn of 731, four years before he died. By then he was around fifty-eight years old – a long life in those days, especially considering the austere physical regime. Bede seems to have recognized himself that this book was the fruition, if not the end, of his achievements as a scholar, a typically striking insight even about himself.

It is Christian history, of course. It shows the working of God through history, the higher truth of the programme of providence which Bede and his contemporaries believed had been inaugurated by the Incarnation. But Bede was also influenced by the classical histories of authors like Suetonius, and their idea of *imitatio*, shunning the bad and following the good. At one point, fascinatingly, he talks about *vera lex historiae*, the 'true law of history'. It is probably going too far to translate this as the 'true principles of history', as some have, but this is still, as Bede says, history based on such principles, on the criticism of sources and their transmissions, on the testimony of innumerable witnesses, on documents, on architectural and archaeological detail: 'from ancient documents, from the tradition of our forebears, and from my own personal knowledge'.

Bede's history starts with Julius Caesar and ends with a remarkable account of the state of Britain as it stood in autumn 731. As Gildas had done before him, Bede made the island of Britain a key character, and began with an almost paradisal description of it as a kind of Promised Land 'before the fall', a land of abundance, richness and a variety of animate and inanimate nature. Bede also lists all the five main races within it, although the chosen race was the English. In this connection his title deserves careful attention: it is a *Historia Ecclesiastica Gentis Anglorum* – an 'Ecclesiastical History of the English people' (or the 'English nation'). The title, no doubt, was considered carefully. It is a Church history, but it is also about what we would call politics, military and social history, even economics. Elsewhere, though, Bede makes slight but interesting modifications to the title which deserve our attention, especially as we have his text in a manuscript of his own lifetime. At the end of the work he twice refers to it in slightly different terms, to which it is tempting to attribute some significance, even as modifiers or qualifiers in Bede's own mind, as he looked back on the work in the last year or two of his life. 'I have assembled these facts concerning the ecclesiatical history of the British, and in particular, the English people.' Then, at the very end, in his summary of his own works, he calls it the Ecclesiastical History 'of our island and people' – which might suggest that Bede realized on completion that its scope had ended up wider than he had originally intended, and that the history of the Celtic peoples of Britain was inseparable from that of the *gens Anglorum*. In the end, the Irish, Scots, Welsh and English have one history.

What was he like? It is not a question which would have concerned him, of course. His friends thought his personality charming, though that doesn't make him one of us. We would find him zealously orthodox, I daresay, rather hostile to British heresies, near the end he speaks of the 'national hatred still born by the Britons for the English'. In that, he was a man of his time. But it is his sweetness of character and his humility which remain in the mind, especially in the touching account of his death written by one of his pupils. As death drew near, he brought out a little box in which he kept a few 'treasures'. Personal possessions, of course, were not really encouraged inside a monastery: just simple dress, simple fastenings, a knife, a whetstone, and so on. But in his box, Bede had a bag of peppercorns (which must have come ultimately from South India), some precious incense and some linen napkins. These he shared out to his friends. Then, sitting on the floor, he whispered a final prayer. The last thing he saw, perhaps, was the divine light flooding through those windows of coloured Frankish glass.

By mid afternoon the storm had subsided. I recrossed the Don from the timber yard and walked back up to Jarrow Hall over the grassy mounds of Simon Westoe's White Cottages. Standing on the promontory looking down the Tyne, it becomes clear why the book was written in this place. It was not just chance: Bede's tale was a product of its landscape, as much as any of the great works of English fiction. It could not have been written by a Londoner or a man from Winchester. They simply would not have known what Bede did, let alone have seen things in the same way.

Just look at the position of Jarrow, and the lie of the land; the location by the Roman wall, which was abandoned to the barbarians after 410. Jarrow's geographical situation led to the assimilation and accretion of many layers of history: its connections with the Picts and the Scots; its deep associations with the Irish (some of the Northumbrian kings were Irish speaking); its long contacts with Celtic Christianity. The book could never have been written in Kent. The character of the Northumbrian renaissance owed much to its position: the meeting in the north-east of various streams of Late Antique civilization – Anglo-Saxon, Irish, Welsh, Roman, Frankish, even Mediterranean and Near Eastern, through Archbishop Theodore and his disciples. There were links, too, with Cumbria, whose sub-Roman civilization survived into Bede's own lifetime: working aqueducts, standing monuments of Romanitas. And then looking out to the North Sea, the Tyne was a thoroughfare as well as a frontier. Some monastic sites only look to eternity – God and nature – renouncing society: Skellig St Michael, for instance. Jarrow was not like that. It was still inside civilization.

It was a brief flowering, though, despite its huge legacy. Bede's monastery lasted little more than a century before it was pillaged by the Vikings. The church remained standing until the eleventh century, when it was burned during William the Conqueror's ravaging of the north in the winter of 1069, and again in the Scottish king Malcolm's great predatory raid during the summer of 1070. It was restored by a pious southerner who had been inspired by reading Bede to 'imitate the holy men of old'. Subsequently the ancient monastery was made a cell of Durham – the smallest a monastery could be, normally inhabited by only two or three monks. But it survived. It had the usual income: corn from other villages in the parish; sheep; a modest industry from sea salt and coal; fishing nets at South Shields. Almost entirely rural now, a far cry from the small industrial town it must have been in Bede's day.

Jarrow continued through the Middle Ages. When the foundations of the Bede's World Heritage Centre were dug recently, traces were found of the fourteenth-century village: a few houses, a surfaced road. The church survived into the sixteenth century as one of Durham's three tiny cells at the ancient Anglo-Saxon sites of Farne Island, Jarrow and Wearmouth. When King Henry VIII's antiquary John Leland visited Jarrow shortly before the Dissolution in 1540, he found three poor monks there, who showed him a little oratory on the north side of the church, and an altar, which they said was that of Bede himself. We know from the Durham records that one of the men who talked to Leland was called John Dove. The master was John Swalwell. I find this one of the most touching scenes in English history. The two Johns may not have brought great glory to Jarrow, but they still served the holy place, a place revered not for miraculous events associated with the lives of the saints, but because of its meaning in history. The monks met by Leland were a continuing presence, living in steadfast observance of the old rule, offering regular divine worship, simply maintaining what one modern scholar has aptly called 'a deliberate self-effacing imitation of the past'.

With Leland's visit, the story of Jarrow as a monastic site comes to an end. Jarrow was surrendered to Henry VIII's commissioners on 31 December 1539, but the half-ruined church remained as the parish church for the villagers. By the eighteenth century, Bede's church was so ruinous that the 'congregation had deserted the nave for some years, perhaps from dread of being buried in its ruins', and only the chancel was used for divine services. Bede's nave was finally demolished in 1782, and its replacement was knocked down by Gilbert Scott in 1866, who built a new church to the west. After the economic depression of the late twenties and thirties, and the Jarrow march, a rehousing programme began. This was when Simon Westoe's old terraces round the church were pulled down, and a new housing estate with a new church was built to the west, but Bede's church, St Paul's, is still used for the main services.

'It seems right to me,' wrote Brother Cuthbert of Jarrow some years after Bede's death, 'that the whole English people, in all their different parts of the country, wherever they may be, should give thanks to God because He has given their nation so marvellous a man, so endowed with various gifts, and so studious in exercising them, and at the same time of such moral excellence . . .'

If Bede could see Jarrow today, he would, I suppose, find it hard to recognize the place at first. But more to the point, would he recognize *us*? Would he see us as descendants of his English? Of course, he lived in a very unequal society which rested on the concentration of wealth into the hands of a few. The beauties of the Lindisfarne Gospels or the Codex Amiatinus were paid for by violence and war and by the enslavement of many. Our society is open, egalitarian, democratic; his was hierarchical, its earthly goals power, wealth and possession. It is easy for us to see his world and ideals as just a primitive step on the road to ours. But history never leads in only one direction; there were many merits in the project of our medieval ancestors, and there are no doubt many lessons still to be gathered from it. As we accelerate away from our past at ever-increasing speed, it may seem that the connection with our ancestors is irrevocably gone. We can only get to them now by making a huge effort to understand what seems to most of us an alien conception of life. That, in however small a measure, is what we do by going to heritage centres like Bede's World. We pick over their ruins; dress our kids in monks' cowls to try to feel what that distant plague year felt like. But in so doing we still recognize them as forebears who played a part in making us what we are. We are, after all, still their descendants.

It would be hard to overestimate the assault by modernism on our sense of history. We are post-industrial, post-modern, post-God, post-everything. Ours are children who have never seen an altar. The ancients created a language: of images, words, symbols, which the people of Britain lived with for centuries. But any religious language, visual or verbal, is doomed by lack of the belief which makes it meaningful. That, clearly, is the fate now of our older language: of signs, words, gestures. But, as Bede knew, religion is only one part of the culture which is given to us by our past: allegiance to the nation and its history and civilization is no less important. In the evolving pattern of British history he would perhaps recognize that the process which he defined is still at work; in the existence of the British state and the continued working out of its relationship with 'our island' and its peoples. Perhaps, too, despite all the revolutions of history, there is some tenuous inheritance in the human dimension, in the life lived. And in his church, there are the pieces of ancient glass reset in the old wall, through which light floods again. And outside there is still the landscape he knew. The promontory with its wide views down the Tyne Valley as far as the strip of sparkling blue, where seabirds rise and wheel in a white cloud above Tynemouth.

15. Epilogue: An English Family

It all started with a small cutting in the *Bath Evening News and Chronicle*. In the summer of 1980, the paper reported that Sir Simon Codrington of Dodington Park, Gloucestershire, then in the throes of an acrimonious divorce settlement, had decided to sell not only the family silver but also the family papers. But these were no ordinary papers. In fact, they were one of the most extraordinary historical archives in British history.

The Codringtons' wealth derived from the exploitation of others. They came from the small hamlet of Codrington in south Gloucestershire, only a few miles from Bath, where their names appear as far back as the fourteenth century. The first Codrington to go to seek his fortune in the West Indies was Christopher, who went to Barbados in 1628. It was his son, another Christopher, who founded the family wealth in sugar estates on Antigua and elsewhere. (*His* son, Christopher the third, was Governor General of the Leewards and founded the splendid Codrington Library at All Souls College, Oxford.) At any rate, in 1684, Christopher number two got the lease of a small island in the West Indies which his descendants owned for the next two hundred years: Barbuda.

Known as Dulcina to the Spanish, who, if their choice of name is anything to go by, may never have set foot on its desolate shores, Barbuda lies thirty miles north of Antigua. A tiny place, sixteen by eight miles at most, and too arid ever to be adopted by sugar planters or by the modern package-holiday industry, it is low, flat and almost waterless, with a great salt lagoon in the north; an unpromising tenure rented from the Crown by Christopher Codrington for 'one fat sheep if demanded'. Over a century after the last Codrington packed his bags, their presence is still everywhere on the island today: the little capital with its corrugated-iron roofs, the lagoon, the bay, all still bear the name of the little Gloucestershire hamlet from which the family haled.

Too dry for sugar cane, Barbuda's sixty-six square miles were used for herding (its scrubby flats are still grazed by a vast population of wandering goats). So the family imported a small workforce of slaves, who looked after the stock and made the Codringtons' money on the side by wreck salvaging. People today say there are still three hundred wrecks on treacherous reefs around Barbudan shores.

Until the abolition of slavery in 1834, the workforce was drawn from Africa. The Codringtons were great record-keepers, and from the 1680s (but in especial detail from 1715) until Emancipation they kept a complete record of all their workers and their families, perhaps the most detailed surviving record of a slave society.

The sale of the Codrington papers was announced by Sotheby's of London in their catalogue, for auction on Monday 15 December 1980. Among several lots of Codrington memorabilia, the key one was this:

Lot 142: SLAVERY. HIGHLY IMPORTANT AND EXTENSIVE ARCHIVE OF SOME 8,000 LETTERS AND PAPERS PERTAINING TO THE WEST INDIAN ESTATES OF THE CODRINGTON FAMILY, PARTICULARLY ANTIGUA AND BARBUDA, FROM THE SEVENTEENTH TO THE TWENTIETH CENTURIES, comprising some 40 maps and plans of the island and plantations, *c.* 130 deeds and mortages, *c.* 250 inventories of slaves and stock and other general estate documents, plantation accounts (*c.* 140 volumes or bundles, and over 700 further documents), nine volumes of commercial papers relating to the sugar trade (invoice books and ledgers, etc), an extensive correspondence between the Codringtons and their attorneys in the Leeward Islands (24 letterbooks containing some 3,000 pages, plus over 1,000 letters), some 400 legal documents, and a number of printed pamphlets, largely about slavery, contained in seventeen cardboard boxes and one tea chest. 1668 to 1944.

Reporting the announcement of the sale on 16 October 1980, *The Times* described the collection as 'probably the single most important collection of West Indian estate papers'. Sotheby's own expert was quoted as saying that this was 'the single most important and comprehensive archive relating to the history of slavery and of the West Indies over a period of some three hundred years'. Although known to historians, Sotheby's said, the papers had 'never formed the basis of a historical study in their own right'. In particular, 'they offer a remarkably detailed picture: from the slave lists and account books it is possible to follow the fortunes and trace the pedigrees [or "roots"] of both individual slaves and entire families . . . a feature which we understand is unique to this archive'.

Not surprisingly, news of the sale of the papers was felt like a bombshell in Antigua and Barbuda. Independence for the two islands had been scheduled for the following summer, and now, said the *Antigua Star*, at the eleventh hour, this 'Caribbean Domesday Book' was to slip through their fingers. The Antiguan government offered thirty thousand pounds, arguing that the least the Codringtons should do was to give them the papers at a knock-down price, considering what they represented to the people of the islands, let alone what the Codringtons had made out of the people's ancestors.

Sir Simon Codrington, however, needed the money, and in the Sotheby's sale of 15 December 1980 the archive went to the highest bidder. For £115,610 the Barbuda papers went to an anonymous purchaser, whose country of origin was not revealed (in fact, we later learned, he was a Swiss-based financier with interests in the oil deposits around Antigua). An export licence was swiftly granted by Mrs Thatcher's government (this was evidently not the kind of history which interested them), but for some reason the papers never left these shores. Early in 1986 they were still in a secret location in England. After a ticklish negotiation with the buyer's lawyers, I managed to get a look at, and film, the papers before they left the country.

We drove out to a bonded warehouse under the flightpath of runway two at Heathrow airport. We passed through security gates and, armed with clearance from HM Customs and Excise, entered the secure zone. There, in a cavernous interior, were hundreds of wooden crates, like the last scene from *Raiders of the Lost Ark*. Among them, in three large wooden packing cases, was the Barbudan archive. With some excitement, we opened the first of the cases to discover mounds of account books, ledgers, letters and indentures, portraying in the most intimate detail the life of the island from the seventeenth to the nineteenth century. Here, carefully noted in copperplate by the Codrington attorneys in the 1760s – the sympathetic Samuel Redhead among them – were lists of slave families: Harris, Beazor, Webber, Teague, Punter, James, Charles . . . surnames shared by virtually all Barbudans on the island still today.

Several factors made this group of slaves a uniquely long-lasting and tight-knit community with a strong sense of identity. First, the Codringtons took care of their slaves and workers in a number of ways which were not typical. Unlike most slave colonies where the families were broken apart, here they were allowed to stay together. Children were not (except for one brief period in the 1780s) separated from parents and sent to plantations on other islands. The slaves also were not involved in sugar production (which was very demanding physically, and a cause of high mortality). They had better food and conditions than most slaves on other islands; there was even a Christmas allowance of pork, whose absence one year, wrote an estate manager, was 'a disappointment they sustained with great patience'. Interestingly enough, the slaves also had their own land, as a disapproving letter of the early 1800s pointed out: 'they have provision grounds of 2–10 acres each, and besides their grounds have hundreds of hogs, and goats, plenty of turkeys, fowls and guinea birds'. (This was later cited by the slaves as evidence that possession of their own land was custom and practice.) The end result of this was that, though they were slaves, the Barbudans were stronger, healthier and lived longer than most, and had families which stayed together. Proof can be seen in the inventories and lading bills: remarkably, the population of the island increased from 196 in 1761 to 503 in 1831, with hardly a new slave being introduced, in contrast to the mass importing of African slaves elsewhere in the Caribbean.

There were whites who disliked the regime on the island. But
even their letters are revealing for their grudging admiration of the
strength and cunning of the slaves. Take this letter from one of the
Codrington agents not long before Emancipation, which almost
suggests the slaves had already set up a tiny island republic:

The Barbuda negroes are a bad set, insolent, ungovernable and almost
outlawed . . . They do not do one third of the work they ought to do,
and steal everything they can put their hands on. They acknowledge no
master, and believe the island their own; any Manager living there now,
and using coercive means to bring them into subjection, I have no doubt
would lose his life . . . They are the strongest, halest People you ever
saw, and yet they would make you believe they were half starved. (Letter
from R. Jarritt, 8 December 1829.)

Some who worked with them, though, spoke admiringly of their
character, as in this letter of John James, 7 September 1824:

They would run into any danger with me, which I have often experienced
in saving lives and property from Wrecks. I have swam off to vessels
surrounded by them when no boat could live, and had never an occasion
to order one. The Negroes generally speaking if left to themselves I could
depend on; many a night have I, surrounded by 100 to 150, slept by the
side of my horse in the woods . . . there are but two white men with
myself on the island, and I frequently leave my wife and daughters
there without fastening the house . . . There are some good head
men on whom I can depend . . . the greater part of the Negroes on
Barbuda would lay down their lives for to serve me when I am with
them . . .

By then, the anti-slavery movement had reached Antigua and
Barbuda, and slaves were agitating to purchase freedom even before
Emancipation. In due course, the slaves of Barbuda not only got
their freedom but inherited the island, which in any case, as the
grumpy Mr Jarritt had noted, they believed to be their own. And
so, by a strange fluke of history, a very tightly knit group of people

from Africa survived over two centuries, and with them their family identity, and their ties and friendships between families, which would be carried to another continent when they undertook their second great migration, this time to Britain in the 1950s, nearly three hundred years after the first.

But before we follow the trail of the Barbudans to the English Midlands, there was a last surprise in the treasure trove of the Codrington papers. For there, in the slave lists in the warehouse at Heathrow, to my astonishment, was also evidence of their place of origin. The Barbudans came from a place on the coast to the west of Accra in today's Ghana. It was one of those extraordinary moments for a documentary researcher. In stories like this, specifics are everything. What we want to know, above all, are the names of real people and real places. And here indeed they were. In the 1970s, Alex Haley's famous book *Roots* had a tremendous impact, especially in the Afro-American community in the US, with its sensational claim to have found the specific place and people; to have traced Haley's ancestry back to Africa, to the Gambia. It was a great idea, and no question it had a poetic truth – for such had indeed been the history of African Americans. But as is well known now, the actual link was not there. Haley concocted his connection with the griots of the Gambia, and in fact was never able to trace his family's ancestry to a particular place and person in West Africa. Perhaps in the long run that didn't matter. But here in the Codrington papers, without a shadow of doubt, was the place of origin of the Barbudans. In Samuel Redhead's handwriting, one could see quite clearly the name of the port from which they had been shipped, a hundred miles west of Accra, on the burning shore of the Gold Coast, dotted with the crumbling ruins of old British forts: *Cormantin*.

I went to see the Ghanaian High Commissioner in London. He rooted out an old map of Ghana in a gilt frame and pointed the place out.

'It's a well-known place on the tourist coast today. In the eighteenth century, the town was part of the old Ashanti kingdom: these were Fante people. Now there's Cormantin: there were settlements all along the coast – British, French, Dutch, Portuguese. Here they shipped gold, slaves and ivory: at Cormantin the fort there, Fort Amsterdam, was built by the British in 1638.'

'So when was the town British?'

'At various times in the eighteenth century. It was later captured by the Dutch and changed hands a number of times. It surrendered to the Ashanti in 1806. Then after Emancipation it was British territory. You had it on your stamps: the Gold Coast Protectorate 1830–74.'

He poured the coffee and stirred sugar in, staring out at the rainy London streets.

'Personally speaking, though, I must say I find these very sad places. You can see chains still attached to the floors and walls. It is a sight to bring sadness and bitterness to the heart. But of course, the Barbudan slaves would not have been from the town itself, that would have been where they were shipped. They must have come from villages inland from Cormantin: villages of the Corromantee tribe. They were victims of war, of slaving expeditions into the interior by African kings. They did the dirty work. The big kingdoms along the coast, like Asante, Dahomy, Benin, all engaged in it. Of course it's a great tragedy in our African history. Well over a million people from this coast alone between the sixteenth and eighteenth century. More than ten times as many from the whole of Africa. Imagine it!'

These slaves from the Gold Coast established a community in Barbuda for nearly three hundred years. Only eight new slaves were recorded as coming over during those years, in which the community grew to five hundred strong. After Emancipation in 1834, they worked as waged labourers for the Codringtons until the 1870s, when the family gave up their lease and the island passed to the administration of the Crown. The next generations grew up as British citizens, with allegiance to the Queen, thinking England was home.

'We had learned English as our first language, of course,' they told me later in the Barbudan centre in Leicester. 'We looked to the Queen as our sovereign and England as our mother country.

We even learned English history at school: Francis Drake and the Norman Conquest. England in a way was "home".'

In the mid 1950s, with the population in Barbuda grown to 1,200, and job opportunities few, the younger generation began to go 'home'. Like many Caribbean communities, they began to migrate to Britain, and by chance the Barbudans ended up in Leicester. The initial connection was entirely fortuitous: an Anglican priest who worked on the island, Father Milburn, came from Leicester, and he told them all about the place and gave everyone who wished to go letters of introduction. So they went to Leicester. Virtually all British Barbudans are there: nearly three hundred people today, they have resolutely stuck together, as is their wont.

'The first address we had was 33 Melbourne Road, a typical English terraced house next to a grocery store,' Railton Beazer continued over dominoes in the community centre. Thin and tigerish, Railton growled occasionally and lounged across his chair, then roared with laughter. At his side, his wife Primrose was large and still, with a great, slow voice. With them were Brillheart James and his wife, Tina.

'I remember the late-night parties, then,' Railton laughed. 'Calypso music blaring out of open windows.'

It spurred the memory and they talked with as great affection about their Melbourne Road house parties as they did about cookups on the beach as kids.

'Well, we still kids, most of us, when we came here. Most of us were sixteen or seventeen. The trip was a great adventure.'

Primrose intervened. 'When we stopped off at Jamaica *en route*, I thought it was England. I had no idea what to expect.'

Railton roared with laughter. 'When we saw the fog at Southampton then we definitely knew we had arrived!

'Whenever anyone new arrived from Barbuda, we held a party as a welcome. A Codrington party we called it. We had a lot of Codrington parties.'

They have kept a close connection with their roots, perhaps because they come from such a small place. They hold meetings of the Barbudan Association on the first Sunday of every month.

They have lectures and slide shows about the island's history. They have had coach trips to the Codringtons' mansion at Doddington Park, where they have picnicked in the gardens designed by Capability Brown: paid for by the sweat of their ancestors, though they would be far too polite to say so.

'The thing is, we are a close-knit community.' Harold Punter had joined us, from another of the old Barbudan families. His wife Linda is white (a number of Barbudans have married white women). 'It's wonderful belonging to it. I couldn't imagine living without the other Barbudans. Our roots go back so far together. We have always been friends, neighbours, and we still are here. I would have to live where they are. They are just the salt of the earth.'

He looked around him: Railton, Primrose, the Jameses, Gilmour Teague, Selwyn Webber. The roots of these people are African but their names are obviously English. Where did they each come from? Again the answer lay in the Codrington papers.

Codrington itself, in Gloucestershire, is a tiny place, in Domesday Book 'Cuthhere's farmstead'. The family took their name from the place. Their estates spread over south Gloucestershire in the seventeenth century just as their Caribbean estates spread across the Windwards after 1628. In both places they employed farmers, labourers and managers to look after their property. From time to time, the papers showed, they sent out Gloucester men to work on their Caribbean properties; these were labourers from their own estates at Sodbury, Marshfield, Doddington and Cold Aston, who would help run the estates and manage the workforce. In 1762, for example, Sir William arranged with 'a farmer of this place to go out to Barbuda, where I expect he will be of use among the cattle and sheep. I will give him 25 pounds sterling per annum for 6 years.' Sometimes men would go out who had experience with horses, which the slaves were not used to handling; in 1783, two grooms went out with colts. Most were evidently young boys, around seventeen years old, without wives or families. There were only ever a few whites at any one time – two or three to a couple of hundred slaves, but some went out young on long contracts and never came back. And according to the Codrington papers, some of them bore surnames by now familiar to us and still well known in Barbuda and Leicester: Beazor, Punter and Webber.

There were Webbers in Antigua, too, on Codrington estates: Thomas Webber worked as a mason in Antigua in the 1750s. But another Webber, Abraham, was on Barbuda, where he worked as a turtler in the 1760s for 40 pounds a year. Abraham made his home there and died in November 1785 leaving two children, Abraham and Mary, who are listed among the slaves in 1766 when they are described as infants. Abraham, who was then four, is later described as 'mustee', i.e., of mixed parentage. In June 1786, Mary was paid the wages due to her father after his death. Abraham was apprenticed to another slave, Daniel Beazor, a shipwright, and much later, in 1805, we find Abraham Webber, aged forty-two, described as a shipwright. So he succeeded in his craft, and he worked in that position till his death sometime around 1820. The family grew. In 1851, seventeen years after Emancipation, there were twenty-two members on Barbuda.

Another famous island family, the Punters, may trace their name to a Codrington estate manager on Barbuda from 1742. One of his descendants was Jack Punter, a shoemaker in 1766, described as a 'very good fellow'; a grandchild, Harry, born in the early 1760s, was a sailor in 1783 and later captain of one of the small sloops which ran between Antigua and Barbuda. In 1851, again, there were twenty-three members of this family on the island.

In the case of most slaves, such names were given to them by overseers or chosen by the slaves themselves from the names of whites they knew. But in the case of the Webbers and the Punters, and possibly others on Barbuda, whites had married blacks. Even the Codrington attorney Samuel Redhead, who was responsible for their Antiguan estates between 1751 and 1779, and for Barbuda from 1761 to 1779, had a black common-law wife, Sarah (Sally) Bullock. Samuel describes their children Joseph and Henry Redhead as 'my natural sons by Sarah Bullock' and he made provision for them in his will. According to Oliver's *History of Antigua* (1899), Sarah returned with Samuel to England and was living with him in his house in London at the time of his death. Such are the hidden human stories behind that terrible time.

There is another clear instance of a white labourer from Gloucester marrying a black woman and of their children bearing his name. The name Beazor is found in south Gloucestershire in the seventeenth century, spelled Beazor, Bezor and even Beagor. The Barbudan Beazors probably derived their name from John Beazor, who went out to Barbuda before 1720. In a document in the Codrington papers dated 3 August 1741, John declared he had been on the island 'above twenty years', and described himself as 'a driver of the negroes'. By the mid 1740s, there were seven Beazors on the island, five men or boys and two women, and they may well all have been descended from John. They all have common English names: Will, Johnny, Tom, Robert, Daniel, Bess and Mary. They were a capable family, as the Codrington attorney dutifully recorded. The papers in the bonded warehouse described Daniel (a child in 1746) in 1783 as 'one of the best slaves in the West Indies', accomplished as a carpenter and shipwright. His son Daniel was apprenticed to his father and became a shipwright himself – and it is Daniel, as we saw, who taught the skill to Abraham Webber. In the last slave list of 1832, just before Emancipation, Daniel is described as 'coloured' and aged sixty-three. By 1851 there were forty-one members of the family on the island. And in the end it would be they and their descendants, not the Codringtons, who would inherit the earth of Barbuda.

This is a story about Afro-Caribbean history, but it is also about the English; the Leicester Barbudans' ancestors were African, and Caribbean, but also English – as are their children. I was curious to tie up the loose ends on this side of the Atlantic too. What about the Gloucestershire origins of the whites who went out to the Caribbean as indentured labourers and who vanished, leaving only their surnames in the black communities of Barbuda and Leicester? Who were they? Even a cursory search through the local archives turns up the old Barbudan names in south Gloucestershire in the area of the Codrington villages: Punters were recorded in 1522 in Dursley and Great Badminton; a Richard Punter was a husbandman in Marshfield in the early seventeenth century. Teagues crop up as labourers at the same time, some distance away in the liberty of St Brevill; and in an earlier 1522 survey at Purton near Lydney. The Beazer name is rare. There are no Beazers in the Gloucester Tudor military survey of 1522. But in the survey of August 1608 entitled *The Names and Surnames of all the Able and Sufficient Men in Body Fit for His Majesty's Services in the Wars, within the County of Gloucester*, in Little Sodbury we find:

John Beaser husbandman
Thomas Beaser husbandman
Edmund Beaser husbandman

Tracing their origin earlier than that is a problem; but a good guess is that they came from Wiltshire. A George Beasser was living near Bradford on Avon in 1576, and the family were still nearby in the eighteenth century, when Beazers were cloth-workers at Melksham (John was executed there for rioting in 1739, according to a colourful narrative in the *Gentleman's Magazine*).

Wherever they originated, the original Barbudan Beazor was probably John Bezor from Little Sodbury, who was sent out by Sir William Codrington towards 1720. Little Sodbury is very near Doddington Park, and the parish registers reveal that Beazors were living there in the seventeenth century. In 1703, they record the baptism of a John Bezor, born to John and Mary Bezor. No other wedding, baptism or funeral record of a Bezor survives from this time at Little Sodbury or anywhere else nearby, so this John may well be the John who goes to Barbuda around 1720, aged seventeen.

Intrigued by the possibility that there might be white Beazors still in south Gloucestershire, I checked the telephone directories, to find one family of Beazors in Marshfield, five miles north of Bath, just off the M4, a village with many Codrington connections. It has to be said that there is no evidence to link them to the Little Sodbury family in 1608, and there are no Beazors in the parish records of Marshfield from 1600–1811. But they were the last white family on the former Codrington estates to bear the name. Their scrapbook of old black-and-white photographs showed hand ploughing there as late as the 1930s. They have one child, a daughter, so the name will die out in Gloucestershire, though it lives on in rude health in Leicester.

One should not romanticize anything to do with slavery. Barbuda was no doubt a very harsh place. But in the story of the slaves of Barbuda there is a kind of redemption. Instead of being an unmitigated nightmare, where everything was stripped from them – dignity, identity, children, roots – in the awful conditions of the slave age, the island was so isolated that for the slaves it became a kind of refuge. Despite its harsh climate and landscape, they were able to establish some faint resemblance of the human relations of free people: they could marry and have children and grandchildren – and see them grow up; and they could cultivate patches of land they called their own. Barbuda was barren, hot and treeless, and they had few freedoms beyond agreed holidays: sheep rustling, fishing in the lagoon, picking wrecks clean. But after Emancipation, they had sufficient education and skills to pass on their crafts as carpenters, shipwrights, wheelwrights and sailors. Poor and isolated as their community was, they had most skills between them, and through cooperation they became a formidable people, in both physical and moral stature. Hard as life on the island must have been, its unusual conditions allowed families to grow from one generation to another, and to develop the strong love of the place which Barbudans today in Leicester feel as strongly as did their forebears.

There's a parable here, especially for those of us, black and white, who lived through the time of Enoch Powell and the 'Rivers of Blood' speech. He died in 1998, and many were affronted that his death should be given such coverage, even on the BBC's main news. What was not made clear, even on the BBC, was that he was wrong. Powell's fantasies of Englishness belonged to another age, as was revealed all too plainly in his absurdly romantic patriotic poems in his book, *Dancer's End*. His was a fatal misunderstanding of the whole course of English history, from a man whose point of view was always that of the Codringtons, and never the Beazors.

In fact, the English are a nation of immigrants. Every wave has added to it and taken on the culture and language of the nation, from the Vikings to the Kenyan Asians. The new generation of Englishmen and women, in their teens and twenties, born and brought up in this world, are capable of taking on more than one history. Despite racist stories in the papers, the occasional terrible injustice, like the Stephen Lawrence case, that's the hope for the future. The country has come a long way in the fifty years since the *Empire Windrush* docked at Tilbury.

There is one more thing I forgot to mention about the Beazors: their name. It's Norman French: Beausire. They're descended from Normans, too. When I talked these things over with the Beazers at the annual Codrington party (reggae, now, rather than calypso, still lots of laughter), Railton was amused to hear that his history – and maybe a tiny part of his ancestry too – may just go back to Domesday Book, Norman knights and medieval husbandmen as well as to the great stream which links Barbuda with the people of Cormantin on the Ashanti coast of Ghana and their deep cultural roots in Mother Africa. What a history! And the point is, the English bit is just as much his history as the next man's, and more so than many. Identity is not something genetic, safe and secure. It is shaped by history and culture: it is about group feeling; allegiance to the state; it is, too, a common sense of culture, custom and language, to be sure, but in an open society that can be wide and inclusive. It is always in the making, never made. When I told him this story, Railton laughed his great laugh and raised his eyebrows: 'Well,' he said, 'we always said we were English!'

Bibliography

A Note on Sources

The sources of these stories range from medieval manuscripts to Victorian paintings; from films and TV to comics and children's books. The stories are about West Indians, Geordies and Devonians – but most are about English local history, and their sources are standard texts, series and compilations which can be accessed by any interested reader. Some obviously require specialist knowledge, but most are accessible to anyone with a little perseverence, especially as more and more material becomes available in translation.

Sources for English Local History

All counties have a local-history magazine and many have a records series which publishes documents: the volumes of the Yorkshire, Wiltshire and Gloucester Record Societies, for example, are cited in these pages. Check the shelves of your local-history library, which should also contain the standard texts for county history. (For an overview, see 'The Rediscovery of England' by W. Hoskins in his *Provincial England* (Macmillan, 1963). County histories started in Tudor times and are still published regularly. The *Victoria County History*, which began in the nineteenth century, is still underway, on a massive scale, with every parish described. Older county histories are often of great value – even if inaccurate in some detail, they frequently notice things missed by later writers. Some are still great: the reader will find Joseph Hunter's *South Yorkshire* (1832) used in these pages, along with Ormerod's *History of Cheshire* (1819), and Nichols's *History of Leicestershire*. For some reason, various other counties, such as Devon, never received this ample treatment.

Other essential tools for local research include Domesday Book, William the Conqueror's county-by-county survey of 1086 (which is published in paperback in parallel text by Phillimore with notes); OS maps, especially the Victorian large-scale ones (photographic reprints can be ordered by many specialist bookshops or from the Survey Office in Southampton); and users' guides, such as *Village Records* by John West (Macmillan, 1962) and a clutch of handbooks published by Phillimore, whose catalogue is a great resource for the local historian, e.g. N. Alcock, *Old Title Deeds: A Guide for Local and Family Historians* (Phillimore, 1994); Denis Stuart, *Manorial Records* (Phillimore, 1992); and W. E. Tate, *The Parish Chest* (Phillimore, 1983). England's unrivalled collection of medieval tax documents is now beginning to be published in translation. From the sixteenth century there is a flood of material which makes it possible to identify every householder who lived in a place from then till now. This can usually be found in your local-history library: parish registers, which as a rule started in the mid sixteenth century; subsidy rolls; protestation lists; military musters; gazeteers (which list shops, crafts and trades); and, of course, voting lists. I find it most helpful to trawl the open shelves of local sections to sample these. There too one may find out-of-print gems like William Hoskins's *Provincial England* and his *Essays in Leicestershire History* (Liverpool University Press, 1950), which contains 'Galby and Frisby', my favourite essay on local history.

Buildings and Monuments

The basic guide is the updated *The Buildings of England* series by N. Pevsner (Penguin); this is very useful but by no means comprehensive. For more detail, see the *Victoria County History* and the volumes of the *Royal Commission on Historic Monuments*: though not available for all counties, some of these are exemplary: e.g. Northamptonshire, or Dorset, where every church, every old house, every earthwork is noted with plans and sketch maps. Again, check the local–history shelves.

Place Names

This is a notoriously thorny topic: local history has been plagued by false etymologies. Two reliable guides are Margaret Gelling's *Signposts to the Past* (Dent, 1978) and her *Place Names in the Landscape* (Dent, 1984). E. Ekwall's *The Concise Oxford Dictionary of English Place Names* is still the best overview. This is based on the massive country-by-county survey undertaken by the English Place Name Society, who also publish an annual journal. Most EPNS volumes are now published. These give immense detail, providing an accurate run of place names as far back as possible, enabling the true meaning of a name to be recovered. As the EPNS volumes also cite dates and sources, they are an invaluable tool to local historians.

Charters

These land documents start from the seventh century, and by the tenth century describe landscapes in great detail. For a list and bibliography, see *Anglo-Saxon Charters*, ed. P. Sawyer (British Academy, 1968; a new edition is in preparation). Sawyer's bibliography provides references for translations and articles in local journals, including reconstructions of the bounds on the ground. The best of these, though, are the more recent books of Della Hooke, published with translations and maps: *Pre-Conquest Charter Bounds of Devon and Cornwall* (Boydell, 1994); *The Landscape of Anglo Saxon Staffordshire* (Keele University, 1983); *Worcestershire Anglo-Saxon Charter Bounds* (Boydell, 1990). These will be the key texts on the Old English landscape.

Landscape

The Making of the English Landscape by W. Hoskins (Hodder, 1986 edition) is a classic; so too is the brilliant *The History of the English Countryside* by Oliver Rackham (Dent, 1986). For aerial photography see: *Medieval Britain From the Air* by C. Platt (G. Philip, 1984) and *Medieval England: An Aerial Survey* by M. Beresford and J. K. S. St. Joseph (Cambridge, 1979). For information on woods, see: O. Rackham, *The Last Forest* (Dent, 1981); *Hayley Wood* (Cambridge, 1975) and *Trees and Woodland in the British Landscape* (Dent, 1981). On fields: *Studies of Field Systems in the British Isles* by P. Baker and R. Butlin (Cambridge, 1973) is a heavyweight; more accessible is *Fields in the English Landscape* by C. Taylor (Sutton, 1987); see too T. Rowley, *Villages in the Landscape* (Dent, 1981). On Laxton, the last working open-field village, see C. S. Orwin, *The Open Fields* (Oxford, 1967 edition) and J. V. Beckett, *A History of Laxton* (Oxford, 1989).

Anglo-Saxon History

For a useful overview, see *The Anglo-Saxons*, ed. J. Campbell (Phaidon, 1982). An excellent handbook is *The Blackwell Encyclopaedia of Anglo-Saxon England*, ed. M. Lapidge and others (Blackwell, 1999). See also D. Hill, *An Atlas of Anglo-Saxon England* (Blackwell, 1981) and *A Companion to Old English Literature*, ed. M. Godden and M. Lapidge (Cambridge, 1991). The key annual publication is *Anglo-Saxon England* (Cambridge), abbreviated here to *ASE*. Lastly, there are two excellent catalogues of Anglo-Saxon art, *The Making of England* (British Museum, 1984) and *The Golden Age of Anglo-Saxon Art* (British Museum, 1991), both edited by L. Webster and J. Backhouse.

Sources for specific chapters are listed below.

The Norman Yoke

F. M. Stenton's *Anglo-Saxon England* (Oxford, 1943) is the classic statement. On the seventeenth-century view, see C. Hill, *Puritanism and Revolution* (Secker, 1958). A great collection of documents on the Levellers is *Puritanism and Liberty*, ed. A. S. P. Woodhouse (Everyman, 1986). The works of Gerard Winstanley are in *The Law of Freedom*, ed. C. Hill (Penguin, 1973); see also Hill's *The World Turned Upside Down* (Penguin, 1975). On the survival of these radical ideas see E. P. Thompson's wonderful book on William Blake, *Witness against the Beast* (Cambridge, 1993), which includes the astonishing story of the survival of the last Muggletonian, Philip Noakes, who died in 1979. On the events of 1066, see A. Williams, *The English and the Norman Conquest* (Boydell Press, 1995), and my *Domesday* (BBC, new edition 1999). On literacy, the fundamental study is M. Clanchy, *From Memory to Written Record* (Dutton, 2nd edition 1993); on language, literature and identity 1290–1340, see T. Turville-Petre, *England the Nation* (Oxford, 1996). Fiction based on the Norman Conquest has mined a rich seam: a recent novel is Julian Rathbone's *The Last English King* (Little, Brown, 1997).

King Arthur: Lost Again?

Gildas' *On the Ruin of Britain* is edited and translated by M. Winterbottom (Phillimore, 1978), on which my translation is based. Nennius' *History of the Britons* and *The Annals of Wales* are edited and translated by John Morris (Phillimore, 1980). *The Gododdin* is translated by Kenneth Jackson in *The Gododdin: the Oldest Scottish Poem* (Edinburgh University Press, 1965); but for new doubts about its authenticity see J. Rowland in *Cambridge Medieval Celtic Studies* 30 (1995). There is an excellent translation of Adomnan of Iona's *Life of St Columba* by Richard Sharpe (Penguin, 1995). The best summary of the historical problems surrounding Arthur is Richard Barber's *King Arthur, Hero and Legend* (Boydell Press, 1961). For the vast medieval literature on Arthur, the bibliography of the specialist publisher Boydell and Brewer should be consulted. Geoffrey of Monmouth's *History of the Kings of Britain* is translated by L. Thorpe (Penguin, 1966). There are countless books available on the 'historical' Arthur, notably Leslie Alcock, *Arthur's Britain* (Penguin, 1971), John Morris, *The Age of Arthur* (Phillimore, 1973), and Leslie Alcock, *By South Cadbury* (Thames and Hudson, 1972). As for fiction, there is no end to it: try Bernard Cornwell's trilogy *The Warlord Chronicles* (Penguin 1996–8).

Glastonbury, the Grail and the Isle of Avalon

There are two popular recent introductions which cannot be bettered: J. Carley, *Glastonbury Abbey* (Boydell, 1988) – just the right blend of scholarship and receptivity, and P. Rahtz, *Glastonbury* (Batsford, 1993) – just the right blend of archaeological rigour and scepticism. See also H. M. Taylor, *Anglo-Saxon Architecture* (3 volumes, Cambridge, 1980): an invaluable catalogue of all surviving AS churches. On early Glastonbury, see B. and J. Coles, *Sweet Track to Glastonbury* (Thames and Hudson, 1986). On the early context on both sides of the Irish Sea, C. Thomas, *Christianity in Roman Britain* (Batsford, 1981) and *Saint Patrick's World* by Liam de Paor (Four Courts Press, Dublin, 1996) are useful. Books on early Somerset include M. Aston and I. Burrow, *The Archaeology of Somerset* (Somerset County Council, 1982); M. Havinden, *The Somerset Landscape* (1981); M. Costen, *The Origin of Somerset* (Manchester University Press, 1992). For the latest summary of Glastonbury's early holdings, see L. Abrams, *Anglo-Saxon Glastonbury* (Boydell, 1996). A useful collection of essays on the same period is *The Archaeology and History of Glastonbury Abbey*, ed. L. Abrams and J. Carley (Boydell, 1991).

On Glastonbury Texts

The *Life of St Dunstan* which I discuss is printed with a most valuable introduction in W. Stubbs, *Memorials of Saint Dunstan* (Rolls Series,

1874). A new edition has now been announced in the Oxford Medieval Texts series edited by Michael Lapidge. An indispensable warning on the faking of Glastonbury's early traditions is 'Ynys-witrin' in *Lucerna*, ed. H. P. R. Finberg (Macmillan, 1964). Other texts include William of Malmesbury's *The Early History of Glastonbury*, translated by J. Scott (Woodbridge, 1981), and *The Chronicle of John of Glastonbury*, edited by J. Carley and translated by D. Townsend (Woodbridge, 1985).

On the Grail and its legends, see R. S. Loomis, *The Grail* (Princeton, 1963). On the Glastonbury legends in general, see R. Barber, *King Arthur, Hero and Legend* (Boydell, 1986).

New Age

No bibliography of this kind should omit the mystical side. For a flavour, see John Michell, *New Light on the Ancient Mystery of Glastonbury* (Gothic Image, 1990). Earlier classics include K. Maltwood, *A Guide to Glastonbury's Temple of the Stars* (1929); and F. Bligh Bond, *The Mystery of Glastonbury and her Immortal Traditions* (1939). For a 1930s vision of Albion, still in print, see D. Faulkner Jones, *The English Spirit* (Rudolf Steiner, 1935). On the 1920s mystics there is Patrick Benham's *The Avalonians* (Glastonbury, 1993). John Cowper Powys's *Glastonbury Romance* (1931) was reissued by Penguin in 1999.

Merrie Englande: The Legend of Robin Hood

For a full modern summary, see J. Holt, *Robin Hood* (Thames and Hudson, 1989 edition), to which I am indebted. An earlier Holt essay is in some respects not superseded by the later work: 'Robin Hood: Some Comments', in a symposium on the outlaw in *Peasants, Knights and Heretics*, ed. T. Aston and R. Hilton (Cambridge University Press, 1976). On outlaws, see M. Keen, *The Outlaws of Medieval Legend* (Routledge, 1977). For fascinating material right up to today, see David Blamires, *Robin Hood: A Hero For All Times* (John Rylands

Library, 1998). The ballads can be found in *Rhymes of Robyn Hood* by R. Dobson and J. Taylor (Heinemann, 1976). Stephen Knight's *Robin Hood: A Complete Study of the English Outlaw* (Blackwell, 1994) is a literary survey from the Middle Ages to the present. On crime, see Barbara Hanawalt, *Crime and Conflict in English Communities 1300–1348* (Harvard, 1979). On the Midlands gangster families, see D. Crook in *English Historical Review* xclix (1984), and on the possible genesis of the legend, D. Crook in *Thirteenth Century England* ii (1989). Too late to be used by me is the bumper omnibus of Hoodiana, *Robin Hood: An Anthology of Scholarship and Criticism*, ed. Stephen Knight (D. S. Brewer, 1999) published after this went to press, which reviews the whole story.

When was England England?

On the origins of the English state, there is an abundance of literature going back to the still interesting *Constitutional History* by William Stubbs (Oxford, 1874). Along with F. M. Stenton's *Anglo-Saxon England* (Oxford, 1943) there are his essays, *Preparatory to Anglo-Saxon England* (Oxford, 1970). For a general introduction on the state, see Joseph Strayer, *On the Medieval Origins of the Modern State* (Princeton, 1970). A classic broad-sweep interpretation is G. Elton, *The English* (Blackwell, 1992). I am especially indebted to C. P. Wormald, 'Englalond: the Making of an Allegiance' in the *Journal of Historical Sociology* 7 (1994); and to James Campbell's Stenton lecture on William Stubbs (Reading, 1989). Wolf's sermon is printed in *Anglo-Saxon Prose*, translated by M. Swanton (Everyman, 1975).

Heritages and Destructions: The Troublesome Journey and Laborious Search of John Leland

The Itinerary of John Leland is edited by L. Toulmin Smith (5 vols., Centaur Press, 1964 reprint) and by John Chandler (Alan Sutton,

1993), a very handy modern-English version which came to my notice after this had gone to proof. My main debt is to James Carley: this chapter would have been much the poorer without his research on John Leland in Paris, and on Leland's visit to Glastonbury, published in *Scriptorium* vol. 40 (1986). For Leland's biography I relied on the *Dictionary of National Biography* and on the introduction by Toulmin Smith; John Chandler (see above) has new details.

For a great overview of the culture of the time, E. Duffy's *The Stripping of the Altars* (Yale, 1992) is already a classic. On the impact of printing on manuscript culture, see *The Coming of the Book* by Lucien Febvre et al. (Verso, 1984). On the possibilities of OE material surviving in the works of antiquarians of the Tudor period and later (a subject whose surface has barely been scratched), see some of Simon Keynes's recent discoveries (e.g. the Abbotsbury cartulary, *ASE* 18 (1989) and the amazing find of a cluster of charters from the seventh to tenth centuries from the archive of the nunnery at Barking, which were copied into a Tudor antiquarian's notebook (see H. Lockwood, *Essex Journal*, spring 1990). The one sure fact in all this is that much remains to be discovered.

Alfred the Great: the Case of the Fenland Forger

The best starting point is Asser's Life, *Alfred the Great*, which is conveniently available in translation (Penguin, 1983) by the two main experts in the field, Simon Keynes and Michael Lapidge. This includes much fascinating ancillary material and a very useful commentary. There is still much of value in W. H. Stevenson's 1904 edition (reprinted by Oxford University Press, 1998), and his notes are full of valuable insights, but Stevenson's text is not easy to use, and new discoveries and changing views mean a new edition is now desperately needed. *The Anglo-Saxon Chronicle* is available in paperback, ed. G. Garmonsway (Everyman, 1972). For a recent view on Alfred, see D. D. Sturdy, *Alfred the Great* (Constable, 1995). More biographies are on the way. On the Asser controversy: the doyen of the older doubters was V. Galbraith, *An Introduction to the*

Study of History (London, 1964). Dorothy Whitelock's reply is *The Genuine Asser* (University of Reading, 1968). Alfred Smyth's *Alfred the Great* (Oxford, 1996) revived the doubts, but has come under withering fire. Two important works came to me after this chapter was written: A. Scharer, 'The Writing of History at King Alfred's Court' in *Early Medieval Europe* vol. 5, no. 2 (1996), and Andrew Prescott, 'The Ghost of Asser' in *Anglo-Saxon Manuscripts and their Heritage*, ed. P. Pulsiano and E. M. Treharne (Ashgate, 1997). In a fascinating piece of detective work, Prescott shows that in all likelihood no trace of the Asser has survived till today. On Humfrey Wanley, see K. Sisam, *Studies in the History of Old English Literature* (Oxford, 1967 edition), and David Douglas, *English Scholars 1660–1730* (Eyre & Spottiswoode, 1951). Simon Keynes recently discovered Wanley's book of hand-painted facsimiles of manuscripts at Longleat, a story told in the *British Library Journal*, 1997. On the Vikings, see R. Page, *Chronicles of the Vikings* (British Museum, 1995). On Alfred's Orosius, see *Two Voyagers at the Court of King Alfred*, ed. N. Lund and translated by C. Fell (York, 1984). On Alfred's towns, see J. Haslam, *Anglo-Saxon Towns* (Phillimore, 1984); on Alfred's plans for defence, see D. Hill and A. Rumble, *The Defence of Wessex* (Manchester, 1996). A useful set of new essays is *Alfred the Wise*, ed. M. Godden and others (Boydell and Brewer, 1997). On Anglo-Saxon medicine, see M. L. Cameron, *Anglo-Saxon Medicine* (Cambridge University Press, 1993). On the Vatican Boethius manuscript, I am indebted to Fabio Troncarelli, *Tradizione Perdute* (Padua, 1981), where the Alfredian commentary is printed with photos. (But see too on this J. Wittig in *ASE* 11 (1983).

The Lost Life of King Athelstan

The best – and most enjoyable – account is still Armitage Robinson's Ford lectures of 1922: *The Times of Saint Dunstan* (Oxford, 1923, reprinted 1969); see too C. Brook, *The Saxon and Norman Kings* (Batsford, 1978) and F. M. Stenton's *Anglo-Saxon England* (1943). Recent interest in Athelstan has been considerable: there are four important academic pieces in particular, all of them very rewarding but unfortunately all rather austere for the non-specialist: M. Lapidge, 'Some Latin Sources' in *ASE* (1980), reprinted in his *Anglo-Latin Literature 900–1066* (Hambledon, 1993); Simon Keynes, 'King Athelstan's Books' in *Learning and Literature in Anglo-Saxon England*, ed. M. Lapidge and H. Gneuss (Cambridge University Press, 1985); D. Dumville, *Wessex and England* (Boydell, 1992); and Mechthild Gretsch, *The Intellectual Foundations of the English Benedictine Reform* (Cambridge University Press, 1999), which came out after my chapter was written. I have published a short account of Athelstan for the general reader in *In Search of the Dark Ages* (BBC, 1980 and later editions), with some further remarks on Athelstan's kingship in *Domesday* (BBC, 1986, new edition 1999) and an essay on him in *Ideal and Reality in Frankish and Anglo-Saxon Society*, ed. C. P. Wormald (Blackwell, 1983). W. Stubbs's edition of William of Malmesbury (Rolls Series, 1885) is still valuable: it is translated in *English Historical Documents*, ed. D. Whitelock (vol. 1, Eyre and Spottiswoode, 1979). See also *William of Malmesbury* by R. Thomson (Boydell, 1987). My unpublished work on the lost Life is used in R. Thomson's new commentary on William's *De Gestis Regum Anglorum* (Oxford, 1999). Lastly, Athelstan has inspired less modern fiction than, say, Alfred or Harold, let alone Arthur, but for a recent Athelstan novel, try *Dark Ages* by John Pritchard (HarperCollins, 1998).

The Story of a Book

This chapter is about reconstructing manuscript history. Though this area may seem forbidding, it is a fascinating and booming field of study and it need not be completely off limits to the patient amateur. For two readable and accessible introductions, see Michelle Brown, *A Guide to Western Historical Scripts* (British Library, 1990) and *Anglo-Saxon Manuscripts* (British Library, 1991): both are beautifully illustrated.

All texts which have come down to us from the past which are not inscriptions on stone or metal are in manuscripts (mss). The learning and literature of the Roman world, for example, mostly survives only in Carolingian mss of the eighth and ninth centuries. So where to look? For an overview of the British situation, see *Medieval Libraries of Great Britain* by N. Ker (British Academy, 1964, supplement by A. Watson, 1987). All pre-AD 800 Western Latin mss (less than 2,000 of them in total) are listed with photos, descriptions and bibliography by E. A. Lowe in *Codices Latini Antiquiores* (11 vols. plus supplement, Oxford, 1934–71; vol. 2 (Britain) new edition 1972). An addendum of new finds appears in the periodical *Medieval Studies* 47 (1985). All surviving mss containing Old English texts (less than 500 in total) are listed in N. Ker, *Catalogue of Manuscripts Containing Anglo-Saxon* (Oxford, 1957; with new finds listed in *ASE* 5 (1976)). All surviving mss and fragments owned in England before the twelfth century (only about 1,000 in total) are in the handlist by H. Gneuss in *ASE* 9 (1980); a revised list is on the way. Lastly, for a master's guide, see B. Bischoff, *Latin Palaeography* (Cambridge, 1998): this is a wonderfully lucid and informative account of the handwritten book and its scripts in the West from the Romans to the age of printing.

On Athelstan's Psalter

One of the most important memorials from English medieval culture, this book had to wait till 1997 for a detailed account of its paintings, by Bob Deshman in *ASE* vol. 26; this appeared after my chapter was written, but I have decided to leave it as it is: my different account of the source of the Galba paintings is based on the arguments of F. Wormald (*England before the Conquest*, ed P. Clemoes and K. Hughes (Cambridge University Press, 1971)). For reproductions of the relevant early Christian art, such as the Ashburnham Pentateuch and the Rabbula and Augustine Gospels, see K. Weitzman, *Late Antique and Early Christian Book Illumination* (Chatto, 1977), and Emmy Wellesz, *The Vienna Genesis* (Faber, 1960). For the North Italian connection I am indebted to Simon Keynes in *Alfred the Wise*, ed. M. Godden and others (Boydell,

1997). On the Greek material in the book, see M. Lapidge, 'Israel the Grammarian' in his *Anglo-Latin Literature* (Hambledon, 1993), after Edmund Bishop, *Liturgica Historica* (Oxford, 1918). Bishop's library is preserved at Downside Abbey: my thanks to Dom. Antony Sutch for letting me peruse it. Bishop's lovely essay 'About an Old Prayerbook' shows it is possible to write entertainingly about manuscripts without making the subject sound like a branch of particle physics!

The Last Bowl-Turner of England

The archive material on William Lailey, including plans, photos and one of his lathes, is preserved at the Reading Museum of English Rural Life. The implications of the sunken workshop are discussed by J. Myres and P. Dixon in the *Antiquaries Journal*, vol. lxviii (1988). The Hawkridge Charter is printed with commentary and translation in M. Gelling, *EPNS Berkshire*, vol. iii (Cambridge, 1976). This story raises the wider question of working peoples' lives in history: for a representative sample, see G. Sturt, *The Wheelwright's Shop* (Cambridge, 1923) – Sturt's *Journals 1890–1927* are edited by E. Mackerness (Cambridge, 1967); G. Ewart Evans's various books about Blaxhall, Suffolk, especially *Ask the Fellow Who Cuts the Hay* (Faber, 1956); *Both Teams at Plough*, an eighteenth-century ploughman's diary from Buckinghamshire (Reading, 1992); and *The Autobiography of Joseph Mayett of Quainton 1783–1839*, ed. Ann Kussmaul (Bucks Record Society, 1986). On the medieval peasant nothing of this kind exists, despite the fascinating hints in Aelfric's dialogue with an Anglo-Saxon (Oxfordshire?) ploughman translated by M. Swanton in *Anglo-Saxon Prose* (Everyman, 1975) and discussed in my *Domesday* (BBC, 1986). The possibilities for the biography of a later medieval peasant, though, are graphically illuminated in *The Taxpayers of Medieval Gloucestershire* by P. Franklin (Alan Sutton, 1993), where, for example, 58 documents are listed on the life of a single peasant, John Pleystud, who died of the Black Death. There is no specific chapter on medieval women in this book, but there is a growing literature: see C. Fell, *Women in Anglo-Saxon England* (British Museum, 1984); D. Baker (ed.), *Medieval Women* (Blackwell, 1978); S. Shahar, *The Fourth Estate* (Methuen, 1983); K. M. Wilson (ed.), *Medieval Women Writers* (Manchester, 1984); and, slightly later, M. Prior (ed.), *Women in English Society 1500–1800* (Methuen, 1985). On families, see *The Ties That Bound* by B. Hanawalt (Oxford, 1986). On children, the field is still open, but see Barbara Hanawalt's *Children Growing up in Medieval London* (Oxford, 1993).

Tinsley Wood

On the Brunanburh mystery in general, the basics are laid out by A. Campbell in *The Battle of Brunanburh* (Heinemann, 1938); see too D. Whitelock in *English Historical Documents* vol. 1 (1979). On the problem of the site, Campbell ably and realistically summarizes the case up to 1938; but his pessimistic conclusion has not stopped the speculation. Currently ahead in the betting is Bromborough in Cheshire (see J. Dodgson in *EPNS Cheshire* vol. iv (1972), which is favoured by the new *Encyclopaedia of Anglo-Saxon England* (Blackwell, 1999): but this was long ago dismissed, it seems to me irrefutably, by the Cheshire historian Ormerod, of all people. My own attempt is 'Brunanburh Revisited' in *Saga-Book of the Viking Society* (1980). Brinsworth/Tinsley was first suggested, as far as I am aware, by A. C. Goodall in *The Place Names of South Yorkshire* (Cambridge, 1913), then by J. Cockburn, followed by several others including A. H. Burne in *More Battlefields of Britain* (Methuen, 1960).

Specifics on Tinsley/Brinsworth

On place names, see A. H. Smith, *EPNS Yorkshire West Riding* vol. 1 (1961). For the excavations, see D. Greene in *Yorkshire Archaeological Journal*, vol. 38 pt 1 (1952) and pt 4 (1955). On the Roman fort, see T. May, *The Roman Forts of Templeborough*

(Rotherham, 1922). For general views of the area and steelworks, see the photographs in Tony Munsford's *Rotherham: A Pictorial History*: a model of its kind (Phillimore, 1994).

A Devon House: to Domesday and Beyond

This chapter is about reconstructing house history. But first, on Devon in general: W. Hoskins, *Devon* (Collins, 1954); W. Hoskins and H. P. R. Finberg, *Devonshire Studies* (Cape, 1952); W. Hoskins, *Old Devon* (David and Charles, 1966) and *Provincial England* (Macmillan, 1963), which contains 'The Highland Zone in Domesday Book'. On Devon housing, see *Devon Building*, ed. P. Beacham (Devon Books, 1995); see also *Devon's Hedges* (Devon County Council, 1997).

County Histories

Devon is poorly served. I used T. Risdon, *Survey of the County of Devon*, written *c.* 1630, published 1714, and T. Westcote, *A View of Devonshire in MDCXXX*, ed. G. Oliver (Exeter, 1845).

Farm Building

There is a vast literature on house building: on my shelf I have M. Wood, *The English Medieval House* (Ferndale, 1981 edition); M. Barley, *The English Farmhouse* (Routledge, 1961); S. Wade Martins, *Historic Farm Buildings* (Batsford, 1991); C. Taylor, *Village and Farmstead* (G. Philip, 1983). On documenting houses, one book stands head and shoulders above the others: *People at Home: Living in a Warwickshire Village 1500–1800* by N. Alcock (Phillimore, 1993). On carpentry, see Cecil Hewitt, *English Historic Carpentry* (Phillimore, 1980), *Church Carpentry* (Phillimore, 1982) and his 'Anglo-Saxon Carpentry' in *Anglo-Saxon England* 7 (1978). Hewitt was an Essex teacher, son of a woodworker, and he was a true pioneer: he recorded and identified medieval carpenters' styles and found pre-Conquest carpentry in several of his home county's villages, such as Little Bardfield, Buttsbury and Hadstock, and further afield, for example in the magnificent spire frame at Sompting, Sussex.

Bury Barton

On the structures, see N. W. Alcock, 'A Devon Farm: Bury Barton, Lapford' in *Transactions of the Devon Association* xcviii (1966). On the Roman site: in the 1985 issue of *Britannia* (the standard periodical on Roman Britain) is 'The Roman Fort at Bury Barton' by M. Todd; the same author wrote *The South-West to AD 1000* (Longman, 1987). On Roman place names I have relied on A. Rivet and C. Smith, *The Place-Names of Roman Britain* (Batsford, 1979). On Nemetostatio and the sacred wood, see C. E. Stevens in J. V. S. Megaw, '*To Illustrate the Monuments . . .*' (London, 1976); on new finds, see F. Griffith, 'A Nemeton in Devon?' in *Antiquity* 59 (1985), and 'Some Newly Discovered Ritual Monuments in Mid-Devon' in *Proceedings of the Prehistoric Society* vol. 51 (1985). On the charters, including that at 'nymed', see Della Hooke, *Pre-Conquest Charter Bounds of Devon and Cornwall* (Boydell, 1994).

Early Tax Documents / Inventories / Parish Registers / Gazeteers

The Devonshire Lay Subsidy of 1332 is edited by A. M. Erskine (Devon and Cornwall Record Society New Series, vol. 14 (1969)). On these documents in general, which are of great value to the local historian, see M. W. Beresford, *Lay Subsidies and Poll Taxes* (1963); an outdated list of published subsidies is in E. L. C. Mullins, *Texts and Calendars* (RHS, 1958). The Devon and Cornwall Record Society New Series 11 (1966) has published sixteenth- and seventeenth-century Devon inventories (ed. M. Cash).

On the Exeter church in the OE period, see Patrick Conner, *Anglo-Saxon Exeter* (Boydell, 1993). The Devon wills quoted here are published in an interesting set of essays: *Devon Documents*, ed. T. Gray (Devon & Cornwall Notes and Queries, 1996).

Photographs

See *Devon's Past: An Aerial View* by F. Griffith (Devon Books, 1988). Last but not least: the photographs of James Ravilious, *A Corner of England* and *An English Eye* (Devon Books, 1995 and 1998) are a remarkable, and at times visionary, record of an upland way of life which survived to the end of the twentieth century.

Peatling Magna: August 1265

The basic narrative is in R. L. Poole, *King Henry and the Lord Edward* (Oxford, 1947). On the background, see J. Holt, *Magna Carta* (Cambridge University Press, 1965) and J. Maddicott, *Simon de Montfort* (Cambridge University Press, 1996). The court case is printed in the Selden Society: *Selected Cases of Procedure without Writ under Henry III*, ed. H. Richardson and G. Sayles (London, 1941). After my book had gone to proofs, Dr David Carpenter kindly sent me his *The Reign of King Henry III* (Hambledon, 1997), in which he looks at peasant participation in politics in the thirteenth century. On peasant literacy, see M. Clanchy, *From Memory to Written Record* (Arnold, 1993). Although this chapter is about a day in 1265, it is also about village histories. On Leicestershire the key collection is G. Farnham's *Leicester Medieval Village Notes*. All Leicester parish registers are on microfiche at the very reader-friendly Leicester Record Office at Wigston. For a classic piece of local village history, see W. Hoskins's 'Galby and Frisby' in his *Essays in Leicestershire History* (Liverpool, 1950). For a pioneering attempt to go even further, and to reconstruct the history and topography of a Leicester village including housing plots between 1086 and the eighteenth century (at Kibworth Harcourt), see C. Howell, *Land, Family and Inheritance* (Cambridge University Press, 1983). This model could be applied in many other places, as Hoskins foresaw: see Charles Phythian Adams, 'Hoskins's England', in *Transactions of the Leicester-shire Archaeological and Historical Society* lxvi (1992). For the possibilities and methods of reconstructing village history in general, a still-useful guide is John West, *Village Records* (Macmillan, 1962 and later editions). For some examples taken at random from my shelf: R. Gough, *The History of Myddle* (Penguin, 1981) and D. G. Hey, *Myddle in Shropshire: An English Rural Community: Myddle under the Tudors and Stuarts* (Leicester University Press, 1974); M. Spufford, *A Cambridge Community* (Leicester University Press, 1965) and *Contrasting Communities* (Cambridge, 1974), both on Chippenham in Cambridgeshire; *Sherington* (in Norfolk) by A. C. Chibnall (Cambridge, 1965). But there are many ways of telling the story: see Ronald Blythe's *Akenfield* (Penguin, 1969), an uncompromisingly stark, realistic – and for that, tremendously moving – portrait of a rural English community in the twentieth century; and *Word from Wormingford* (Penguin, 1996), an elegiac portrait of a vanishing world expressed in the old language of the seasons and the liturgy.

Jarrow and English History

There are two very readable introductions by Peter Hunter Blair: *The World of Bede* (London, 1970) and *Northumbria in the Days of Bede* (London, 1976); and two interesting volumes of essays: *Famulus Christi*, ed. G. Bonner (S.P.C.K., 1976) and a massive and beautifully produced new study with essays on many themes: *Northumbria's Golden Age*, ed. J. Hawkes and S. Mills (Sutton, 1999). On Jarrow church, see H. M. Taylor, *Anglo-Saxon Architecture* (Cambridge, 1980), which contains a summary of the excavations by Rosemary Cramp. On the recent discovery of Bede's handwriting in the Jarrow Bibles, see R. Marsden in *ASE* 27 (1998). As yet, most of Bede's works are untranslated; but several, including his *Calculation of Time*, are planned in a new series, Translated Texts for Historians, which already runs to over thirty volumes (Liverpool University Press). Bede was born only two or three generations after Pope Gregory's mission to convert the English in 597: it is worth remembering that the epic poem *Beowulf* may be from the same time (translation published by Penguin, 1957). On this, see C. P. Wormald, 'Bede, Beowulf, and the Conversion of the Anglo-Saxon Aristocracy' in *Bede and Anglo-Saxon England*, ed. R. T. Farrell (British Archaeological Reports, Oxford, 1978): a typically challenging view of the cultural laminations of the time.

Epilogue: an English Family

The raw material for this story starts with the catalogue from Sotheby's: it is to be hoped that this remarkable archive will eventually be published in full. The history of black people in Britain is a vast area, in which I can pretend no special competence. Two general introductions are P. Fryer's brilliant *Staying Power* (Pluto Press, 1984), and N. File and C. Power, *Black Settlers in Britain 1555–1958* (Heinemann, 1981). See also two works by F. O. Shyllon: *Black Slaves in Britain* (Oxford University Press, 1974) and *Black People in Britain 1555–1833* (Oxford, 1977). On black Britons in the eighteenth century, see P. Edwards and J. Walvin, *Black Personalities in the Era of the Slave Trade* (Macmillan, 1983). The works of several black writers of that time are now published, for example the autobiography of Olaudah Equiano. On the slave trade in general, see H. Thomas, *The Slave Trade* (Macmillan, 1998).

Last of all, a word on the construction of Englishness. A truly vast field, this, in which you pay your money and take your choice. There is of course a wide range of literature which takes a different tack from my chapter five: try P. Wright, *On Living in an Old Country* (Verso, 1985) and Tom Nairn, *The Breakup of Britain* (Verso, 1981). In general, *Writing Englishness* (Routledge, 1995) is a good introduction to the sources; it includes excerpts from many famous texts such as Stanley Baldwin's *On England*, H. V. Morton's *In Search of England*, and George Orwell's *The Lion and the Unicorn*. Guide books are another fascinating source on Englishness, from the Murray's Handbooks to Arthur Mee's *King's England*, and, immediately after the Second World War, the County books, the Batsford England series, and Pevsner. On the mainstream 'official' construction of English identity in our time, see *Imperialism and Popular Culture*, ed. John MacKenzie (Manchester University Press, 1986); and for details on its various manifestations – school texts, lantern slides, magazines and cigarette cards – see *Propaganda and Empire* by J. Mackenzie (Manchester University Press, 1984). On painted images of England in the nineteenth century there is C. Wood's *Paradise Lost* (Barrie and Jenkins, 1988). From the mid nineteenth century, the popular image of England was created also by photographs. For a broad overview, see John Taylor, *A Dream of England* (Manchester University Press, 1994), a fascinating study in the use of photography, from Emerson's 1880s portrait of the Norfolk Broads, and the photographic survey of Shakespeare's Warwickshire, to *Picture Post* and modern accounts of Englishness by the likes of Martin Parr and John Kippin. For a different approach, see two photographers whose work appears in this book: James Ravilious (*A Corner of England* and *An English Eye*) and John Davies, *Green and Pleasant Land* (Manchester, Corner House, 1986). This is a vast and entertaining field through which, as always in such quests, it is enlightening to wander at random and make one's own discoveries.

Index

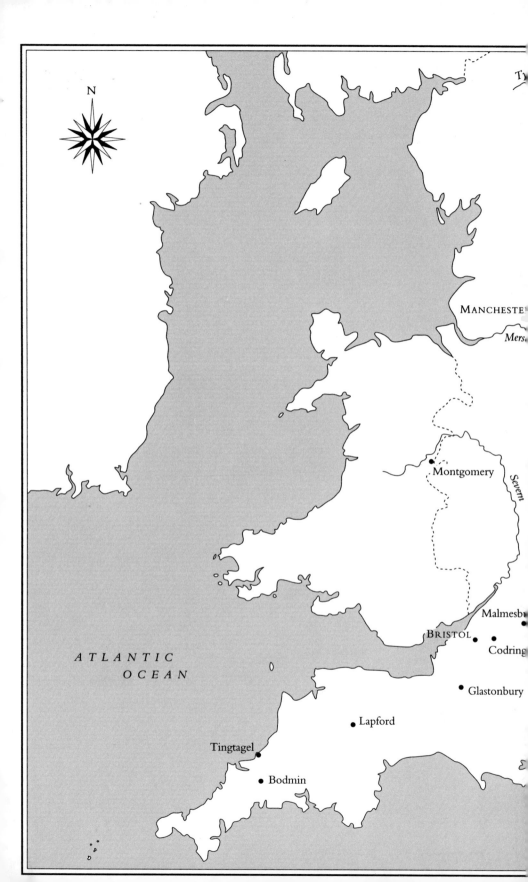